GEORG SIMMEL

Essays on Interpretation in Social Science

translated and edited with an introduction
by Guy Oakes

ROWMAN AND LITTLEFIELD
TOTOWA NEW JERSEY

Introduction and translation © 1980 by
Rowman and Littlefield

First published in the United States, 1980
by Rowman and Littlefield, Totowa, New Jersey

The translations of *"Vom Wesen des historischen Verstehens,"*
"Das Problem der historischen Zeit," and *"Über die Geschichte
der Philosophie"* are published by arrangement with K.F. Koehler
Verlag, Stuttgart; the translation of *"Die historische Formung"*
by arrangement with Drei Masken Verlag, Munich.

Library of Congress Cataloging in Publication Data

Simmel, Georg, 1858-1918.
    Essays on interpretation in social science.

    Includes index.
    1. Social sciences—Addresses, essays, lectures.
    2. Social sciences—Methodology—Addresses, essays,
lectures. I. Title.
H61.S584 1980   300'.1'8   79-15460
ISBN 0-8476-6193-8

Printed in the United States of America

Contents

Introduction

Introduction

THE TEXTS AND THE THEMES

In his first major methodological study, Max Weber devotes considerable space to the problem of criteria for interpretation in the sociocultural sciences, focusing specifically upon the status of this problem in the German philosophical literature between the work of Dilthey in 1883 and the work of Theodor Lipps in 1906. In this discussion, Weber claims that the elements of a theory of interpretation are most fully developed in the second edition of Georg Simmel's book *The Problems of the Philosophy of History* (Weber, 1975, p. 151). The first edition of this book was published in 1892 as a monograph of 109 pages. In a brief and incomplete autobiographical fragment—undated, but written between 1914 and 1918—Simmel himself offers some illuminating comments on the circumstances under which it was written. In particular, he acknowledges his debt to Kant and indicates how he attempted to generalize Kant's fundamental insight in his own philosophical and methodological studies.

I began my work with studies in epistemology and Kant scholarship, studies which were combined with work in history and the social sciences. The initial result of these studies—set out in the book *The Problems of the Philosophy of History*—was the following basic idea. In exactly the same sense that the categories of the understanding constitute the perceptually given material world as the concept of nature, so the a priori categories of the intellect constitute the events that are objects of immediate experience as the concept of history (Gassen and Landmann, 1958, p. 9; Wolff, 1974, pp. 35-36).

In the autobiographical sketch, Simmel explains how this distinction between form—the a priori categories of the mind—and content or process—the raw material of events, actions, and

3

experiences—became the fundamental methodological principle of his work, the basic assumption on which his idea of reciprocity and his concepts of truth, value, and objectivity were grounded.

Both his contemporaries and later intellectual historians have sometimes represented Simmel as a neo-Kantian thinker. However, as one acute commentator has noted, the neo-Kantian thought of this period took an extraordinarily complex and sublimated turn in the work of Simmel (Oesterreich, 1923, p. 467). In fact, Simmel's relationship to Kant is complicated and ambiguous. On the one hand, the elements of Kant's epistemology are among the presuppositions on which Simmel's own philosophy and methodology rest. On the other hand, Simmel was inclined, especially in his later works, to reject some of Kant's basic premises. However he did not explicitly repudiate the Kantian problematic of his own conceptual framework. The ambivalence of Simmel's attitude toward Kant is nicely illustrated in a letter to Count Hermann Keyserling, dated October 31, 1908. Simmel mentions his preoccupation with epistemological and metaphysical problems. However he suspects that there is a sense in which we remain limited by an epistemology that is grounded on Kantian foundations. "What did this man not inflict upon the world when he explained it as an idea! When will the genius appear who will emancipate us from the spell of the subject in the same way that Kant liberated us from the constraint of the object? And what will this third category be?" (Simmel, 1968a, p. 239).

In his published lectures on Kant—*Kant: Sixteen Lectures Delivered at Berlin University*—Simmel attempts to elucidate the basic strategy that Kant employs in the *Critique of Pure Reason*. According to Simmel, Kant begins by establishing that any empiricist theory of knowledge must be unsatisfactory. Knowledge of nature or scientific knowledge is not possible on the grounds that the empiricists think: it is not a copy or a reproduction of perceptions or sense impressions. If experience does not provide an adequate foundation or criterion for knowledge then the following question, the main issue of Kant's first critique, obviously arises: under what conditions is knowledge of nature possible? Kant attempts to answer this question by means of an epistemological critique, an inquiry into the presuppositions of knowledge. In order to resolve the main problem of the first critique, Kant poses the question: on what presuppositions does knowledge of nature rest? What are the a priori conditions for the possibility of knowledge of nature? Kant's answer to this question considers the experience on which knowledge of nature is grounded. It is only possible as a form that is constituted by the fundamental categories or a prioris of the human intellect. It follows that the structure of the intellect establishes the conditions for the possibility of experience and all knowledge based on experience.

In the third lecture of the Kant volume, Simmel scrutinizes the fundamental assumption of Kant's theory of knowledge. According to this assumption, the categories of the human mind are logically prior to all experience. They function as presuppositions on which experience rests. Therefore they constitute the ultimate epistemological foundation on which knowledge of nature is grounded. Simmel notes that Kant's seminal insight is so simple and obvious that its relatively late appearance in the history of philosophy is astonishing. Kant himself restricted his original insight to the domain of the natural sciences. However Simmel claims that the potential fertility of this idea is not exhausted in the philosophy of Kant. He suggests that we also examine the a priori presuppositions of the entire psychological and historical world. This examination, he believes, will establish the following conclusion: in the same sense that the facts of the natural sciences are not pure sense impressions, so historical facts are not reproductions of immediate experience. Like the natural sciences, the historical sciences are also grounded on constitutive forms. These forms structure the brute data of reality by means of a variety of categories: affective, intellectual, political, psychological, and moral. The constitutive function of these categories is the indispensable condition under which the raw material of historical existence can be structured in a meaningful and intelligible fashion. The same point also holds for our understanding of law, art, psychology, religion, and the entire domain of culture: the world of culture is a possible object of experience and knowledge only insofar as it is constituted by the forms of the mind.

The Kantian turn of Simmel's thought is unmistakable in the second edition of *The Problems of the Philosophy of History*. Simmel himself repeatedly stresses the intimate relationship between this essay as a critique of historical reason and Kant's *Critique of Pure Reason*. In his philosophy of history, Simmel attempts to refute an empiricist theory of historical knowledge which he calls historical realism, naturalism, or empiricism. His method is to employ the same strategy that Kant used to refute the empiricism of Locke and Hume. Historical knowledge is not possible on the grounds that the historical empiricist supposes: it is not a reproduction of the event as it actually happened. If historical realism fails to provide a foundation for historical knowledge, then what follows? The main problem of Simmel's book, a Kantian question: under what conditions is historical knowledge possible? In other words, Simmel believes that the principal issue of his critique of historical reason, like the main question of the *Critique of Pure Reason,* also has its source in the refutation of empiricism.

Simmel also thinks that the inquiry in which he attempts to answer this question can be described as Kantian. He claims that it is necessary to emancipate the mind from history in the same way that Kant freed it from nature. How did Kant achieve the emancipation from nature? By means of an epistemological critique. Perhaps, Simmel suggests, the same epistemological critique will also succeed within the domain of the theory of historical knowledge. In other words, Simmel proposes to deal with the main issue of his essay by posing the problem: what are the presuppositions of historical knowledge? If historical knowledge is possible, on what grounds must it be based? Or, as Simmel also formulates the question, what are the a priori conditions for the possibility of history? How does the mere event become history?

As Simmel sees it, the import of his answer to this question also qualifies as an extension of the work of Kant. Man conceived as a datum or an object of a theoretical discipline may be produced by the causal forces of both nature and history. But suppose that man is conceived as "the congitive subject": the investigator who raises questions about nature and history, the scientist and the historian. From this perspective, man "produces both nature and history" (Simmel, 1977, p. ix). History, Simmel argues, is possible only as a form of experience and knowledge. The definitive properties of this form are products of the categories or a prioris of the human mind. These categories are among the conditions for the possibility of history. It follows that there are a priori presuppositions which state the conditions under which it is possible to experience reality historically and think historically. These presuppositions define the sense in which historical experience and knowledge are possible, and they determine the limits of history as a form of experience and knowledge.

Simmel, therefore, conceives *The Problems of the Philosophy of History* as an attempt to extend the Kantian concept of form as an a priori presupposition of experience and knowledge in order to consider a question that Kant himself did not pose. However Simmel claims that in the first edition of the book, this basic problematic—the refutation of historical realism and the defense of the proposition that he calls epistemological idealism, the thesis that historical inquiry is grounded on a priori categories—was not yet clear to him. In the second edition, Simmel represents the fundamental issue of the philosophy of history as the question: how does the mere event or phenomenon become constituted as an historical fact, an object of historical experience and knowledge? In the first edition, this problem only arises in a diffuse and implicit fashion. In order to eliminate this defect and present his views on the philosophy of history in a more articulate and coherent fashion, Simmel prepared a second edition in 1904. Between 1892 and 1904, the idea of history as a constitutive category had become a theme of major importance in Simmel's thinking. For this reason, he conceived this second edition as an essentially new book (Simmel, 1977, p. ix). This shift in the basic purpose of the book was a consequence of Simmel's insight that not only the natural sciences, but also the historical or sociocultural sciences are products of the immanent principles of the intellect.[1]

In 1907, Simmel reprinted the second edition of *The Problems of the Philosophy of History,* adding only a few notes which were intended to clarify the basic problematic of the book. However Simmel's thinking on the philosophy of history continued to change. For this reason, he made plans as early as 1913 to produce a fourth edition, which would again qualify as an entirely new book.[2] In a letter of Christmas and New Year greetings to Heinrich Rickert dated December 26, 1916, Simmel describes his plans.

I am working on the fourth edition of my philosophy of history. However this will not be a new edition, but rather a completely different book, with a different title also. In the course of the years, my views and attitudes on these problems have completely altered. They have become much more radical and atrociously complicated. In consequence, I have no idea at all when this work will be completed, especially since the hours which make complete concentration possible are relatively infrequent these days[3] (Gassen and Landmann, 1958, pp. 116-117).

This book was never written. In the spring of 1918, Simmel discovered that he had terminal and inoperable liver cancer. At that point, he suspended his research on the philosophy of history and also gave up plans to complete ambitious works on individuality and freedom, the sociology of art, and aesthetics. Simmel spent the final months of his life completing his last book on metaphysics, the *Lebensanschauung*. However three essays which constitute preliminary studies for the new book on the philosophy of history were completed and are translated in this volume: "The Problem of Historical Time" (1916), "The Constitutive Concepts of History" (1917-1918), and "On the Nature of Historical Understanding" (1918). These essays provide a more comprehensive and detailed analysis of three doctrines which are only sketched in *The Problems of the Philosophy of History*, doctrines which state the definitive theses of Simmel's philosophy of history: (1) the theory of the categories or a prioris that constitute history as a form of experience and knowledge; (2) the theory of the extratheoretical interests of historical knowledge that define the threshold of historical consciousness; and (3) the theory of interpretation that provides a hermeneutic on which historical knowledge is grounded. Also included is a translation of Simmel's brief essay "On the History of Philosophy" (1904). In this paper, Simmel applies the main doctrines of his philosophy of history to the problem of understanding a specific province of historical phenomena: the history of philosophy.[4]

THE THEORY OF FORMS[5]

All of the work for which Simmel is remembered is based on the assumption that the world as a whole and specific aspects of it become possible objects of experience and knowledge only if they are constituted by some form or forms. Therefore it would not be an exaggeration to describe the concept of form as Simmel's fundamental methodological instrument. The immense range of problems and themes that Simmel introduces into his lectures, papers, and books reduced many of his contemporaries to bewilderment and sometimes created doubts about the authentic value of his contributions. This is hardly surprising. Simmel's contemporaries were the heirs of the most creative era in the history of German academic sociocultural science. A generation of dazzling innovation—the period of Wilhelm von Humboldt, Hegel, Niebuhr, and Ranke—was followed by a generation of scholarly demigods—the period of Mommsen, Burckhardt, Treitschke, and Dilthey. It is not astonishing that many of their successors within Simmel's generation acquired the retrospective and wistful gaze of epigones whose creative energies seemed to be exhausted, the perspective of mannerists cursed by a fate of increasingly sterile specialization and purely technical virtuosity. An academician of the Wilhelminian period who attempted to transcend the boundaries of a conventional academic discipline inevitably exposed himself to the damning charges of dilettantism and sensationalism. Throughout his career, Simmel worked in a variety of disciplines and became famous for the scope of his research interests. Some of his major books deal with problems in moral philosophy, Kant scholarship, sociological theory, the sociology of modernity, metaphysics, aesthetics, and the philosophy of history. He also did work that simply defies classification within the terms of conventional academic discourse. His books on Kant and Goethe (1906), Schopenhauer and Nietzsche (1907), Goethe (1913), and Rembrandt (1916) seem to create a new intellectual genre or style of thought: the metaphysical biography, which explores the unique individuality of a specific mode of existence and its expression in a particular person. Although the heterogeneous and kaleidoscopic impression created by an initial acquaintance with Simmel's writings is undeniable, an analysis of his concept of form will reveal order in the apparent chaos of his writings and establish that the seemingly incoherent fragments are intimately related. Put another way, it can be shown that all of Simmel's mature works are produced by the use of this same basic concept. However it is also difficult to resist the conclusion that this fundamental concept remains obscure. Simmel's own remarks on his idea of form are metaphorical and illustrative rather than analytical. Form is perhaps the most problematical component of Simmel's entire conceptual apparatus: opaque and elusive, but also essential and axiomatic.

Simmel describes the dichotomy of form and content or structure and process as an irresistible necessity of thought. A form, Simmel claims, may be conceived as a category or a collection of categories. He also describes forms as languages into which the world or aspects of it may be translated. These languages may be conceived as general schemata which constitute conditions for the intelligibility of the world as a whole or specific aspects of it. Reality—the raw material of the cosmos—is a qualitatively and quantitatively infinite manifold of indistinguishable phenomena. Reality as such is unintelligible because of its status as a continuous and homogeneous process. Aspects of reality can be grasped as possible objects of experience and knowledge only if they fall under some constitutive form. It follows that a form may be represented as a taxonomy, a system of classification, or a conceptual scheme that performs an epistemological function: it defines the conditions under which the world can be experienced and represented in a certain way, the conditions under which it can become the object of a certain kind of experience and knowledge. A form, therefore, identifies the conditions under which a certain kind of cognitive status can be ascribed to a given item. Science, for example, is a form because its presuppositions state conditions under which it is possible to conceive any phenomenon as an object of scientific knowledge. History is a form for the same reason: a phenomenon can be represented as an object of historical knowledge only if it is comprehended by the constitutive categories of history. The same point also holds for art, religion, death, and eroticism: they are forms in the sense that they specify conditions under which it is possible to have a certain kind of experience and acquire a certain kind of knowledge. Form, therefore, is an epistemological category.

As Simmel employs it, the concept of form is systematically ambiguous. It has at least three referents: the constitutive category itself; the constitutive activity or the process of constitution whereby forms are created; and the products of this constitutive activity, the world as represented from the perspective of a certain formative category. History, for example, is a form in each of these three senses. "History" may designate the categories by reference to which the world is experienced as an object of historical knowledge. It may refer to the activity of historical constitution itself. Or it may refer to the world of historical phenomena that is formed by the a prioris of history.

According to Simmel, the categories, criteria, and principles that define any form are distinctive properties of the form itself.

They cannot be derived from reality as such. Put another way, they cannot be deduced from any description of the process or the concents on which the form is imposed. This essential property of forms may be described as their immanence or autonomy. Any form, Simmel claims, is governed by "its own immanent and objective logic." Every form has "a self-sufficient and autonomous existence" (Simmel, 1922a, pp. 29-30). Commenting on the forms generated by aesthetic, intellectual, practical, or religious activity, Simmel observes that they may be conceived as empires or kingdoms each of which functions according to its own intrinsic laws. Each form has its own definitive modes and its own characteristic language. Each form produces a representation of the world that is unique to the form itself.

Simmel's most comprehensive account of the immanence of forms is contained in his work on the philosophy of history. In these writings, one of Simmel's major purposes is to establish that the properties of history as a form cannot be derived from reality, life, or experience. The states and contents of life are fluid, homogeneous, and inextricably interrelated. Historical knowledge is possible only if this manifold is structured in such a way that specific aspects within it can be discriminated. The manifold of life is structured into distinguishable aspects, such as science, art, and religion. Phases of these aspects are discriminated, such as the Renaissance, the Scientific Revolution, and the Reformation. Periods of growth and progress, inactivity and stagnation, genius and decadence are discriminated within the life of a single individual. Simmel claims that these discriminations are superimposed upon life. They have their source in "values and concepts that do not lie within life itself." Nor can they be identified "within the natural rhythm of life."

Put another way, these concepts are formed when we represent life—including our own lives—from the perspective of history, when life is conceived in terms of the a priori of historical form (Simmel, 1967, p. 204).

According to Simmel, history as a form necessarily abrogates or suspends the definitive qualities of the process of life itself. Simmel bases this claim on two considerations. First, history synthesizes discontinuous, fragmentary, and discrete data into continuous wholes. Consider, for example, the period of European music which extends from the early compositions of Karl Maria von Weber to the symphonies of Mahler and the operas and tone poems of Richard Strauss. Musicologists have identified this massive outburst of musical creativity—which includes the compositions of Berlioz, Wagner, Chopin, Schumann, Liszt, and Brahms—as "the romantic period." In Simmel's view, however, the continuity of this synthesis cannot be derived from reality, the specific compositions that constitute European music from Weber through Richard Strauss. On the contrary, the continuity of the synthesis is an exclusive property of the historical construct itself. Second, history also fractures "the real continuity which subsists within any given temporal process." Consider distinctions such as classical and romantic, Gothic and Renaissance, revolution and reaction. "These distinctions," Simmel claims, "destroy the smooth transitions of life itself"(Simmel, 1967, p. 204). The destruction of the continuity of life and the introduction of distinctions which make reality intelligible, therefore, are a consequence of the immanent requirements of history as a form.[6]

Therefore we are obliged to conclude that the properties of forms are immanent in the sense that they cannot be derived from any description of the contents on which these forms are imposed. However Simmel's remarks concerning this property of forms occasionally betray a curious uncertainty or equivocality. Sometimes his comments on specific forms imply that the relationship between the categories of a form and the raw material of reality is more intimate than the foregoing paragraphs suggest. In his essay on "The Adventure," for example, Simmel analyzes adventure as a form of life and claims that life as a whole can be constituted as an adventure. Although it is in principle possible for any experience to become an adventure, Simmel indicates that certain events—erotic experiences, for example—are more accessible to this form other than phenomena.[7] Simmel makes the same point about fashion in his essay on "Fashion." Although it may seem that any mode can become fashionable, this is actually not the case. Certain modes—Simmel mentions the unusual, the odd, and the extreme—"show a special disposition to live themselves out in fashion." Other phenomena, however—he mentions the classic—resist this form (Simmel, 1971, p. 321). Simmel suggests that in this respect, art is comparable to fashion. "The forms of art," Simmel argues, "bear a closer relation to some facts than they do to others" (Simmel, 1971, p. 320). Although certain objects assume the form of art "without apparent effort," others "avoid all transformation into the given forms of art" (Simmel, 1971, p. 320). Simmel makes the same claim about the relationship between history as a form and its subject matter. History encounters its data "as a kind of half-formed or proto-product." The raw material of history is "already constituted by a priori forms of comprehension. The categories which constitute this material are already present in the material itself, at least in an embryonic or modified form" (Simmel, 1977, p. 62).

Are the categories of any form immanent and autonomous? Or is there some extremely intimate relationship between a form and the raw material that it constitutes? Or is there some sense in which these alternatives are not mutually exclusive? In other words, is there a sense in which a close relationship can be established between the immanent and autonomous categories of a form and the material that they structure? This third possibility seems to represent Simmel's position. Although the categories of a form do not reproduce the properties of real life nor can they be deduced or derived from life, forms themselves are created by the incessant energies of life. In the *Lebensanschauung,* life and form are described as "the ultimate constitutive principles of the world" (Simmel, 1922a, p. 16). Simmel makes the same claim in his book on Rembrandt: life and form are the "ultimate" or "final categories of a weltanschauung" (Simmel, 1919, p. 67). In his book on Schopenhauer and Nietzsche, Simmel offers a number of comments on Nietzsche's "completely novel concept of life," a concept which represents "the literary and philosophical reification of Darwin's idea of evolution" (Simmel, 1923, p. 4). Three of Simmel's comments in this context may also be applied to his own concept of human life.

First, life as a homogeneous and undifferentiated process remains inaccessible to analysis. Life as such is not a possible object of experience or knowledge. This is why forms are necessary conditions for the intelligibility of life. Second, the manifold of life is in a state of perpetual flux. It is constantly creating, increasing, and intensifying its own potentialities and energies. Simmel sometimes describes this definitive feature of life by claiming that life is essentially "more-life." Life has the disposition to renew or reproduce itself by creating new poten-tialities and forces. Third, life not only exhibits the tendency to renew itself by producing more life; it also has the capacity to transcend itself by creating new entities that are "more-than-life." In what sense are the entities produced by life "more-than-life"? According to Simmel, these entities have properties which are distinguishable from life conceived either as an undifferentiated manifold of potentialities or as the disposition to regenerate its own energies. They become detached from the rhythm and flux of life. In consequence, they acquire stable properties which become juxtaposed to the constantly changing process of life. This is why Simmel represents these entities as being more than life itself. Although they are products of life, they develop characteristics that are independent of life. In order to articulate both of these properties of forms—their ultimate source in the energies of life and their eventual emancipation from these energies—Simmel calls forms "objectifications" of life.

Simmel provides many illustrations of the manner in which life as undifferentiated process and more-life creates forms which are more-than-life. In perpetually renewing itself, life also creates a new generation of human beings. This aspect of life is manifested in the forces of attraction between the sexes, energies that create forms of eroticism in which human sexual desires are expressed. When they begin to function more autonomously, these forms of eroticism may be transformed into forms of love—Christian and platonic love, as well as the modern sentimental or romantic mode of love. These forms of love can become completely detached from the original erotic energies of life that produced them. The same holds true for science. Consider the autonomy and sovereignty of its methods and norms. Ultimately, these methods and norms have their source in the practical needs of everyday life. The exigencies of life generate a proto-form of knowledge on which the capacity to adapt to the environment of life is dependent. The forms of science, therefore, are originally created by the requirements of life itself. The proto-forms of utilitarian knowledge are transformed into the forms of science when knowledge becomes independent of the needs of life and begins to function according to its own intrinsic norms. In its continual flux, life also creates feelings and modes of conduct to which a religious status can be ascribed. In this context, Simmel identifies the feeling of love, our emotional response to nature, and our sense of community with other human beings as proto-forms of religion. Religion does not have its source in an independent transcendental domain that lies beyond life. On the contrary, religion as an autonomous form is a consequence of the incipient religiosity implicated in the contents of life itself. According to Simmel, this property of the forms of love, science, and religion can be ascribed to every form: the origin of all forms may be traced to the energies of life and its disposition to recreate itself.

Economics and painting, sexuality and marriage, prostitution and the drama, flirtation and the bourgeois household, Simmel tells us, are all forms. However law, society, morality, history, art, science, religion, and love are also forms. The same holds for reality, knowledge, existence, and value. If prostitution, morality, and value are all forms, if history, science, and knowledge are forms, then there must be relationships of logical dependence among forms. In other words, there are forms which have the following property: a content can be constituted by this form only if it is already constituted by some other form. An item can fall within the conceptual scheme of history, for example, only if it falls unders the form of knowledge. It follows that a certain aspect of reality as constituted by one form may have the status of "raw material" or "brute fact" from the perspective of another form. Language, for example, is the raw material of literature. From the perspective of history as a form, the world as structured by the forms of meaning and existence is a collection of mere data.

As these remarks suggest, Simmel believes that the world is constituted by a multiplicity of forms. The same content may be embraced by many different forms, and the same form may be realized in many different contents. In *Schopenhauer and Nietzsche,* Simmel speculates that multiplicity or diversity may be the genuinely definitive human characteristic. The immense variety of human energies and potentialities is mirrored in the multiplicity of images or objects that man produces. Because man is a "heterogeneous being," his relationship to the world is mediated by a plurality of conceptions, perspectives, and conceptual schemes. Any given aspect of the world appears in more than one sequence of interests and concepts, images and meanings. Because man is constituted by a plurality of perspectives, it follows that the same homogeneous manifold is constituted by a plurality of forms. Therefore any given phenomenon may be not only an object of desire, but also of theoretical knowledge, aesthetic evaluation, and religious significance (Simmel, 1923, p. 14). Simmel considers the color blue as an example of a phenomenon that may be constituted by a variety of forms. In optics, blue is a wave length. In lyric poetry, it symbolizes a mood of depression.

In religious symbolism, it represents the kingdom of heaven. In the first chapter of his *Soziologie,* Simmel argues that in the same way that matter may be represented in the most diverse spatial forms imaginable, so the same interests may be constituted by entirely different social forms. Economic interests, for example, may be realized either through competition among producers or through a planned organization of producers. The same religious interests may be embodied in a relatively free and diversified community or in an authoritarian and centralized form of religious organization. According to Simmel, every aspect of reality exhibits this same property: it can be comprehended by a variety of forms.

The world, therefore, is constituted by a multiplicity of forms. According to Simmel, these forms are radically different from one another in the sense that no form can be reduced to any other form. Forms are not only immanent in the sense that the categories of a given form cannot be derived from a description of the contents on which this form is imposed; this thesis is a basic premise of Simmel's critique of the empiricist or positivist tendencies of modern thought. In addition, forms are also immanent in the sense that the categories of a given form cannot be derived from the categories of any other form; this thesis is a basic premise of Simmel's critique of the reductionist tendencies of modern thought, tendencies exhibited in the doctrines of mechanism, biologism, psychologism, historicism, and sociologism. In his essay on "The Philosophy of Landscape," Simmel makes a contemptuous reference to the "banality of the view of the Enlightenment" and its disposition to reduce ideal provinces of value to base instincts and motive forces of life. On this reductionist view which Simmel criticizes, religion is derived from fear, hope, and ignorance; knowledge is derived from the contingencies which serve the needs of perception; and art is derived from an imitative drive or a play instinct. Simmel represents this view as a foolish oversimplification and claims that each of these provinces represents an autonomous and irreducible source of the energies of life. Sometimes he calls them "Ur-phenomena": they are among the original and irreducibly different energies of life. Since these energies generate the forms of religion, knowledge, and art, it also follows that these forms cannot be reduced to more basic or elementary forms.

Simmel claims that there are certain forms which can comprehend "the entire infinity of logically possible contents" in such a way that a single integrated world or universe is produced (Simmel, 1922a, p. 29). As examples of such *Weltformen*—universal or cosmic forms—Simmel mentions art, knowledge, value, and meaning. The different worlds that are constituted by these cosmic forms "all lie on the same ontological plane." In other words, they are ontologically autonomous and irreducible. None of these forms is more or less relative, contingent, or subjective than any other. It follows that no form—including the "real world" of practical, everyday, quotidian existence—has a privileged ontological status (Simmel, 1922a, p. 34). Simmel claims that it is logically possible for any phenomenon to become an object of knowledge, art, or religion. The worlds constituted by these forms are juxtaposed and isolated from one another. Although Simmel acknowledges the possibility of "borderline uncertainties in specific cases"—cases in which there may be legitimate doubt whether a given content is embraced by a given form—there is no possibility of intersection or overlap between these worlds. This is because each of these forms "expresses the totality of the raw material of the cosmos in its own special language" (Simmel, 1922a, p. 29).

Since forms create autonomous and irreducibly heterogeneous worlds, it is not surprising to learn that no form is exhaustive. No conceptual scheme can provide a complete classification of reality. The language of every form is incomplete. Why is this the case? Simmel's discussion of this issue is always provocative and illuminating. In the final analysis, however, it remains inconclusive. Convenient access to this problem is provided by his brief essay "On Aesthetic Quantities." Attacking the theory of aesthetic realism which conceives art as an image or reproduction of reality, Simmel defends the thesis that art cannot represent all contents. Why is art as a form incomplete? This is a consequence of historical variations in art and artistic media. Because of these variations, "art must have different relations to objective being" at different points in history (Simmel, 1968c, p. 81). Because of the variability of all artistic activity and every object of art, it follows that there are contents that cannot be embraced by the form of art as it is constituted at a given stage of history.

Simmel introduces a number of variations on this argument. In the *Lebensanschauung*, he claims that there is no art as such. Only historical forms of art exist: "art as conditioned by its techniques, its possibilities of expression, and the peculiarities of its style."

According to Simmel, it is obvious that art in this historical sense cannot comprehend the entire universe of possible contents. The belief that this is possible—the fundamental assumption of aesthetic naturalism—is a species of "artistic megalomania." The methods of Giotto or Botticelli cannot encompass the impressionistic style in which Degas's ballerinas are represented (Simmel, 1922a, p. 32). Simmel presents the same argument in *The Main Problems of Philosophy*. Arguing in opposition to the Kantian view of the timelessness of a priori categories, Simmel claims that forms are subject to historical variations and transformations. Consider, he suggests, conceptual schemes and criteria for observation and the classification of observations; the translation of perceptual data into the constructs of the natural sciences or the human sciences; or criteria for truth and falsity. In other words, consider all the forms in which the world and its aspects become objects of knowledge. Simmel claims that all of these forms have evolved in the course of intellectual history, a process that will undoubtedly continue (Wolff, 1969, pp. 289–90). Because of this perpetual process of variation and transformation, the constitution of reality within the limits of any given form is incomplete, fragmentary, and impermanent. Recalling Fichte's remark that the kind of philosophy one has depends upon the kind of man he is, Simmel claims that the same point holds much more generally. "The kind of knowledge that humanity has at any given moment is dependent upon what humanity is in this moment" (Wolff, 1959, pp. 289-90).

Should we infer that although forms are incomplete for what could be called contingent historical or sociological reasons, the completeness of forms is a logical possibility? On occasion, Simmel takes—or appears to take—this view. "In principle," Simmel claims, "every form can embrace the totality of existence" (Wolff, 1959, p. 289). Given the import of the concept of form, each important or comprehensive form—in this context he mentions science, art, religion, sensuality, meaning, and value as examples of such forms—can comprehend every existing phenomenon.[8]

Although it is in principle possible for each of these forms "to translate the entire world into its language," in fact this ideal state of completeness is never actually realized. This is because forms never function "in abstract purity and absolute exhaustiveness" (Wolff, 1959, p. 289). On the contrary, they only function within the limits defined by the specific historical disposition of intellectual forces. At this point, Simmel repeats the above argument which establishes that any historical instance of art is inevitably incomplete. It follows that any historically given form of art "can only embrace *specific* contents." Other contents resist inclusion within this form, "even though, *in principle,* it is possible for them to be constituted as contents of art" (Wolff, 1959, p. 289). Simmel claims that this is a property of all forms: each form is based on an ideal claim that the totality of contents can be structured within a complete and comprehensive world. It is legitimate to characterize reality, knowledge, art, and religion as "worlds" or "universes" precisely because it is logically possible for these forms to comprehend the totality of the raw material of the cosmos. In fact, however, this ideal claim can only be realized within the limits of specific historical conditions.

Therefore Simmel's position on the completeness of forms seems to be the following: the exhaustiveness of forms is a logical or conceptual possibility, but—due to historical variations and sociological transformations—an empirical or contingent impossibility. Forms conceived as constitutive categories are exhaustive in principle. Forms conceived as formed contents—the historical structures in which these categories are embodied or realized—are not. This position could also be articulated in the following way. The exhaustiveness of forms is logically possible in the sense that a statement of the conditions specified by the a priori categories of any given form does not entail that any given content fails to satisfy these conditions. The exhaustiveness of forms is empirically impossible in the sense that a description of the conditions which are satisfied by the empirically existing contents that are formed in a certain way—for example, the art or the science of a specific historical period—entails that some aspects of reality fail to satisfy these conditions.

Although this solution to the problem of the completeness of forms is logically satisfying, it is otherwise objectionable. Most important, it is apparently inconsistent with the import of Simmel's concept of form. Simmel claims that the categories which constitute a form necessarily establish some distinction. They imply criteria for distinguishing contents that fall under this form from contents which do not. Therefore incompleteness seems to be a logically necessary property of forms, an essential component of the concept of form itself. This conclusion is obviously inconsistent with Simmel's remarks concerning the logical possibility of the completeness of forms. However Simmel apparently commits himself to this conclusion in several different essays. Recall that in the essay on "The Adventure" he claims that certain experiences are more accessible to this form than others. And in the essay on "Fashion" he argues that not all modes are equally disposed to become fashion. Simmel even generalizes this point. "None of the forms by which the human mind masters the material of existence and adapts it to its purpose is so general and rational that all objects, indifferent as they are to their own structure, should uniformly conform to it" (Simmel, 1971, pp. 320-321). In the essay "On Aesthetic Quantities," Simmel defends precisely this position in some detail and with specific reference to the form of art.

It seems to follow that there are occasions on which Simmel argues that forms are logically complete and empirically incomplete and other occasions on which he argues that forms are both logically and empirically incomplete. Simmel's position on the exhaustiveness of forms, therefore, is typically Simmelian: provocative, ambivalent, and inconclusive. Should we conclude that the more limited forms of poetry and sociology are essentially incomplete and the higher forms of art and science are not? Or should we conclude that art and science are also essentially incomplete, although the still more universal forms of value and knowledge are not? Simmel—faithful to his wonted playful and elusive style—offers no instructions concerning what conclusions, if any, should be drawn. In any case, forms conceived as the historical structures of formed contents that actually exist are impermanent and incomplete. Perhaps—although Simmel's texts seem to be irredeemably ambivalent concerning this point— forms conceived as constitutive categories are also incomplete.

A further property of forms which is closely related to the properties of immanence and irreducibility is their incomparability or incommensurability. A religious commitment cannot be understood by employing the criteria that are appropriate to an experiment in chemistry. A piece of music cannot be judged according to the standards appropriate to a geometrical proof. Nor can an historical interpretation be appraised by employing the criteria for truth on which physical theories are grounded. Forms are incommensurable in the sense that criteria for truth, validity, adequacy, or appropriateness are relative: they are immanent properties of the form to which they apply, and they vary from one form to another. In addition, these criteria also vary from one problematic or collection of issues to another within the same form. Simmel claims that the criteria for the appraisal of a portrait are not the same as the criteria for the evaluation of a photograph. He also argues that criteria for truth in history vary from one branch of history to another. "If we are sufficiently careful about how the import of this remark should be understood," Simmel warns, "we can say that each history—each individual branch of historical science—has its own peculiar criterion for truth" (Simmel, 1977, p. 83). In order to support this claim, Simmel analyzes the logical properties of interpretation in various branches of history: philological history and the history of ethics, the history of technology and the internal political history of a nation, ecclesiastical history and the history of art. He tries to establish that each of these historical problematics is grounded on its own distinctive criterion for historical truth. Within each branch of history, Simmel claims, truth can be ascribed to "the propositions which satisfy *its own* immanent criteria for truth" (Simmel, 1977, p. 84).

Simmel's most complete and detailed account of the incommensurability of forms is presented in his various analyses of philosophy as a form and its relationship to other forms in the economy of intellectual life. From Simmel's perspective, a philosophy cannot be represented as a collection of doctrines and arguments. A philosophy is a form of life or a way of experiencing the world. The results of philosophical activity are not propositions that have truth value in some straightforward sense—such as the propositions which describe historical data or the results of a scientific experiment—or even in some very extended or metaphorical sense—such as the propositions which works of art are sometimes said to express. The results of philosophizing are not propositions at all. They are the attitudinal expressions of a typical kind of human being. The philosophy of Kant, for example, is not constituted by the theses and arguments contained in his books. It is the systematic response of a certain type of human being to the world, a response which is expressed in these books. In that case, the refutation of all the theses and arguments in Kant's books would not actually constitute a refutation of Kant's philosophy. Nor could it be represented as a critique of Kant's philosophy. According to Simmel, it does not even make sense to suppose that the expression of a form of life could be refuted. This would make no more sense than the attempt to refute an emotion, a moral commitment, or a desire. It follows that criteria for the evaluation of the products of philosophical activity—expressions of forms of life—are not comparable to criteria for the evaluation of the products of scientific research—empirically verifiable propositions.

Philosophy as an activity which expresses a certain view of the world, Simmel claims, is comparable to art. "If art is a world view as experienced by a certain temperament, then philosophy could be called the temperament expressed by a certain world view" (Wolff, 1959, p. 294). It obviously follows that there is a sense in which the products of philosophy and the arts are incommensurable with the conclusions of the sciences. Moreover Simmel claims that each philosophy contains its own immanent criteria for the adequacy of expression. In his writings, Simmel frequently returns to the consideration of philosophers who illustrate juxtaposed and incommensurable human types: Plato, Meister Eckhart, Spinoza, Kant, Schopenhauer, Marx, and Nietzsche. The products of any given species of philosophical activity, therefore, can only be judged by reference to its own immanent criteria for truth, adequacy, or appropriateness.

Metaphysical value and empirical truth value, philosophy and the sciences, and even individual philosophies are incommensurable. These views apparently entail a complete relativization of philosophy. The concept of truth seems to be eliminated from philosophy. Or perhaps philosophy as an inquiry is eliminated. According to Simmel, however, this is only appearance. In reality, philosophy replaces one criterion for truth—truth as correspondence between a proposition and its object—with another—truth as the coherence of expressions. If there is some sense in which it is appropriate to speak of criteria for truth in philosophy, then the criteria for truth on which philosophy is grounded are not comparable to the criteria for truth on which the other sciences and scholarly disciplines rest. In the latter domain, there is a sense in which true propositions correspond to the objective properties of the subject matter of these disciplines. However consider the conditions that define correspondence. In view of Simmel's theory of the relativity of criteria for truth, these conditions presumably vary, both from one science and discipline to another and also from one problematic to another within the same science or discipline. In philosophy, on the other hand, truth cannot be represented as correspondence in any sense. The issue of the adequacy or soundness of the claims made in philosophy is not germane to the question of the agreement between these claims and some object. On the contrary, this issue concerns the question of whether these claims function as "the adequate expression for the being of the philosopher himself and the type of humanity that he represents" (Wolff, 1959, p. 297). Simmel suggests that this conception of philosophy can be summed up in the idea that philosophical thought objectifies the personal and personifies the objective. In the claims that a philosopher makes, "a possible response of the spirit as a whole and as such to the world and life as a whole is expressed" (Simmel, 1921, p. 2). Suppose that such an expression is "immanently or intrinsically true, exhaustive, and convincing." In that case, the philosophical claim is of "timeless significance, regardless of whether it is confirmed or refuted as an objective claim about things" (Simmel, 1921, p. 2). It follows that there is a sense in which the claims of philosophy "lie beyond all proof" (Simmel, 1921, p. 125).

In view of this thesis, consider what is at stake in the choice between different philosophies. Presumably one should not speak of alternatives in this context. From Simmel's standpoint, different philosophies express different responses to the world. For this reason, they constitute different, but not necessarily alternative or mutually inconsistent intellectual commitments. It apparently follows that the choice between different philosophies is ultimately determined by the differences that distinguish types of human beings from one another.

In *Schopenhauer and Nietzsche,* Simmel illustrates his position that the choice between different philosophies is not a conclusion that can be validly deduced from premises, but rather a decision or a commitment that is existentially motivated. In a discussion of the relationship between Nietzsche's theory of value and an egalitarian or democratic theory, Simmel claims that proof and refutation are only possible in disputes in which common standards are acknowledged by both parties to the controversy. Under this condition, the agreement or lack of agreement with these standards could be recognized by both disputants as a conclusive method for resolving the dispute. In such a case, the controversy has a purely intellectual or theoretical nature: if there are common standards acknowledged by both parties, then in principle it is always possible to resolve such a controversy. Simmel claims that this is a consequence of the following consideration: given a determinate criterion for truth, it is always logically possible to decide whether a given proposition satisfies it. However the controversy between the Nietzschean theory of value and the democratic theory is more radical than this. The foregoing condition is not met: there is no mutually acknowledged standard to which both parties can appeal as an ultimate reason or conclusive ground. It follows that these two theories of value are not related as thesis and antithesis or argument and counter-argument. On the contrary, they represent two juxtaposed modes of being. A decision between them cannot be based on logical grounds. In a case of this sort, it is not possible to draw a conclusion since there are no jointly accepted premises from which a conclusion could be derived. In such a case, it is necessary to make a choice between the two positions. This choice is not grounded on the force of reasons, but rather upon rhetorical, psychological, and practical considerations (Simmel, 1923, p. 157).

Consider the claims in which philosophical responses to the world are expressed. From the perspective of the criteria for truth employed in the other sciences and scholarly disciplines, these claims may be conclusively refuted and discredited. However this does not necessarily affect their adequacy as philosophical expressions. Simmel asks that we consider the following intriguing possibility: a theory which is objectively false and conclusively refuted may constitute a more profound and perspicuous expression of a certain type of mind than a theory which is objectively true. Further, the source of its philosophical clarity and profundity may even be responsible for its objective or empirical defects. The mystical view of the world as embodied in the philosophy of Meister Eckhart is one of Simmel's favorite examples of such a philosophy. In view of these considerations, Simmel concludes that truth may not really be the proper concept to employ in interpreting and evaluating a philosophy.

Simmel attempts to articulate what is involved in this issue by introducing a distinction between truth value and what might be called existential value. The concept of truth is invariably grounded on some relationship of correspondence or agreement between a proposition and some object to which it is juxtaposed. In philosophy, however, it is the intrinsic or immanent character of the conceptual scheme itself that is decisive, the clarity, profundity, and authenticity of its expressions. It follows that the ultimate criterion for the adequacy of a philosophy is not the objective truth of its propositions, but rather the type of being that animates these propositions and is exhibited in them. Who really cares, Simmel asks rhetorically, whether Plato's theory of ideas or the pantheism of the Stoics and Spinoza is "correct," whether Nicholas of Cusa's conception of God as the convergence of contradictions or Fichte's theory of the ego really "corresponds to the facts," whether Schelling's doctrine of the identity of nature and mind or Schopenhauer's metaphysics of the will is really "true"? All of these doctrines have been repeatedly and conclusively "refuted." Nevertheless, the human types which express their response to existence in all of these "errors" have survived and continue to outlive these refutations. In other words, an existential value may be ascribed to these philosophical positions, a significance that is independent of the question of whether their assertion as propositions satisfies a correspondence criterion of truth. These considerations, according to Simmel, establish that philosophy cannot be evaluated by reference to the standards which apply to other intellectual enterprises (Wolff, 1959, pp. 198–199).[9]

Simmel's position on the immanent and incommensurable properties of philosophy as a form also applies to all other forms. Forms are not only autonomous and irreducibly different modes of experiencing and conceptualizing the world or specific aspects of it. Their criteria for truth or standards of adequacy are also peculiar to the form itself. It follows that the acts and artifacts that are constituted by one form cannot legitimately be appraised by reference to the criteria of another form. No form has a privileged ontological, epistemological, or logical status. In defending this position, Simmel's main interest is to dispute a thesis that he sometimes calls "intellectualism": the claim that there is some sense in which natural science is a preeminent or exhaustive form. Simmel holds that natural science does not occupy the status of a privileged form in relation to which all other forms are subordinate, inferior, or derivative. His view of the autonomy, irreducibility, and incommensurability of forms is nicely summarized in the following passage from his posthumously published journal.

One of the most pernicious aspects of intellectualism is that it regards "objections" to works of art, religions, metaphysical schemes, and so on as "refutations." Let us suppose that they even exhibit thousands of errors, defects, and contradictions. This fact alone does not necessarily have any bearing on their value. On the contrary, their value is based exclusively on the positive aspects of their significance. Why should these positive features not remain, in spite of these inadequacies? Only within the domain of theoretical claims does a valid objection or counterexample constitute a fatal blow. This is because it is only *theoretical* claims to which truth and falsity can be ascribed (Simmel, 1967, pp. 28–29).

If history is a form, then all of the definitive properties of forms may also be ascribed to history. (1) Like other forms, history may be represented as a language, a taxonomy, or a collection of categories. History is a conceptual scheme constituted by the a prioris of history. (2) The categories which constitute the form of history have an epistemological status. The a prioris of history are conditions for the possibility of representing the world historically. These a prioris function as logical conditions— "transcendental presuppositions," as Simmel sometimes puts it—for the possibility of historical experience and knowledge. (3) The form of history is immanent in the sense that the a prioris of history do not reproduce the properties of the homogeneous manifold of reality, nor can they be derived from any description of unformed reality. (4) Like other forms, however, history is a product of life. History is an artifact created by the process of life. As a form, it represents an objectification of the energies of life. (5) History is logically dependent upon other forms. A given content can fall under the form of history, for example, only if it is already comprehended by the forms of existence and meaning or significance. (6) The same homogeneous manifold of reality that is constituted within the form of history is also comprehended by other forms. The universe exhibits a plurality of forms which function as different perspectives from which the same raw material may be represented. (7) History is a distinctive form, irreducibly different from every other form. The a prioris of history, therefore, cannot be derived from the categories of some other form. (8) Since forms are products of life, they are affected by the incessant flux of life. It follows that forms are susceptible to variations and transformations. There are no timeless or eternal forms. Therefore Simmel's theory of history, which entails that history is a form, and his theory of forms, which entails that forms are variable, together imply the impermanence of history as a form. It would even make sense to ascribe an end—a final or conclusive state—to history. The ineluctable process of genesis, growth, maturity, decline, decay, and collapse in which all forms are implicated also affects history. A form is destroyed when the energies of life can no longer be contained within its limits. In this context, Simmel yields to a metaphor from fluid dynamics: the forces of life burst the antiquated and petrified forms that confine them. For this reason, the form of history will be destroyed when the energies of life can no longer be comprehended by its a prioris. (9) Like other forms, history is incomplete. Simmel develops two theses concerning the incompleteness of forms. According to the first, forms conceived as the structures of formed contents which actually exist are incomplete. This thesis ascribes empirical or contingent incompleteness to forms. According to the second, forms conceived as constitutive categories are incomplete. This thesis ascribes the property of logical or conceptual incompleteness to forms. Simmel is unambiguously committed to the empirical incompleteness of forms. However his views on logical incompleteness are ambivalent and perhaps ultimately inconclusive. History, therefore, is incomplete in the sense that its categories do not in fact comprehend all contents. History may also be incomplete in the sense that it is logically impossible for the a prioris of history to provide an exhaustive representation of reality. (10) Forms are incommensurable in the sense that the products of one form cannot legitimately be understood or evaluated by reference to the standards or criteria of another form. Simmel admits that history shares some of its properties with other forms—art, philosophy, and sociology, for example. In the final analysis, however, history, like every other form, is grounded on its own distinctive criteria for truth.

THE THEORY OF FORMS AND THE CONCEPT OF CULTURE

The import of Simmel's theory of forms may be clarified by considering how he employs this theory to develop an analysis of culture. As Simmel conceives it, culture is a form, and the world of cultural artifacts is a collection of forms. In *The Main Problems of Philosophy,* Simmel claims that the process of history develops a large number of entities which have a certain property that he finds intriguing: although they are products of intentional mental activities—"artifacts created by subjective psychological invention and energy"—they acquire "a definitive, objective, intellectual or spiritual existence" which transcends both the persons originally responsible for their creation and also the persons who subsequently recreate or interpret them (Simmel, 1911a, p. 71). As examples of these objectified mental entities, Simmel mentions the propositions of a legal system, moral precepts, tradition, language, religion, and the artifacts of the arts and the sciences. Neither the external forms on which these entities are dependent—spoken or written words, for example—nor the specific persons who are responsible for their creation can exhaust the import of these entities and their peculiar form of existence. In order to elucidate the definitive mode of the existence of objectified entities, Simmel considers the mind or spirit that is invested in a book. Since the reader can identify this spirit in the book, there is no doubt that the book contains it. But in what sense? On the one hand, it seems to be the spirit of the author himself, the expression of his mental processes. Since the author may no longer be alive, however, the book cannot contain his psychological processes. On the other hand, it seems that the reader is responsible for the spirit that is embodied in the book. But this alternative is not acceptable either, since the import that the reader manages to derive from a book is dependent upon the book itself. Simmel claims that the import that the reader comprehends is present in the book "in an objective form" (Simmel, 1911a, pp. 71-72). The fact that a given book has a specific objective import is not dependent upon how often it is read or understood. It is not even dependent upon whether it is read or understood at all. Simmel claims that this same form of existence can be ascribed to all of the entities that make up the history of culture. This is why he describes the structures of culture as embodiments of "objective spirit."

This category makes possible the dialectical transformation of the supermaterial into the material and the supersubjective into the subjective. It determines the entire historical development of mankind. This objective spirit makes it possible for the artifacts of the energies and activities of individuals to be preserved independent of each individual and every single production (Simmel, 1911a, p. 72).

The "dialectical transformation of the supermaterial into the material and the supersubjective into the subjective"? This is a characteristically Simmelian expression of the following idea. In the structures of culture, the contents of psychological processes—the "supermaterial"—are expressed in forms that are independent of the subjective or psychological conditions of their genesis. These same objective or "supersubjective" expressions are translated back into the domain of the subjective when the norms of culture are incorporated into the personal culture of specific individuals.

As Simmel understands it, the origin of culture is situated in the following condition: categories that are generated by the process of life and are created in order to sustain the energies of life acquire the status of autonomous structures which have their own intrinsic import and value. Although these categories have their ultimate source in the energies of life, they are transformed into objectified domains which acquire a relative independence from life. Paraphrasing Goethe's remark that everything which is perfect or complete in its own way transcends itself, Simmel claims that this is a definitive characteristic of life itself. As noted in the foregoing discussion of the theory of forms, creativity or the capacity to produce more-life is an essential quality of life. However self-transcendence is also one of its definitive properties. Life has the characteristic disposition to create entities that are more-than-life. "From its own material, life constitutes or creates forms or structures—cognitive as well as religious, artistic as well as social, technical as well as normative—which represent a surplus or excess of the actual life process and the instruments that perpetuate this process" (Simmel, 1967, p. 24).[10] These structures are the objective conditions for the possibility of culture: "objective" in the sense that their properties are independent of individual persons. Simmel devotes considerable attention to the relationship between the structures of culture and the personal life that originally created them. On the one hand, these structures may enrich and intensify the contents of life. On the other hand, they may become juxtaposed to life as ossified forms which petrify its creative energies. In this latter case, there is a sense in which these structures conflict with the process of life that created them: they stabilize, rigidify, and, ultimately, terminate the energies of life. Therefore an antagonistic relationship between personal life and culture can be identified. In the final analysis, however, these structures are produced by life and are comprehended within its limits.

It is the essential nature of life to transcend itself, to create from its own material what no longer qualifies as life, to creatively juxtapose the course of its development and its own inherent laws to the antithesis of life (Simmel, 1967, p. 24).

This process, which Simmel calls the self-transcendence of life, creates the superpsychological or trans-subjective structures that constitute the objective conditions for the possibility of culture. The development of culture, therefore, is a consequence of the relationship between life and form.

The distinction between life and form also provides the foundation for two other distinctions that are crucial to Simmel's analysis of culture: the distinction between cultural value and objective value and the distinction between subjective and objective culture. In the essay "On the Nature of Culture," Simmel claims that we have an unreflective habit of ascribing cultural value to the worlds generated by the forms of art, morality, and science. Although they may, in fact, qualify as cultural values, this is not a consequence of their "purely objective or immanent import" or their "autonomous and indigenous significance" (Simmel, 1957, p. 90). From the fact that a given objective value can be ascribed to a given item, it does not follow that it has a specific cultural value. Nor from the fact that it has a particular cultural value can it be inferred that this item also has a corresponding objective value. Although this sort of correspondence cannot be established between objective values and cultural values, Simmel does not argue that these two axiological domains are independent. On the contrary, his theory of culture entails that cultural value can be ascribed to an item only if it has some objective value. In other words, Simmel attempts to establish two theses: (i) there is a distinction between cultural value and objective value, and (ii) cultural value is dependent upon objective value.

In order to support these two theses, Simmel considers some examples which are intended to show how the cultural value and the objective value of different forms may vary. He suggests that we consider the norms and criteria which apply to an artwork insofar as it is conceived as an object of art history or aesthetics. They are quite different from the norms and criteria which apply to this same artifact insofar as its cultural value is at stake. From the perspective of aesthetics, an artifact has an immanent value that is a consequence of the a priori categories of this particular form. Culture, on the other hand, constitutes an autonomous form that cannot be reduced to the form of art. Since forms are not only irreducible but also incommensurable, it follows that the value ascribed to an artifact from the perspective of the a prioris of the form of culture does not necessarily correspond to the value ascribed to it from the perspective of aesthetics. The musicological value of Wagner's *Tristan and Isolde,* for example, can only be determined by reference to the categories that constitute music as a form. In order to establish its musical value, it would be important to describe the place of this opera in Wagner's theory of chromaticism and the crisis in classical harmonics and tonality that this theory produced in the early years of the twentieth century, a crisis which led to the development of theories of atonal music in the works of Schoenberg, Berg, and Webern. In principle, these considerations are irrelevant to the cultural value of the opera, which is determined by its contribution to the formation and development of the character of individuals (Simmel, 1957, p. 91; 1978, pp. 452–53). If the cultural value of an artifact is determined by its influence on the formation of character, it obviously follows that the cultural value of an artifact may vary considerably. For example, the extent of the cultural value of Wagner's music during the years 1860-1920 can be estimated by its profound effect on men as different as Nietzsche, Baudelaire, Zola, Mallarmé, Valéry, Proust, Cézanne, Renoir, Verlaine, Joyce, D. H. Lawrence, T. S. Eliot, Thomas Mann, and Hitler. Since that period, however, the cultural value of this music has waned considerably.

Simmel, therefore, makes the distinction between objective or immanent value and cultural value in the following way. Consider the value which can be ascribed to a given artifact from the perspective of the categories of a specific form; for example, the import of Newton's *Principia* from the perspective of natural science, the value of Monteverdi's madrigals from the perspective of music, the significance of Kant's first critique from the standpoint of philosophy. This is the objective value of the artifact, the value which can be ascribed to the artifact insofar as it is constituted by the categories of a certain form. On the other hand, consider the value which can be ascribed to a given item from the perspective of its contribution to the formation of the character of individual persons. This is the cultural value of the artifact, the value which can be ascribed to the artifact insofar as it has some role in constituting specific personalities.

It follows that there is no essential correspondence between objective and cultural value. The most sublime works of art, the most original scientific theories, and the most profound philosophical arguments may remain utterly inaccessible to the culture of individuals. In spite of their immense objective value from the perspective of the forms of art, science, and philosophy, their contribution to our total existence may remain inconsequential. On the other hand, an item which has an insignificant objective value may "produce exactly what our existence needs for the harmony of its components, for its mysterious unity, which transcends all of its specialized requirements and energies" (Simmel, 1957, p. 91). Presumably Simmel would ascribe this property to phenomena that fall within the domain of the popular: although their objective value may be negligible, they may have considerable cultural value because of the contribution they make to the development of the total personality of many individuals. In this context, the Goethean influence on Simmel's concept of culture—especially Goethe's theory of personality and culture as set out in the Wilhelm Meister novels—is unmistakable. Culture produces a synthesis of the contents of life. It is the point at which the subject—the individual personality as constituted by the energies and forces of life—and the object—the world as constituted by autonomous, irreducibly different, and incommensurable forms—intersect.

Given the distinction between cultural value and objective value, Simmel claims that it is also legitimate to distinguish two different senses of the concept of culture: subjective and objective culture. Simmel conceives objective culture as the domain of objects which function as instruments for the cultivation of the individual. It constitutes the path that the individual is obliged to take in order to acquire culture: the process of culture requires that he traverse the world of objectified forms. Simmel conceives subjective culture as the state of the individual personality that is the product of this process. Objective culture is constituted by the world of cultural forms and their products. Subjective culture is constituted by the life of the individual personality insofar as it represents a synthesis of these autonomous forms. Simmel comments on the properties of this synthesis in the essay "Feminine Culture." He claims that there is a sense in which subjective culture is the dominant aim of objective culture. The ultimate significance of culture lies in the consummation or perfection of individuals. This is possible only if the contents of objective spirit become autonomous. They must be emancipated both from the original creators of the form and also from the eventual consumer of its values. This process of emancipation and estrangement is essential if the contents of objective culture are to serve as instruments for the subjective culture of individuals. Subjective culture is differentiated from objective culture by posing the following question: to what extent and with what intensity do individuals appropriate the contents of objective culture? The definition and the limits of subjective culture are determined by the extent to which the life of the individual participates in these objective forms. It follows that subjective culture is impossible independent of objective culture. Put another way, the subjective culture of individuals presupposes the objective culture of the world of autonomous forms and their products. This is because a given state of the personality or a given phase in the development of the person qualifies as culture only to the extent to which it incorporates the products of objective culture. However the domain of objective culture cannot be completely independent of subjective culture. This is because the genesis of the forms of objective culture depends upon the creative energies of life. Nevertheless, objective culture can acquire a relative autonomy. According to Simmel, the process of the emancipation of objective culture transpires in the following way. Suppose that objects which formerly contributed to the subjective culture of individuals acquire new properties. And suppose that these objects can only be incorporated into the subjective culture of individuals in an incomplete and fragmentary fashion. Under these conditions, the products of objective culture become detached from the energies and interests of the individuals who originally created and appropriated them (Simmel, 1978, pp. 448–50, 453–62)

Because the energies of life are incessant, the interplay between the forces of life and the forms of culture is unceasing. Cultural change is the consequence of this interplay. There is one particular form of cultural change that provides the principal focus of Simmel's analysis of culture. He regards this process as the distinctive feature of the culture of the modern West. Simmel claims that with every advance in objective culture, the domain of objective value becomes increasingly complex, extensive, and inaccessible to the subjective culture of individuals. In this phase of culture, the domain of objective value expands, and the disposition to conceive all value as objective value becomes predominant. Under these conditions, the discrepancy between subjective and objective culture inevitably increases. The consummation and perfection of individuals is no longer regarded as the definitive aim of culture. On the contrary, it is represented as a culturally insignificant, private, subjective, and psychological epiphenomenon. Objective values no longer seem to have the status of mere instruments for the cultivation of individuals. On the contrary, individuals become instruments for the realization of objective value. Simmel's theory of forms entails that there is a profound contradiction between life and form. In his analysis of culture, the doctrines of the general theory of forms are applied to the domain of cultural forms. Therefore this same contradiction will also appear in the domain of culture. In the province of culture, the contradiction between life and form is exhibited as the conflict between subjective value and objective value, the antagonism between the subjective or private culture of the person and the objective or public culture of the artifacts that he creates, the tension between the energies that generate the process of culture and the forms in which this process is objectified. Simmel claims that the "revolutionary" struggle between the evolving flux of the process of life and the abstract rigidity of the cultural forms in which this process is structured is "the fundamental motive force of cultural change" (Simmel, 1922a, p. 17).

In a brief essay published in 1916, Simmel sketches the principal elements of a theory of cultural change. He suggests that we consider how the Marxist schema of economic development illuminates the phenomenon of cultural change. On this view, the economic forces in every historical period create a form of production and exchange which corresponds to them. However these same forces continue to develop within the limits of the forms they create. At some point, the inconsistency, antagonism, or conflict between the evolving forces of production and the rigid structures of the economy becomes intolerable. When the new forces of production can no longer be confined within the limits of these archaic forms, the old forms are shattered and new forms are created. Simmel notes that the valid implications of this schema extend far beyond the province of economics. The conflict between the energies of life and the structures in which they are expressed is inevitable and universal. Although Simmel notes that there are periods in which this conflict is latent—phases of apparent cultural harmony or equilibrium in which there seems to be a correspondence between life and form—the history of culture is constituted by the interaction and contradiction between the process of culture and the forms in which this process is structured. Simmel argues that this conflict has reached an unprecedented level in the present phase of culture. Both extensively and intensively, the contradiction between life and form has reached a hitherto unattained peak. The contemporary stage of this conflict is extensively unprecedented because more of the forms and energies of life are embraced by it than ever before. It is intensively unique because the antagonism between life and form within any given province of culture has become more uncompromising and radical than ever before. The thesis that the conflict between life and form in contemporary culture has reached novel proportions and developed to an unprecedented intensity leads Simmel to the conclusion that modern culture is gripped by a protracted crisis. Because this crisis is both inevitable and irresolvable, it is also tragic.

The theory of forms entails that life can only be expressed in forms. It follows that the process of culture can only be embodied in the forms of culture. However the theory of forms also entails that any form has its own peculiar import and autonomous structure. A form functions according to its own immanent logic and is governed by its own distinctive laws. Therefore it also follows that the forms of culture inevitably become detached from the energies of life that originally created them. The objective culture of artifacts becomes independent of the subjective culture of individuals. The energies of life create a product that can no longer be described as life. The forms of culture are more-than-life, artifacts of life in which its energies are congealed. As a result, the properties of these artifacts—the world of objective culture—become juxtaposed to the properties of life—the domain of subjective culture. Simmel, therefore, notes that the ultimate result of the process of culture is paradoxical: life can only be expressed in forms, however these forms have an intrinsic significance and an autonomous existence that remove them from the domain of life itself. This contradiction is the source of the tragedy of culture. Although culture is an inevitable product of life, the conflict between life and culture is also inevitable. In the development of culture, the contradiction between life and form is expressed in the objectification of culture and its estrangement from the culture of the individual. As Simmel analyzes it, objectification is constituted by two intimately related processes. Simmel neither names these processes nor clearly distinguishes them. For analytical purposes, however, it will be useful to distinguish reification and instrumentalization as the constitutive elements of objectification.[11]

In his 1909 essay on "The Future of our Culture," Simmel notes that pessimism as a prevalent response to contemporary culture is grounded in the perception of the widening abyss that separates the culture of things from the culture of persons. A bewildering variety of different kinds of devices and techniques, forms of knowledge and art, possible styles of life and sources of interest develop. As a result, extensive domains of the world of objective culture become incomprehensible to the individual. At this point, Simmel employs a comparison favored by German intellectuals ever since Winckelmann's pioneering work on Greek art: the relationship between the allegedly integrated and harmonious Greek culture of Classical Antiquity and the fragmented and incoherent culture of the modern West. Simmel claims that in the culture of Periclean Athens, politics and science, military strategy and the fine arts, and the entire universe of culture exhibited a coherent structure and a uniform style. In consequence, it could be incorporated into the subjective culture of every individual. Subjective and objective culture developed in a harmonious fashion, a harmony which has been shattered by the emancipation of objective culture. The process by which objective culture becomes independent of subjective culture is a result of the reification of forms and their emancipation from the subjective culture of the individual (Simmel, 1957, p. 95).

Simmel's theory of the reification of culture is a consequence of the theory of forms. Cultural forms become detached from the interests and energies of life. The world as constituted by the categories of a given form is subjected to a logic that is immanent to the form itself. For this reason, objective culture becomes detached from subjective culture. Moreover, there are intrinsic limits upon the development of the subjective culture of the individual, limits defined by the conditions for the integrity of his personality. However there are no intrinsic limits upon the development of objective culture. From the perspective of the individual, therefore, the world of objective culture begins to assume the appearance of a collosal domain of uncanny, threatening, and oppressive objects which he can neither appropriate nor dismiss. Simmel notes that the subjectivism, narcissism, and solipsism of the denizen of modern culture, his irrational capriciousness and serendipidity, can be interpreted as a response to the process of reification. It is an expression of despair which is based on the perception that it is impossible to incorporate the increasingly heterogeneous world of objective culture into the culture of his personal life (Simmel, 1957, p. 96).

The other aspect of the objectification of culture is intimately related to the process of reification. In the first chapter of his book of lectures on Schopenhauer and Nietzsche, Simmel notes that the evolution of culture produces a curious result: as man becomes more cultivated, his life becomes more oblique and opaque. This is because the relationship between his conduct and its purposes is mediated by an increasing number of instruments, tools, and techniques. Simmel claims that in simple cultures, the relationship between desire, means, and satisfaction is direct, uncomplex, and transparent. In advanced cultures, however, this relationship is no longer so straightforward and unproblematical. The middle link in this sequence proliferates and is reproduced. The use of one technique becomes dependent upon the use of another, which requires still another technique. The result is the instrumentalization of culture: the creation of an incomprehensible maze of techniques, mastery of which requires an apparently infinite chain-like sequence of actions. Simmel notes that there are many situations in which it is impossible for the denizen of modern culture to acquire a clear grasp of the ultimate stage of this sequence during every phase of his conduct. This is a consequence of two considerations. First, the dimensions of the entire sequence have become so vast and unmanageable that he can no longer acquire a perspicuous view of the sequence as a whole. Second, each new technique becomes so complex and demanding that its mastery requires specialization and the complete concentration of the energies of the individual. As a result, the modern consciousness becomes focused exclusively on techniques and instruments. The person becomes locked within a grid of projects, enterprises, and institutions for which he can identify no ultimate value or purpose. Purely utilitarian interests and activities which have no intrinsic significance are regarded as if they were definitive values. The result of this process can be described as the instrumentalization of values, or the axiological reification of objective culture. Put another way, intrinsic values disappear from culture, and instrumental values—items to which no intrinsic value can be ascribed—apparently take their place.

Simmel's favorite illustration of the instrumentalization of values and the axiological reification of intrinsically worthless techniques is the role of money in modern culture. Money is nothing more than an instrument of exchange and a means of standardizing values in such a way that they can all be compared by reference to the same standard. Independent of these purely instrumental functions, money has no value. However Simmel notes that in modern culture, money has acquired the status of an ultimate purpose. It is the process of economic development itself that makes this otherwise irrational dislocation of value comprehensible. If all cultural values acquire the status of commodities the value of which can be measured monetarily and if all commodities are in principle accessible at every time and place to every potential consumer, then the satisfaction of most human desires will depend exclusively upon whether the potential consumer of cultural values possesses the necessary money. From the perspective of the consciousness of modern culture, therefore, need or deficiency does not signify a lack of objects, but only a lack of money. As a result of this process, money, which was nothing more than an instrument for the standarization and exchange of values, acquires the status of the paradigmatic value: the value by reference to which the worth of every other product of culture is determined.[12]

Simmel describes the instrumentalization of values and the reification of cultural forms as self-contradictions of culture. They both rest on the same foundation: the increasing discrepancy between subjective and objective culture. The result of these two self-contradictions is the "typically problematical predicament of modern man: the feeling of being oppressed by an infinity of elements of culture because he can neither incorporate them into his own personal culture nor—because they are potential objects of his subjective culture—can he simply ignore or reject them" (Simmel, 1917, p. 47). The uneasy feeling that modern culture faces an impending crisis can be understood as a consequence of these two processes. The hectic pace of modern life, its sensuality and greed, the conflation of technological progress with cultural advancement, the fact that purely methodological criteria have acquired a privileged and quasi-sacred status in many intellectual disciplines and are regarded as more significant than substantive results, the fact that more importance is ascribed to money than to the things it can buy—all these phenomena are "symptoms of a diseased culture," a disease which reaches its crisis as a result of the extension and intensification of these two processes (Simmel, 1917, p. 48).

Simmel argues that the crisis of modern culture is an inevitable product of cultural development. Because this crisis is an inevitable consequence of the process of culture itself, culture is tragic. The processes of reification and instrumentalization, therefore, produce the tragedy of culture.[13] In what sense is culture tragic? What is the import of Simmel's theory of the tragedy of culture? Although Simmel never devoted an entire essay exclusively to the phenomenon of tragedy, many of his writings present a fragmentary analysis of tragedy and an interpretation of culture as tragic. In a passage from his posthumously published diary, Simmel considers the distinction between tragedy and pathos. Suppose that a shingle falls off the roof of a house and kills a young man who is full of hope and the will to live. This event is pathetic or sad, but it is not tragic. It would qualify as tragic only if there were some sense in which the young man's death is both a consequence of his nature and also antagonistic to it. The criterion of the tragic is situated in the scope and intensity of the tension which is exhibited in the following paradoxical relationship: the forces which destroy life are a necessary consequence of the fundamental nature of life itself. In the phenomenon of the tragic, there is a "profound harmony" between life and the forces that threaten to destroy it (Simmel, 1967, pp. 38–39).

In the posthumously published "Fragment on Love," Simmel remarks on the "overtone" of tragedy that hovers over every great lover and every great love. The tragedy of Romeo and Juliet, for example, is intimately related to the immeasurable depth and profundity of their love. An erotic relationship of these dimensions cannot be accommodated within the limits of the empirical world. However the relationship between Romeo and Juliet was a product of this world and remains inextricably emeshed in its

interests and conflicts—the family interests and conflicts of the
Montagues and the Capulets, for example. From the outset,
therefore, the relationship between Romeo and Juliet is implicated in a "fatal contradiction." Tragedy is not simply constituted
by the collision of juxtaposed energies or ideas, desires or
demands. On the contrary, the property of tragedy can be
ascribed to phenomena only when the following condition is
satisfied: the force that destroys life is created by the immanent
necessities of life itself. In the final analysis, therefore, the tragic
conflict between life and the world is an instance of self-
contradiction. According to Simmel, all cultural forms are involved in this conflict. In other words, culture is inherently tragic
because forms, which become juxtaposed to the energies and
interests of life, are necessary products of the process of life.[14] The
process of culture is tragic because the objectification of cultural
forms exhibits the two essential features of tragedy. On the one
hand, the objectification of forms is a consequence of the nature
of life. As an essential condition for the possibility of culture, it is
also a necessary condition for the realization of the creative
energies of life. On the other hand, the discrepancy between
subjective and objective culture which is the result of objectification demonstrates that cultural forms, although artifacts of life,
ultimately become antagonistic to the vital energies that created
them. In the final analysis, they threaten to destroy the subjective
culture of the individual, the end for which they originally served
as instruments.[15]

Simmel interprets the consequences of the tragedy of
culture—the ossification, proliferation, and fragmentation of the
forms of culture—as a crisis that reduces modern culture to a state
of incoherence and chaos.

Mere instruments have acquired the dignity of ultimate values. This
completely transposes the natural order of our spiritual and practical
existence. Objective culture develops to an extent and according to a
tempo which increasingly transcends the level of subjective culture, even
though the authentic significance of the perfection of objective culture
lies in its contribution to subjective culture. The individual domains of
culture develop along divergent paths, with the result that the different
provinces of culture become juxtaposed and estranged from one
another. Culture as a whole is really approaching the fate of the tower of
Babel. As a result, the most profound value of culture, which consists in
the interconnection and coherence of the structures of culture, seems to
be threatened with destruction (Simmel, 1917, p. 62).

As Simmel represents it, the crisis of culture is a crisis of the spirit of modern man, a crisis of conscience. In several of his writings—and especially in *The Philosophy of Money*—Simmel provides an interpretation of the sociopsychological correlates or manifestations of this crisis in the mentality of the natives of modern culture. The reification of culture leads the individual to retreat into a private and increasingly solipsistic world of personal values. The result is a subjective and narcissistic culture. Because the enrichment of subjective culture is dependent upon the incorporation of objective forms, this private culture is also embraced by the tragedy of culture: modern subjectivism is an inevitable product of cultural development, but it is also inconsistent with the possibility of culture. The instrumentalization of cultural values produces a state of aestheticism in which all values seem to have the same axiological status. If it is impossible to make any distinction between values, the suspicion arises that no intrinsic values can be identified. In that case, none of the artifacts of culture seems to be more or less valuable than any other. The instrumentalization of values, therefore, leads to the trivialization of values, an axiological relativism and skepticism that ends in a cultural nihilism which constitutes the ultimate stage of the crisis. The proliferation of cultural forms creates the impression that any given cultural form is meaningless. The hyperexcitability and overstimulation of the sensibilities of the modern individual produce a hypersensitivity that ends in exhaustion, banality, and boredom. This is Simmel's sociological interpretation of the ontological state that Freud later called *"Das Unbehagen in der Kultur"*: malaise in the state of culture, conventionally translated as "Civilization and its Discontents."[16]

Simmel's theory of the tragedy of culture is a form by means of which he attempts to provide an interpretation of the definitive features of modern culture. Since the empirical reality of culture is also constituted by an indefinite number of other irreducibly different and incommensurable forms, neither the form of tragedy nor any other form can provide a complete representation of modernity. In view of this consideration, it should not be surprising that the most cogent illustration of Simmel's theory may be provided by a literary *Gedankenexperiment* which selects certain aspects of reality for representation and exaggerates them in the interest of interpretation. From this perspective, Hermann Hesse's final novel *The Glass Bead Game* is an extremely useful interpretive document.

The novel is set in the indefinite future, in the period that follows an age of "frightful wars and civil wars," an era in which men "dwelt anxiously among political, economic, and moral ferments and earthquakes" (Hesse, 1970, p. 13). In the novel, Hesse imagines a tranquil province called Castalia, "the pedagogical province," located in the mountainous region of a larger state. In Castalia there are elite schools devoted exclusively to the education of only the most gifted students. These schools supply new members of "the Order," the class of scholars and intellectuals that is responsible for the intellectual culture of the country. The elite student is obliged to progress through a series of academies until he is admitted to the Order and becomes free to pursue any course of research that he may choose. The rules of the Order include bachelorhood, poverty, and the renunciation of a career or profession in the ordinary sense. The vocation of the elite student is to be a teacher or scholar. As regards the circumstances of life in Castalia, we are presumably asked to imagine perfect intellectual freedom and magnificent resources. Amenities include quasimonastic living arrangements and superb libraries, collections, and laboratories.

The ultimate aim of Castalian culture may be described in some Simmelian language as the desubjectification of the individual by means of the de-objectification of cultural forms. The novel is written in the form of a biography of a master of the Glass Bead Game Joseph Knecht, compiled by an anonymous Castalian scholar. The narrator notes that the mere project of collecting biographical data seems to be inconsistent with the values of Castalian culture. This is because Castalia attempts to obliterate individuality and subjectivity by completely integrating the individual into the domain of objective culture. Put another way, its aim is the elimination of the dichotomy between subjective and objective culture by exhaustively incorporating the domain of objective culture into the subjective culture of the individual. As a result, the narrator notes that it is extremely difficult, in some cases quite impossible, to collect information germane to the subjectivity of the Castalians. Because of the ideal of personal anonymity to which Castalia is committed, even the original names of its members may have disappeared.

In the narration of the origins of the Glass Bead Game, we learn that Castalian culture was preceded by the Age of the Feuilleton, an era which was distinguished by a profusion and proliferation of the artifacts of culture. The result was confusion and chaos, a culture of disorder which had lost its bearings. The Age of the Feuilleton was named after its most popular and characteristic literary genre. The style of the feuilleton also formed the mentality of the epoch. The Age of the Feuilleton generated a culture of "mental pablum." "A torrent of zealous scribbling poured out over every ephemeral incident, and in quality, assortment, and phraseology all this material bore the mark of mass goods rapidly and irresponsibly turned out" (Hesse, 1970, p. 12). The response to this proliferation of cultural artifacts was a retreat to privacy and subjectivity, which the narrator sees epitomized in the modern popularity of crossword puzzles. The denizens of this culture devoted themselves to the solution of intrinsically insignificant puzzles in the attempt to escape the axiological vacuum produced by the chaos of cultural values. "The music of decline" had sounded, the prelude to the collapse of outmoded forms of culture. The narrator notes that the Glass Bead Game had its origins in an "ascetically heroic countermovement" which created a new kind of intellectual discipline and adopted a new and courageous attitude of resignation and serenity toward the aging of cultures. The most salient aspect of this new mentality was that serious men no longer produced new artifacts of objective culture. These intellectuals accepted the fate of belonging to a culture past its peak. Like the Hellenistic culture of late antiquity, the new ascetic culture which succeeded the Age of the Feuilleton was an expression of cultural Alexandrianism. This formed the origins of a new "monastically austere intellectual discipline" that achieved its mature expression in the Glass Bead Game.

The synthesis of subjective and objective culture represented by the Glass Bead Game is an attempt to transcend the tragedy of culture by forestalling it. Its strategy is to eliminate the cause of the tragedy of culture, the process of objectification. The ultimate aim of the Game is the cultivation of the player. In the words of the Music Master of Castalia: "We should be so constituted that we can at any time be placed in a different position without offering resistance or losing our heads" (Hesse, 1970, p. 69). The project of the Game is to perfect subjective culture by freezing objective culture. In this way, it attempts to reverse the increasing gap between subjective and objective culture by creating a new cultural synthesis. This new synthesis is the Glass Bead Game player. The player's aim is not to create new things, perfect artifacts, or enrich the world of objective culture, but rather to perfect himself and consummate his subjective culture by incorporating the complete and unchanging domain of objective culture within the limits of his personality.

The adepts of the Glass Bead Game conceived the life of the mind in the Age of the Feuilleton as a degenerate plant which had exhausted its vital energies in excessive and uncontrolled growth. The culture of the Age of the Feuilleton was a culture of decadence. The new synthesis of subjective and objective culture introduced by the Glass Bead Game represented a way of pruning a plant back to its roots. The innovations of the Game, therefore, represented a form of radical surgery on an organism whose health had been mortally endangered by its own excesses. These reforms rested on a new asceticism. Students no longer regarded education as a desirable and profitable commodity. Young people who devoted themselves to the life of the mind no longer flocked to those intellectual supermarkets, the universities, where they would receive "a nibble of this or that from the dainties offered by celebrated and loquacious professors who without authority offered them the crumbs of what had once been higher education" (Hesse, 1970, p. 24). Geographically and culturally isolated in the province of Castalia, they were subjected to a rigorous program of study, the aim of which was to purify and strengthen the mind. Renouncing a career, success, celebrity, and possessions, they abandoned the bankrupt professions of the universities, the academies, and the feuilleton factories and devoted themselves to re-establishing culture on a new foundation. This new foundation was the Glass Bead Game. The Game is compared to a great organ on which the entire universe of music can be played. The adept of the Game plays with the total values of culture like a virtuoso organist who has an ideally perfect instrument at his disposal. The manuals and stops of this organ range over the entire intellectual canon and the total cosmos of culture. As a result, it is possible in the Game to reproduce "the entire intellectual content of the universe" (Hesse, 1970, p. 7). The rules of the Game are fixed. Variations and alterations are subject to the strictest control. In other words, objective culture has become static. Within this rigid structure, however, the capacities of every player enjoy the freest possible creative expression. The project of the Glass Bead Game is commited to the assumption that a static objective culture is a condition for the possibility of a rich and dynamic subjective culture.

The Game is the symbol of Hesse's vision of a new intellectual and moral order that would be built upon the the ruins of the Age of the Feuilleton. The details of the Game itself are only sketched. Its secret language is taken from several arts and sciences, predominantly from mathematics and music. By employing this language according to the rules of the Game, the adept is capable of "expressing and establishing interrelationships between the content and conclusions of nearly all scholarly disciplines" (Hesse, 1970, p. 6). By employing these rules—the precise content of which Hesse never identifies—new dialectical and synthetic relationships are established between components of culture which seem to be utterly heterogeneous and independent: for example, the movement of a sonata, a law of physics, and a line of Greek verse. The purpose of these exercises, which constitute the playing of the Game, is to create new and increasingly universal syntheses of the apparently disparate fragments that constitute the total capital of culture. The Glass Bead Game player does not create new music or new literature. Nor does he establish new sciences, or even make new scientific or scholarly discoveries. On the contrary, the domain of objective culture is regarded as a constant ensemble of meanings and values. Creativity conceived as the production of new artifacts of objective culture is regarded as impossible. In any case, the attempt at this sort of cultural creativity is expressly forbidden by the laws of Castalia. The player creates new syntheses of existing meanings and values. The quality of a synthesis—the result of any given Glass Bead Game—is determined by aesthetic considerations: simplicity, elegance, universality, harmony, and integrity. The purpose of such a synthesis is to incorporate the contents of objective culture into the domain of subjective culture in a novel fashion. Castalia, therefore, is a cultural world constituted by an aesthetic order which the mind attempts to impose upon reality. It is an attempt to eliminate the tragedy of culture by reconciling the conflict between subjective and objective culture. This is why Castalia represents an attempt to de-objectify and de-instrumentalize culture by limiting the intensity and the consequences of the process of objectification. This is the purpose of freezing objective culture and incorporating all cultural forms into the subjective culture of the Castalians by means of the syntheses of the Glass Bead Game.

According to Simmel, however, any such attempt is doomed to failure. It is a consequence of Simmel's Heraclitean ontology that life is perpetually in flux, constantly creating new energies and forces that eventually cannot be incorporated within the limits of any existing ensemble of cultural forms. These energies can be realized in the subjective culture of individuals only if they are first expressed in the creation of new forms of objective culture. Without this new objective culture, it is impossible for the individual to incorporate these forces into the domain of his subjective culture. Castalia, on the other hand, is an expression of cultural Eleaticism: an attempt to maintain the existing collection of cultural forms as a timeless and permanent cultural canon. From Simmel's perspective, the Castalian project is inconsistent with the possibility of subjective culture precisely because the perfection of subjective culture depends upon the enrichment of objective culture. Therefore Castalia itself is an expression of the inevitable tragedy of culture. As a response to the crisis of culture, Castalia is a product of the creative energies of life. In its heroic effort to terminate the cultural variation and flux responsible for the crisis, however, the culture of Castalia becomes inconsistent with the possibility of culture. The result is a new kind of sterility that destroys both subjective and objective culture.[17] The tragedy of culture, therefore, is inevitable because it is a consequence of the perpetual conflict between life and form, a conflict which, in Simmel's view, is constitutive of human existence.

THE THRESHOLD OF HISTORICAL CONSCIOUSNESS

Because history is one of the multiplicity of forms in which reality is constituted, history as a form of experience and knowledge is defined by reference to certain categories or a prioris which are epistemological conditions for the possibility of history. According to Simmel, history is also grounded on ontological requirements. Because history is not co-extensive with reality and "history" does not refer to everything that exists, there are also ontological conditions for the possibility of history. Since reality is an infinite manifold of events that are constantly in flux, "history" only identifies a certain province of reality. "The historical perspective," Simmel argues, "is only applicable to certain aspects of reality; it only applies to certain modes of classifying these aspects. The objective properties of the elements of reality are not, as such, historical" (Simmel, 1977, p. 207). Simmel introduces a concept in order to identify the aspects of reality which qualify as history: the idea of a threshold of historical consciousness. In his analysis of this concept, Simmel formulates ontological conditions for the possibility of history.

Simmel identifies the threshold of a quality by reference to conditions which are both necessary and sufficient for the ascription of that quality. If a given condition or set of conditions is necessary but not sufficient, then the threshold of this quality has not yet been reached. In his essays on art and aesthetics, Simmel often stresses the importance of aesthetic thresholds. He suggests that we consider a phenomenon which is so large that the significance of its dimensions cannot be represented. One of his favorite examples of such a phenomenon was the scene of many of his most pleasant vacations: the Alps. Such a phenomenon is not the possible object of a painting, Simmel argues. Phenomena which exceed a certain magnitude are not possible objects of visual art. This is because they transcend the limits of the threshold of this sort of art. The same holds for objects which are too small. Unless an object attains certain minimum dimensions, it is not a possible object of visual art. Objects smaller than this may have reached the threshold of perception or observation, but they have not yet crossed the threshold of art. It follows that the necessary conditions for the threshold of some qualities may be sufficient conditions for the threshold of other qualities. On this point, Simmel notes that the thresholds of the various arts may not be the same. For example, the minimum dimensions which would qualify a phenomenon as a possible object of a painting would not necessarily be large enough to qualify it as an object of architecture. Aspects of human life appropriate for representation in a comedy may not have the dimensions required for a tragedy. Also the dimensions which would situate a phenomenon within the threshold of one art might be too large for the threshold of another art. The dimensions of the themes of Wagner's operas, for example, exceed the threshold values of the sonata.

It follows that a threshold is reached when heretofore existing phenomena are conceived or experienced in a new way. The result is the constitution of a new kind of entity. This entity has a significance that could not be ascribed to these phenomena before the threshold in question is reached. At a certain threshold, Simmel claims, a change in quantity or degree produces a change in quality or significance. Beneath this threshold, a given increment of change in quantity will not produce a proportionate increment of this quality. If the threshold of this quality has not yet been reached, a given increment of change will produce no effect at all. Below a certain decibel level, a sound is inaudible. Beneath a certain point on the spectrum of light waves, color is invisible. Put another way, beneath the limits defined by these thresholds, there are no perceptible colors or sounds.

In order to illustrate this point, Simmel employs various examples. In *The Philosophy of Money,* he considers the idea of a threshold of justice. From the perspective of logic or semantics alone, the theft of an ordinary pin may qualify as theft. However Simmel suggests that it is "quantitatively too trifling and insignificant to set in motion the complex psychological mechanism of the consciousness of justice" (Simmel, 1978, p. 264). This is because the threshold of justice is in part constituted by the principle *minima non curat praetor:* the magistrate does not concern himself with trivia. Beneath this threshold, no judicial status can be ascribed to a phenomenon. It may, of course, attain other thresholds, for example the thresholds of taste or morality.[18] In his essay on fate, Simmel argues that our personal fate is not determined by every phenomenon that we encounter. There are innumerable events which impinge upon the purely external or superficial aspects of our lives without having any bearing upon what Simmel calls the authentic core of the personality. In view of this consideration, Simmel claims that it is possible to speak of a threshold of fate which is defined by reference to a certain "quantum of meaning" that can be ascribed to events. Beneath this threshold or quantum level, a phenomenon does not lie within our fate (Simmel, 1957, p. 11). It follows that the threshold of a quality is determined by what might be described as a basic fact of philosophical anthropology: qualitative differences in our reactions or responses are dependent upon quantitative differences.

In Simmel's theory of thresholds, therefore, the conditions which define the threshold of a quality invariably have the following property: they describe both the maximum and the minimum limits—the threshold values—of the reaction or response which a phenomenon must elicit in order to lie within a specific threshold. It follows that thresholds are products of mental acts. They are objects of consciousness. Put another way, thresholds are determined by ascriptions of meaning. What is actually described in the statement of the conditions that define a certain threshold? It is the significance that we attribute to phenomena. Reality exhibits thresholds only because we ascribe meaning to certain phenomena. If there were no acts in which meaning is ascribed, then there would be no thresholds or threshold phenomena. It follows that the threshold of history must be defined by reference to meanings that we ascribe to certain aspects of reality but not to others. Phenomena fall within the domain of history because we conceive them as having certain properties. These events qualify as history only because we represent them from a certain perspective.

Thresholds, therefore, are intentional properties of objects: properties which they possess because meanings can be ascribed to them. Thresholds are constituted in acts of the ascription of meaning. Independent of these acts, no thresholds can be defined. This is because thresholds are logically dependent upon the significance that can be differentially attributed to phenomena. The conditions which define a threshold identify a phenomenon insofar as it is the object of an intentional act. Both the existence and the structure of threshold phenomena are determined by mental acts or processes. Simmel's theory of thresholds is an important component of his general philosophical position. This position rests on the assumption that there is a sense in which reality presupposes consciousness. Subjectivity, as Simmel sometimes puts it, is a condition of objectivity. Because constitutive acts of consciousness are necessary conditions for the existence of threshold phenomena, it follows that these phenomena cannot be identified independent of consciousness. The existence of threshold phenomena is dependent upon consciousness. There is a sense in which consciousness is a basis for certain provinces of objective fact. One of these ontological domains is history. Consciousness is an essential presupposition of history for the following reason: only a finite spectrum within the infinite manifold of phenomena constitutes history, a spectrum which we conceive in a certain way or represent from a certain perspective. The threshold of the historical interest, therefore, lies within consciousness. This is why Simmel calls this interest the threshold of the historical consciousness.

In Simmel's analysis of the threshold of historical consciousness, historical reality is constituted by reference to two distinguishable interests. These interests are fundamental and autonomous in the sense that they are both axiomatic or primitive:
they are not interdependent, nor can either of them be derived
from other more basic interests. One of them is the interest in the
content of historical reality, an interest in the importance or
significance that can be ascribed to historical facts. As Simmel
represents it, the ascription of this interest is a necessary condition
for the ascription of the historical interest. Therefore it is a
necessary condition for the threshold of historical consciousness.
Because reality is an infinite manifold of processes that are
constantly in flux, history as an ontological category must be
grounded on some criterion for identifying the historical
phenomenon within this manifold. It must be based on some
principle which differentiates the event to which historical
significance can be ascribed from the mere event as such.

In the essay "The Problem of Historical Time," Simmel considers the relationship between interpretation and historicity. He
argues that the understanding of a phenomenon—which depends upon the ascription of meaning to it—is a necessary
condition for the identification of that phenomenon as historical.
Simmel suggests that we consider a report concerning the alleged
conduct of someone whose character we know quite well. Suppose that this report has the following property: although it is
logically possible, we find it unintelligible or uninterpretable in
virtue of all we know about the person. In that case, Simmel
claims, we would hesitate to accept this report as an historical fact.
We would hesitate because the report does not seem to identify a
possible object of interpretation, an item to which significance can
be ascribed. Imagine, for example, a letter signed "Richard
Wagner" in which the moral and spiritual qualities and the
aesthetic sensibilities of Jews are praised. Or imagine an essay in
defense of Christian ethics attributed to a certain "Friedrich
Nietzsche." According to Simmel, we would be reluctant to accept
these documents as the historical facts they appear to be. We
would be inclined to regard them as forgeries because they cannot
be interpreted consistently with what we know about the charac-
ters of Wagner and Nietzsche. If the interpretation of a
phenomenon or the ascription of meaning to it is a necessary
condition for its historical status, then a phenomenon to which no

meaning can be ascribed does not lie within the domain of history. Simmel claims that "even the mere identification of an entity or an event—the identification of its potential historicity—depends upon a certain degree of understanding. In the absence of this measure of understanding, the item would remain an unqualified and undifferentiated variable, a complete unknown" (Simmel, 1957, p. 44). Under these conditions, such an event would not fall within the threshold of history because the interest in significance could not be ascribed to it.[19]

However Simmel does not identify the domain of history with the domain of significance. Not all of the meaningful, interpretable, or intelligible acts and artifacts of human beings have an historical status. Consider a diary entry by an otherwise unknown person of the eighteenth century which documents his friendship with an equally obscure contemporary. From a logical point of view, Simmel claims—from the perspective of the a priori categories that constitute history as a form of experience and knowledge—this diary entry is an historical fact. From an ontological standpoint, however—from the perspective of the threshold of historical consciousness—it is not. Why do these facts fail to qualify as history in what Simmel calls "the substantively important sense" or the ontological sense of this concept? Simmel suggests that the reason may be the following, adding the reservation that this is only a hypothetical and speculative suggestion. The facts constituted by the diary entry do not qualify as history because we are not able to determine whether they have any consequences that influence human conduct. Consider, Simmel proposes, the mere quantum—the weight or number—of these effects.

Perhaps this provides the criterion for the feeling of historical interest with which we react to certain causal factors. The causal factors that we designate as "important" are precisely those which have consequences that are, in comparison with "unimportant" events, more observably determinable or quantitatively estimable (Simmel, 1977, p. 164).

Suppose that this diary entry did not concern two anonymous figures of the eighteenth century. Suppose that it was written by Hegel and recorded the beginning of his friendship with Hölderlin. In this case, according to Simmel, the diary entry would satisfy our interest in the significance of historical content. That is because we would have some appreciation of the bearing of the facts reported in the diary upon certain aspects of the lives of specific persons. In this case, the diary entry might shed light on the development of Hegel's thought and the genesis of romanticism. The historical interest in significance, therefore, can be ascribed to a phenomenon only if it is not conceived as an isolated event, only if it is possible to make some estimate—even a purely subjective or speculative estimate—of its consequences that influence human conduct.

A diary entry by an anonymous person which lies unread in some provincial archive has no historical significance. A diary entry by Hegel noting that his work was going badly because of indigestion might have some historical significance. A diary entry by Napoleon noting that his military planning for the Russian campaign was going badly might have considerably more historical significance. It follows that what Simmel calls the quantum of historical significance of an event is determined by the number of consequences of this event to which an influence upon human conduct can be ascribed. Suppose that the consequences of an event cannot be estimated. Or suppose that, although they can be estimated, they have no identifiable bearing upon human conduct. In that case, the event in question does not lie within the threshold of the interest in historical significance: from the perspective of this interest, it is meaningless. Simmel notes that this is why it may not be possible to ascribe historical significance to persons and events of the recent past: it is because we are not yet able to estimate their consequences. He also notes that historical significance should not be confused with any other species of value or significance. An anonymous diary entry might have both moral and aesthetic significance. But it would not follow that historical significance can be ascribed to it.

According to Simmel, the interest in significance is independent of the existence of the phenomenon to which this significance is ascribed. In other words, the following two questions are logically independent. Can significance be ascribed to a given entity? And does this entity in fact exist? From the exclusive perspective of the interest in significance, it is of no importance that the man named Oedipus who murdered his father and slept with his mother is a product of the poetic imagination. The fact that Oedipus is only a mythical or fictional character is irrelevant to this interest. According to Simmel, this is why the interest in significance, although necessary, is not sufficient to define the threshold of historical consciousness. In order to complete the definition of the threshold of history, another element is essential. Simmel calls this other element the existential interest, or the interest in the reality of historical content. He argues that many phenomena interest us even though no value or significance of any sort can be ascribed to them. Phenomena of this sort are interesting only insofar as they exist or only because they happened. Simmel identifies this as the principal source of our interest in the mundane events of the quotidian world. Much of the subject matter of journalism, for example, would lose whatever interest it has if it were established that the alleged events that the journalist describes did not really happen. This is presumably what is meant when events of this sort are described as "trivia": our interest in them is completely exhausted by the fact that they happened. Although this is hardly surprising, Simmel holds that a phenomenon falls within the domain of historical reality only if its existence can be established. Somewhat less commonplace is Simmel's insistence that the existential interest of history is also an interest in the unique temporal location of phenomena.

Suppose it were established that a certain phenomenon occurred at some unspecified and undeterminable time. Simmel considers the possibility of discovering the remains of an archeological site the antiquity of which cannot be identified. Under these conditions, Simmel argues, no historical status can be ascribed to these ruins. Other kinds of value and significance might be attributed to the contents of the site. They might contain aesthetically interesting objects of art or technological devices of a utilitarian interest. And the site itself might have a certain value from the perspective of arousing curiosity and providing a source of amusement. It might even constitute a tourist attraction of considerable economic value. But suppose that this site cannot be located within a definite time-frame. In that case, Simmel claims, it exists in an historical vacuum. The existential interest, therefore, is also an interest in temporal location. An event falls within the domain of history only if it is possible to establish its existence and its temporal location: the historicity of an event entails that the event can be located at a determinate point in time.

In order to illustrate the import of this condition, Simmel considers a scientific experiment of the following sort: although it was actually performed and has a beginning and an end, no relationship can be established between this experiment and the events which precede or follow it. Simmel argues that an experiment which is conceived from this perspective—a standpoint from which the temporal location of the experiment is irrelevant—is not an historical event. Consider an oxidation reaction as described in an elementary chemistry textbook, for example the heating of mercury in the presence of oxygen to produce mercuric oxide. Such an experiment has no historical status. Consider, on the other hand, the first performance of this experiment. Suppose that this particular experiment had a revolutionary effect upon the development of chemical theory. In that case, it would be possible—and also essential—to situate this experiment within what Simmel calls a determinate time-frame. A determinate time-frame specifies a unique location for the experiment within our system of temporal coordinates. Such a specification would provide a temporal framework that identifies the relationship between the experiment and the state of chemical theory that precedes and follows it. Consider, for example, the first oxidation reaction experiment that Lavoisier performed with mercury, an experiment that has a classical status because it led to the overthrow of the phlogiston theory and the development of a new theory of combustion. Conceived from this perspective—a perspective which situates the experiment within a determinate time-frame—the experiment satisfies the existential interest in temporalization. This is because it is possible to locate the experiment within a system of temporal coordinates. As Simmel puts it, the historical experiment can be identified as occurring at a certain temporally defined point. The ascription of such an identity to the experiment is a necessary condition for ascribing an historical status to it.

Although the interest in the temporalization of a phenomenon is a necessary condition for the ascription of the historical interest, it is not a sufficient condition. In view of Simmel's ontological assumptions, it is not difficult to appreciate why this is the case. If reality is an infinite manifold of qualities constantly in flux, then a criterion for distinguishing history from the mere event is essential to the possibility of historical knowledge. This criterion cannot be derived exclusively from the existential interest. That is because this interest is solely concerned with temporally defined existence as such. Its domain is not limited to those aspects of existence to which significance can be ascribed. The existential interest, therefore, is only a necessary condition for the constitution of the threshold of historical consciousness. It follows that the criterion for distinguishing history from the mere phenomenon must also be determined by the interest in the significance of content. The threshold of historical consciousness is located at the intersection of these two interests. "Where these two criteria mesh—the existential interest and the interest in content—we find the specific interest in the facticity of certain distinctive sequences of events, persons, circumstances and states that provides the foundation for history" (Simmel, 1977, p. 173). In consequence, a phenomenon falls within the ontological domain of history if and only if it satisfies the interest in the reality of content—the existential interest—and the interest in the content of reality—the interest in significance. Put another way, the threshold of historical consciousness may be defined by reference to a certain set of predicates. The predicates that constitute the ontological domain of history are those which truly apply to an object if and only if that object has the following two properties: it can be located within a determinate time-frame and the interest in significance can be attributed to it.

Simmel's account of the threshold of historical consciousness seems to be confusing—or perhaps even paradoxical—in the following respect. On the one hand, he claims that the ascription of the interest in historical significance is independent of the existence of the item to which this interest is ascribed. Therefore it seems that an item can have historical significance even though it does not exist. On the other hand, he claims that there is a definitive difference between historical significance and every other kind of value or significance. The historical significance of an item—as opposed to its moral, logical, or aesthetic significance, for example—is dependent upon the number of consequences that can be attributed to it. But if it can be said that a certain item produces a certain number of consequences, then it follows that this item exists. Therefore it seems that the interest in historical significance is not independent of the question of existence, and the historical significance of a given item is not independent of its existence.

Why does Simmel's philosophy of history require a theory of the threshold of historical consciousness? The problem which

creates the necessity for a threshold of history is a consequence of
Simmel's ontology. If reality is an infinite manifold, then historical knowledge is possible only on the basis of a criterion for
distinguishing within this manifold items which have historical
significance from items which do not. The threshold of historical
consciousness defines a limited domain of reality as having
historical significance. The apparent contradiction created by
Simmel's solution to this problem is a consequence of his criterion
for the historical threshold, the definition of historicity. The
threshold of the historical consciousness is defined by reference
to the intersection of two criteria which, Simmel claims, are
logically independent. The interest in significance is independent
of the interest in existence and vice-versa. However Simmel sees
that historical significance should not be conflated with other
kinds of meaning. The domain of axiology is affected by an
irrationality of its own: history, aesthetics, logic, and ethics
constitute autonomous and irreducibly different provinces of
value. Therefore Simmel distinguishes historical significance
from other kinds of significance by arguing that the historical
significance of an item—unlike its moral, logical, or aesthetic
significance—is determined by the number of consequences that
can be attributed to it. From this analysis of historical significance
—which is based on the necessity of distinguishing the domain of
historical meaning from other domains of meaning and value—it
apparently follows that historical significance is not independent
of existence after all: in order to produce consequences, an item
must exist.[20]

Like all threshold phenomena, Simmel notes, there is a sense in
which the threshold of history is subjective. The threshold of the
historical consciousness is not an objective property that can be
ascribed to events independent of their relationship to acts of the
ascription of meaning. On the contrary, it is an intentional
property of events, a property which they possess insofar as they
are objects of mental acts. As Simmel puts it, the threshold of
historical consciousness is a property which the events produce in
us (Simmel, 1977, p. 167). In other words a premise which
Simmel apparently regards as a primitive and axiomatic datum of
philosophical anthropology is an ontological condition for the
possibility of history: consciousness is constituted in such a way
that a theoretical interest in both existence and significance is
generated.

THE THEORY OF INTERPRETATION

Consider the following two postulates of Simmel's philosophy of history. First: the a priori categories which constitute history as a form of experience and knowledge entail that historical knowledge is grounded on an understanding of mental processes and their relationship to human conduct and its artifacts.[21] Second: the threshold of historical consciousness which defines the ontological status of history entails that historical reality is grounded on an understanding of the significance of certain kinds of events. Both of these propositions—the epistemological postulate and the ontological postulate—entail that history is based on the possibility of understanding or interpretation. According to Simmel, what constitutes an interpretation, and under what conditions is interpretation possible?

Simmel's various contributions to the problem of interpretation appear in a variety of writings published between 1892 and 1918. Readers familiar with Simmel's style of work will not be surprised to learn that he never attempted to articulate these views into a systematic theory of interpretation. Like much of Simmel's work on the philosophy and methodology of the sociocultural sciences, his writings on interpretation retrace a path taken by one of his older philosophical contemporaries: Wilhelm Dilthey.[22] Many of the major ideas and theses that later appear in Simmel's writings can be identified in Dilthey's earlier works. Simmel's preoccupation with certain problems in metaphysics, epistemology, the philosophy of history, and aesthetics corresponds very closely to Dilthey's interests. Both Dilthey and Simmel began their careers apparently committed to positivist epistemological assumptions. Both shift to the neo-Kantianism of a middle period which stresses the importance of a critique of historical reason. And, like Dilthey, Simmel also moves away from Kant to elaborate a novel philosophical position in which an undeveloped theory of interpretation occupies a crucial status. In the work of both Dilthey and Simmel, however, this position was final only in the sense that it was the last position that they adopted, the position that immediately preceded their deaths. It cannot be represented as a definitive solution to the major problems with which both men grappled. The last writings of Dilthey and Simmel remain fragmentary, unsystematic, and, above all, eclectic, for the earlier positivistic and neo-Kantian elements are still identifiable in their final works. In spite of these parallels between the earlier writings of Dilthey and the later works of Simmel—and, again, devotees of Simmel's writings will betray no surprise here—Simmel never mentions Dilthey in his published work.

Within the domain of the theory of interpretation, the path that Dilthey took between 1883 and 1910 may be reconstructed as follows. In his *Einleitung in die Geisteswissenschaften* (1883), Dilthey is chiefly concerned with the psychological presuppositions of interpretation. Understanding is analyzed as a recreation or empathetic intuition of mental states and processes. Beginning in 1894-86, however, Dilthey moves to a radically different conception of understanding as an interpretation of objective meanings. The import of these objective meanings is logically independent of any description of the psychological processes that originally produced them. Dilthey's most complete published statement of this later theory of interpretation as the understanding of the content of "objectified mind" is presented in *Der Aufbau der geschichtlichen Welt in den Geisteswissenschaften* (1910). In order to identify this basic shift in Dilthey's thinking, it may be useful to distinguish a psychologistic hermeneutic from a cultural hermeneutic. In a psychologistic hermeneutic, understanding is concerned with the psychological reconstruction of mental processes. In a cultural hermeneutic, understanding is concerned with the interpretation of artifacts that are originally generated by mental processes. However these artifacts become detached from the conditions of their psychological genesis. They acquire an autonomous structure which can be understood independent of any description of the psychological conditions responsible for them. Given this distinction, it would be accurate to describe Dilthey's work on interpretation between 1883 and 1910 as turning from a psychologistic to a cultural hermeneutic.

Simmel's research on interpretation between 1892 and 1918 parallels this same shift. The first edition of *The Problems of the Philosophy of History* offers a psychologistic theory of interpretation. Like many of the neo-Kantians of that period, Simmel in this early phase of his development ascribes an ontological and quasi-empirical status to Kant's epistemological categories. The a priori categories of the Kantian epistemological subject become real entities situated in an empirical psyche. These entities are psychological forces and energies. They are represented as the principal causal factors in the explanation of human conduct. Beginning with the second edition of this book, Simmel moves from a psychologistic view of understanding to a radically different conception. In this new conception, interpretation is principally concerned not with causal relations between psychological processes, but rather with logical relations between conceptual entities. This later view of interpretation was an important component of the new position on the philosophy of history which Simmel mentions in his letter to Rickert dated December 26, 1916 (Gassen and Landmann, 1958, pp. 116–17). Simmel's most complete sketch of a cultural hermeneutic is presented in two of the essays translated in this volume: "On the Nature of Historical Understanding" and "The Problem of Historical Time."

In the writings of both Dilthey and Simmel, a preoccupation with the psychological underpinnings of interpretation and the assumption that there is some sense in which understanding is essentially a psychological process never disappear completely. Although Dilthey and Simmel begin to abandon a psychological and genetic analysis of understanding in order to develop a logical or conceptual analysis in which the import and validity of interpretation are detached from genetic and psychological considerations, this move is never actually consummated. The psychologistic hermeneutic is never decisively repudiated and replaced by a cultural hermeneutic. In consequence, traces of their earlier psychologism can still be identified in their last works. From this perspective, the careers of both Dilthey and Simmel clearly exemplify the transitional, eclectic, and dynamic quality of the Wilhelminian intellectual era as a whole.

In the second edition of *The Problems of the Philosophy of History,* Simmel's preoccupation with the psychological presuppositions of interpretation is obvious. Roughly the first third of the book is devoted to this issue. The first condition of historical understanding, Simmel claims, is the following: the historian must be able to recreate the mental processes of the historical person. As Simmel analyzes it, this process of "recreation"—which he often places within quotation marks, indicating that he had suspicions about its status—is based on the following analogical reasoning. As a result of observing the concomitance or covariation between my own behavior and my mental states, I know that whenever my conduct has the observable property X, then I am experiencing the mental state Y. Suppose I observe that the conduct of some other person has the property X. In that case, I infer that he is also experiencing the mental state Y. That the mental life of other persons corresponds to our own, Simmel claims, "is an a priori of all practical and theoretical relations between one subject and another" (Simmel, 1977, p. 45). The possibility of interpretation, therefore, seems to be grounded on a certain kind of psychological isomorphism. It apparently presupposes that there is a certain sense in which the person who interprets and the person who is interpreted have the same nature: the relationship between the interpreter's mental states and their observable expression is the same as the relationship between his subject's mental states and their observable expression.

Simmel returns to this point in the important essay on "Feminine Culture," first published in the *Archiv für Sozialwissenschaft und Sozialpolitik* in 1911. In a discussion of the sociology of medical diagnosis, Simmel claims that there is a sense in which both diagnosis and therapy are dependent upon an ability to empathize with the condition of the patient. Objective, clinical methods of diagnosis, he argues, often lead to premature conclusions if they are not supplemented by this sort of "subjective knowledge" of the condition and feelings of the patient, a variety of knowledge which invariably functions as an a priori of the art of medicine (Simmel, 1911b, p. 290). Simmel claims that one of the conditions for the possibility of this kind of knowledge is "a certain constitutional analogy" between the physician and the patient. There is a sense in which the doctor and the patient must have the same "nature." Otherwise it would not be possible for the diagnostician to recreate the condition of the patient by means of the psychological process of empathy. Simmel draws some interesting conclusions from this assumption of psychological isomorphism. He believes it follows that female physicians can often be more accurate than male physicians in their diagnoses of female patients. They could also discover symptomatic relationships that are inaccessible to the male physician. Why is this the case? It is a consequence of what Simmel apparently regards as a fundamental fact of philosophical anthropology. In relation to female patients, the female physician possesses a diagnostic instrument that her male counterpart lacks: she has experienced states similar to the states of her female patients. On the basis of this same reasoning—"that a different kind of knowledge is a consequence of a different mode of being"—Simmel also concludes that women could make uniquely feminine contributions to the enterprise of interpretation in the sociocultural sciences (Simmel, 1911b, p. 291).

However Simmel repeatedly stresses that "recreation" should not be conceived as an exact reproduction of the mental states of the other person. Applying his remarks on empathy and psychological recreation to the problem of historical interpretation, Simmel claims that the project of understanding historical persons is not a question of merely recreating their mental states and processes, nor can it be represented as an intuitive process of the same sort. On the contrary, interpretation seems to be a primitive and irreducible process that cannot be analyzed into simpler constitutive elements or causal factors.

During this period, therefore, Simmel's writings betray a curious ambivalence concerning the essential properties of interpretation. On the one hand, the psychological isomorphism between the interpreter and his subject seems to be a condition for the possibility of interpretation. There must be a certain "basic identity or equivalence" between the knower and the object of knowledge. For this reason, Simmel claims, it would perhaps be impossible for an earthling to understand an inhabitant of another planet, even if there were some sense in which a complete description of its observable behavior were available. This is also why we can usually understand our fellow citizens better than foreigners and members of our own family better than strangers. It is why we can understand people who share our temperament more easily than we can understand persons with a character diametrically opposed to our own. Simmel summarizes these observations by claiming that insofar as understanding represents an inner or psychological recreation of a mental process that cannot be directly apprehended, our ability to understand the mind of another person is a function of the extent to which his mind resembles our own. On the other hand, Simmel also introduces the following reservation: this relationship between the mental processes of the interpreter and the mental processes of his subject should not be conceived as a mechanically reproduced form of congruence. One does not have to be Caesar in order to understand Caesar, nor does one have to be Augustine in order to understand him. On the contrary, a certain diversity or heterogeneity between the interpreter and his subject—a certain psychological detachment or reserve—is often a condition which favors interpretation more than an exact psychological isomorphism. Simmel concludes these remarks on interpretation in the essay on "Feminine Culture" with the equivocal observation that interpretation is constituted by an extremely variable relationship between the interpreter and his subject, a relationship that does not seem to be accessible to further analysis.

This is also the position that Simmel takes in the second edition of *The Problems of the Philosophy of History*. Repeating the now famous remark about Caesar, he adds that one does not have to be another Luther in order to understand him either. Although a certain degree of psychological distance between the interpreter and his subject may render understanding impossible, Simmel nevertheless claims that it is still possible for us to understand mental states which we have never experienced for ourselves. In other words, reproduction of the mental states of another person is not a necessary condition for interpretation. Nor is it a sufficient condition. Imagine, Simmel suggests, an exact correspondence between the mental states of the historian and the mental states of the historical person.

For example, let us suppose that love and hate, thought and desire, pleasure and pain as subjective states have exactly the same essential properties in the minds of both. Even if this were the case, this direct equivalence of subjective states would not constitute historical knowledge (Simmel, 1977, p. 68).

On the contrary, Simmel claims, historical knowledge requires the reconstruction or transformation of the mental states of the historical person from the perspective of the a priori categories that constitute history as a form. However Simmel also admits that interpretation rests upon an "intimate relationship" between the mental states of the historian and those of the historical person. There is apparently some extremely unobvious sense in which the psychological possibility of recreating the mental states of other persons is a necessary condition for historical knowledge (Simmel, 1977, pp. 66, 87). Exactly what is this intimate relationship? What is the import and status of the claim that, in some sense, psychological intuition, or the recreation of mental states, is a necessary condition for interpretation?

Simmel considers this issue within the context of some comments on Schopenhauer's theory of art. When a mental entity is understood, Simmel claims, there is a sense in which the interpreter "makes this psychological process his own. He immerses himself in knowledge of this process. And—insofar as the person can be identified with his mental states—it can be said that at this moment he really *is* this psychological process" (Simmel, 1977, pp. 92–93). However Simmel adds the following crucial reservation. "The identity that is at stake here—between the mental states of the historian and the mental states of the historical person—is not a mechanical copy of the primary event. On the contrary, the interpreter comprehends—or shares in—the content or meaning of the event insofar as it is intelligible" (Simmel, 1977, p. 93). The interpreter, therefore, does not reproduce the experience of his subject. On the contrary, he only grasps the meaning or import of this experience. At this point, Simmel introduces a comparison between his theory of interpretation and the Platonic theory of ideas. The Platonic ideas "participate" in the data of the observable world not insofar as the latter are phenomena, but only insofar as they are intelligible entities or possible objects of knowledge. In the same way, the interpreter "participates" in the mental states of his subject not insofar as these states are psychological processes or experiences, but only insofar as they are understandable entities or possible objects of interpretation.

In *The Problems of the Philosophy of History,* therefore, the problematical relationship between interpretation, psychological recreation, and the psychic identity or psychological isomorphism between the interpreter and his subject seems to be the following. Interpretation presupposes a psychic identity between the mind of the interpreter and the mind of his subject in the following sense: the interpreter can establish the import or content of the mental processes of his subject. In other words, he can identify these mental processes and their putative objects. But it does not presuppose that the interpreter can reenact or recreate the process itself.

Husserl employs a distinction that Simmel would have found useful in this context. He differentiates the noetic properties of mental acts from their noematic properties. The noetic properties of a mental act are the qualities which are ascribed to it insofar as the act is a mental process of a certain sort: a belief, a wish, or an intention, for example. The noematic properties of a mental act are ascribed to it insofar as the act has a specific objective import or content. The noetic properties of acts may be described independent of their noematic properties. For example, the properties of wishes and feelings may be described simply insofar as they are mental processes and independent of the object that is wished for or felt. Also the noematic properties of mental acts may be described independent of the properties which these acts have as mental processes. The object of a wish or the content of a belief, for example, can be described without considering the process of wishing or believing. Descriptions of noetic and noematic properties, therefore, are logically independent. Put another way, the identification of the noetic properties of an act is logically independent of the identification of its noematic properties, and the identification of the latter properties is also logically independent of the identification of the former properties. Given Husserl's distinction, Simmel's view of the significance of psychological isomorphism for interpretation can be stated as follows. Interpretation rests on the possibility that the interpreter can discover both the noetic and the noematic properties of the mental acts of other persons. But it does not presuppose that he can reenact or reproduce their noetic properties.[23] Interpretation does not rest on the presupposition that the sociologist of culture can in some sense reproduce the anti-Semitic emotions of the German middle class of the 1880's and 1890's. It is only based on the assumption that he can establish what these emotions were and identify their content. Interpretation does not require that the military historian recreate Nelson's state of mind during the Battle of Trafalgar. But it does require that he identify both Nelson's strategic intentions and their putative objects. Interpretation does not rest on the possibility that the art historian can embrace the beliefs of Renaissance architects concerning the relationship between urban design and the metaphysics of the human personality, but it does assume that the historian can discover these beliefs and their import.

This position approaches Simmel's later views on interpretation as they are sketched in two of the essays translated in this volume: "The Problem of Historical Time" and "On the Nature of Historical Understanding." In these essays, Simmel retreats further from a psychologistic analysis of interpretation. He develops the elements of a cultural hermeneutic in which interpretation is principally concerned with semantic import, logical relationships, and conceptual structures that are independent of any consideration of their psychological genesis or causation.

In the essay "On the Nature of Historical Understanding," Simmel describes understanding as a relationship between one mind and another. It is a fundamental or primitive process of human life in the sense that neither the conditions for its possibility nor its definitive properties can be analytically reduced to simpler constitutive elements.[24] Simmel claims that the interpretations which are developed in order to serve the theoretical interests of the sociocultural sciences have their ultimate source and prototypical forms in the interests and needs of everyday life. The process of understanding is generated by the energies of life itself. This is why Simmel thinks that an account of the concept of historical understanding is dependent upon an analysis of the concept of understanding that is employed in everyday life, an analysis of the circumstances surrounding the fact that it is possible for one person to understand another. This is also why "ultimately our understanding of the Apostle Paul and Louis XIV is essentially the same as our understanding of a personal acquaintance" (Simmel, 1957, p. 60).

In this essay, Simmel analyzes the concept of understanding by distinguishing two components which the act of understanding combines in an "integral synthesis." The first element is the object of interpretation or the interpretandum: a given empirical datum which has not been understood. The second element is the "interpretive conception" or the interpretans: the interpretive idea or schema which the interpreter imposes upon the uninterpreted datum. In the process of understanding, the interpretive conception "penetrates the given phenomenon and transforms it into an object of interpretation" (Simmel, 1957, p. 60). Simmel claims that there are three typical forms of this relationship between interpretans and interpretandum. All three forms have their source in the interests of everyday life, and all three are essential to the theoretical interests of the sociocultural sciences.

In the first form of this relationship, the observable conduct of a person is interpreted by reference to the mental processes which it supposedly expresses. Or, alternatively, these hypothetical mental states are inferred from the person's observable conduct, which is conceived as their manifestation. In either case, observable conduct is understood as an expression of mental processes. Or, in the historical case of this form of the relationship, the artifacts which document the actions of the historical person are understood as manifestations of his state of mind. Simmel describes the observable conduct or expressions of another person as a bridge and a symbol which we employ to produce a hypothetical reconstruction of what may have transpired in his mind. Simmel's analysis of this form of the relationship between interpretans and interpretandum also suggests that understanding is grounded on the principle of psychic identity or psychological isomorphism which was the subject of the equivocal discussion presented in the first chapter of *The Problems of the Philosophy of History.* Suppose that I interpret the conduct of another person as expressing a certain state of mind. On what grounds can such an interpretation be based? Apparently the basis for this interpretation is the following. In my own case, this conduct is associated with a certain state of mind which it expresses. Therefore I infer that the conduct which I observe also expresses the same state of mind in the other person. In other words, understanding apparently presupposes that the relationship between mental states and conduct which obtains in the case of the interpreter also holds in the case of the subject of the interpretation.

At least this seems to be a necessary condition for interpretation. Experience seems to indicate that the petit bourgeois cannot understand Napoleon or Goethe, the European cannot understand the Oriental, and the modern man cannot understand the medieval man. Should we conclude that understanding is based on an identity between the interpreter and his subject? Simmel claims that this inference would be premature. The analogical reasoning on which understanding is based has a purely negative force. "In other words, a certain degree of disparity or dissimilarity between the nature of the historian and the nature of the historical person makes understanding impossible. But it certainly does not follow that understanding is a product of this sort of identity" (Simmel, 1957, p. 62). Therefore a certain isomorphism between mental processes and their expression in both the interpreter and his subject is a necessary condition for interpretation. Simmel, perhaps following his own admonition that understanding is a fundamental and irreducible process that resists analysis into simpler elements, never attempts to identify the precise nature of this alleged psychic identity. This sort of isomorphism, however, is not a sufficient condition for interpretation. Suppose that the historian and the historical person have the same nature. This condition alone would not constitute an adequate basis for understanding. Interpretation, therefore, is not a logical consequence of psychological isomorphism. Like Max Weber, Simmel thinks that it is essential not to confuse the conditions under which it is possible to have an experience with the conditions under which it is possible to understand this experience. Satisfaction of the former set of conditions does not entail satisfaction of the latter. From this consideration, Simmel draws the following conclusion:

It may be true that we can only comprehend a mind that resembles our own in one way or another. The conduct of beings on a distant star like Sirius, for example, may remain unintelligible to us. From the fact that my mind has exactly the same nature as the mind of another person, however, it does not follow that I understand this person (Simmel, 1957, p. 65).

Consider the assumption that the knower and the known—the historian and the historical person, for example—must have essentially the same properties. Simmel suggests that this assumption is ultimately grounded on a belief in the existence of timeless forms or eternal substances, a Greek mode of thought perhaps exhibited most clearly in the early dialogues of Plato. Simmel rejects this mode of thought as a "naively mechanistic" dogma. The critique of psychological isomorphism as a basis for interpretation which Simmel develops between 1905 and 1918, therefore, may be understood as a critique of a psychologistic hermeneutic, a psychologism to which Simmel himself seems to have been committed in his early work.[25]

In the second form of the basic relationship between interpretans and interpretandum that Simmel considers, an act which has been interpreted in the foregoing psychological sense is understood by reference to another act "on the same psychological plane" (Simmel, 1957, p. 69). The latter act, which constitutes the interpretans, has also been interpreted psychologically. As an illustration of this relationship between interpretans and interpretandum, Simmel considers the intense hatred which a Hanoverian Legitimist exhibits toward Bismarck during the war of 1866 and the subsequent Prussian annexation of Hanover. The conduct of the Hanoverian—once it is psychologically understood as an expression of an emotion—may be interpreted as an instance of a type of emotion, namely hatred. Simmel claims that this sort of interpretation is "transhistorical" in the sense that it is independent of both the conditions for its genesis and the character of the person that it affects. According to Simmel, the Hanoverian's attitude toward Bismarck, Brunhilde's feelings toward Kriemhilde, and the tenant's feelings about his dishonest landlord may all be understood as expressions of the same psychological process. In everyday life, Simmel claims, this form of interpretation functions in the following way. A specific mental process is understood when it is placed within a framework or context. This is achieved by representing the given mental process as an individual case or instance of a more general type of the same process. In the historical use of this form of interpretation, a mental process is understood when it is identified as a component of what Simmel calls a temporal network. The Hanoverian's hate for Bismarck, for example, is understood historically when it is placed within the context of the war of 1866 and the annexation of Hanover.

In his discussion of this second form of the relationship between interpretans and interpretandum, Simmel claims that two different modes of understanding can be identified. One mode he calls "ahistorical," "immanent," or "objective." The other he calls historical. This is perhaps the crucial distinction on which Simmel's theory of interpretation is based. Simmel explains the differences between these two modes of interpretation by distinguishing two different kinds of question which may be raised about the object of interpretation. On the one hand, an interpretation may represent an answer to a question about the conditions for the genesis or the production of the interpretandum. In that case, the question is historical and the interpretans produces an historical interpretation. On the other hand, the interpretation may represent an answer to a question about the intrinsic properties of the interpretandum itself. According to Simmel, there is a sense in which a description of these properties is independent of any description of the genesis of the interpretandum. In this latter case, Simmel calls the question immanent or objective. Perhaps it is not difficult to grasp approximately what Simmel intends by this language. The question is immanent in the sense that it concerns properties of the interpretandum which are intrinsic to it or constitutive of it. This sort of question could be called objective in the sense that it poses a problem about the properties of the object of interpretation itself, not a question about the properties of its antecedent psychological conditions. This is, of course, what Simmel means when he calls this sort of question "ahistorical." It follows that the interpretans which provides an answer to such a question could be called immanent or objective in the same sense.

Simmel, therefore, supposes that a distinction can be made between two kinds of properties which may be ascribed to an interpretandum. On the one hand, the interpretandum may be identified as having immanent properties. To claim that these properties are immanent is to claim that there is a sense in which they are independent of the conditions for the genesis or production of the object: no description of the genesis of the interpretandum will entail any consequences germane to its immanent properties. An understanding of its genesis, therefore, is irrelevant to an understanding of its immanent properties. It follows that the truth or falsity of any description of the immanent properties of the interpretandum is logically independent of the truth or falsity of any description of the conditions for its genesis. On the other hand, the interpretandum may be identified as having historical properties. To claim that these properties are historical is to claim that they are dependent upon the conditions for the genesis of the object. A description of the historical properties of the object, therefore, is dependent upon a description of its genesis. In order to understand its historical properties, it is necessary to identify the conditions for its genesis. Further, the truth or falsity of any description of its historical properties is a logical consequence of the truth or falsity of some description of its genesis. Assuming that this is the basic distinction that Simmel intends, an immanent interpretation may be conceived as an attempt to understand the immanent properties of an interpretandum, and an historical interpretation may be conceived as an attempt to understand the historical properties of an interpretandum.

In order to explain the import of Simmel's distinction, suppose we consider a literary artifact that has repeatedly been subjected to a variety of interpretations, Thomas Mann's novel *Doctor Faustus*. Consider the following questions about the novel. Does it present a theory of music as a synthesis which mediates and reconciles the following polar oppositions: intellectuality and sensuality, order and chaos, the esoteric and the popular, aestheticism and barbarism, objectivity and subjectivity, health and disease? Does the conflict between these polar oppositions transpire within the life and character of its principal figure, the composer Adrian Leverkühn? Is the music of Leverkühn—and perhaps all music—presented as a species of demonic creativity that betrays an extremely intimate but nevertheless paradoxical relationship to theology? Does the novel shed some light on the history of Germany from Luther to Hitler? Does the novel illuminate the conditions under which a culture of esotericism and aestheticism can lapse into decadence and collapse into barbarity? Given Simmel's distinction, these issues are all immanent in the sense that their resolution is logically independent of the question: what were Mann's intentions in writing *Doctor Faustus*?

According to Simmel, it is possible that Mann's literary intentions were completely irrelevant to these issues. It is also possible that Mann may have failed to write a novel that realizes his own literary intentions. Simmel claims that an interpretandum—an artifact, for example—has immanent properties which are independent of the intentions of its creator, properties which he did not intend and could not have intended. A technician, for example, may invent a device which functions according to principles that are completely unknown to him. Such a device may have uses that the inventor did not anticipate and—if he remains ignorant of the principles according to which it functions—could not have anticipated. Laws, Simmel claims, often have properties which the legislators themselves are unaware of, features which are only discovered through the execution and interpretation of the laws. However these additional possible meanings should not be regarded as errors or distortions simply because they were not intended by the legislators. On the contrary, they are immanent in the following respect: although they are independent of the conditions under which this body of law was instituted, there is a sense in which they are logical consequences of these laws. Consider the emotions with which a man of the twentieth century responds to a Gothic cathedral or to a sonata written in the classical style. Simmel claims that there is no sense in which these emotions and the interpretations they generate are dependent upon the feelings of the architect or the composer. On the contrary, they represent objective and immanent properties of the interpretandum itself. "The relationship between the creator and his work," Simmel infers, "invariably betrays this curious property. The autonomous artifact contains elements that cannot be explained by reference to the intentions of the designer" (Simmel, 1957, p. 74). In Simmel's view, this aspect of the distinction between immanent interpretation and historical interpretation locates a crucial difference between these two forms of interpretation. In principle, it is possible for an indefinite number of immanent interpretations of the same object to be correct or true. However no more than one historical interpretation of this object can be true.

In order to illuminate this fundamental difference between immanent and historical interpretation, Simmel considers the following illustration. Suppose that the author of a riddle constructs the puzzle around a certain solution which he has in mind, a specific word. Suppose that another solution is discovered which works just as well as the author's own solution: from the perspective of both logical and aesthetic criteria, it solves the riddle equally well. Simmel claims that under these conditions, no privileged status can be claimed for the author's solution. There is no sense in which his solution is superior to the other solution, or to any other solution which satisfies the same criteria equally well. In principle, there is no limit on the number of possible and equally legitimate solutions that might be constructed. According to Simmel, the historical question "What solution did the author of the riddle intend?" has, at most, only one correct answer. However the question "Objectively, what qualifies as a solution to the riddle?" may be answered by all those solutions that satisfy the same criteria equally well. How do these remarks about the riddle illuminate the distinction between immanent and historical interpretation?

Suppose that a creative process has assumed the form of objectified mind. Consider all the extremely diverse forms in which this process can be understood. Each form of understanding is equally legitimate or justifiable to the extent that it satisfies the criteria of precision, logical coherence, and material sufficiency. The identification of the real intention which lies behind the creative process in the mind of the creator is not a necessary condition for this sort of understanding (Simmel, 1957, p. 73).

Simmel attempts to elucidate this point by considering how it applies to the difference between an immanent interpretation and an historical interpretation of Goethe's *Faust*. The former interpretation is independent of any account of the intentions that

Goethe may have had in writing *Faust*. Consider the criteria by reference to which an immanent interpretation would be evaluated: internal consistency and coherence; logical and aesthetic simplicity, symmetry, and completeness; consistency with the text of the drama itself and the ability to explain otherwise problematical relationships; and so on. Suppose that different immanent interpretations of *Faust* satisfy these criteria equally well. In that case, Simmel claims, each of these interpretations is equally correct or sound. Consider, for example, the different interpretations of Oedipus, Faust, and Hamlet that have been proposed: moral, theological, Marxist, Freudian, Jungian, expressionist, existentialist, formalist, and structuralist name only a few of the best known. Consider the implausible but logically possible condition in which all of these interpretations satisfy the same criteria equally well. Under this condition, Simmel argues, each of these interpretations is equally valid. However this does not hold true for an historical interpretation. In an historical interpretation, this sort of systematic ambiguity is logically impossible. In fact, the creative process of the composition of *Faust* transpired in one specific way. Either we can identify the process responsible for the genesis of the drama, or we cannot. However the genesis of *Faust* cannot be the object of several different but equally legitimate historical interpretations.

According to Simmel, this analysis identifies a fundamental difference between an objective or immanent interpretation and an historical interpretation.

A variety of equally legitimate objective interpretations of *Faust* is possible. However a variety of equally legitimate historical interpretations of *Faust* in the mental processes of Goethe is an absurdity (Simmel, 1957, p. 75).

Simmel recognizes that there may be a variety of hypotheses concerning the historical interpretation of a given phenomenon. Ultimately, however, only one of these hypotheses can be true, and all the others must be false. Immanent interpretation does not entail these mutually exclusive alternatives. It follows that a "completely definitive" historical interpretation of a given phenomenon is possible, but not a completely definitive immanent or objective interpretation of "all the possible meanings implicated in this phenomenon" (Simmel, 1957, p. 76).

It follows that there are two basic and closely related differences between immanent and historical interpretation. (1) Immanent interpretations are concerned with properties of the interpretandum that are independent of its production or genesis. Historical interpretation is concerned with properties of the interpretandum that are dependent upon its genesis. (2) Only one historical interpretation of a given phenomenon can be true. In principle, however, there is no limit upon the number of equally legitimate immanent interpretations of a given phenomenon. Simmel presumably thinks that these differences are intimately related for the following reason. Only one historical interpretation of a given datum can be true because only one interpretans will be confirmed by a description of the unique genesis of the interpretandum. Since immanent interpretation is independent of any description of the genesis of the interpretandum, its legitimacy is not determined by reference to this consideration. In the domain of immanent interpretation, Simmel claims, this requirement is replaced by other criteria: consistency, coherence, completeness, simplicity, and symmetry, for example. It is logically possible for more than one interpretation to satisfy these criteria equally well. Therefore the same legitimacy may be ascribed to all these immanent interpretations.

Simmel's theory of immanent interpretation is worth examining in some detail. On this view, the criteria for immanent interpretation include the possibility of a variety of irreducibly different interpretations of the same phenomenon which are not mutually exclusive. In the final analysis, this aspect of Simmel's theory of interpretation seems to be a consequence of an important assumption to which his philosophical anthropology is committed. Recall that forms are generated by the incessant energies of life. Irreducibly different existential commitments and modes of being produce autonomous, irreducibly different, and incommensurable forms. The above discussion of the relationship between Simmel's theory of forms and his theory of culture analyzed the process in which forms become objectified as the structures of culture. Simmel's theory of immanent interpretation is intimately related to the theory of forms and the theory of culture. It is essential to distinguish immanent interpretation from psychological and historical interpretation precisely because forms become objectified in structures that acquire properties which are independent of their genesis. The diversity of cultural forms is a consequence of the plurality of distinctively different energies of life which cannot be derived from one basic and uniform cause or source. The possibility of different but equally legitimate immanent interpretations also seems to be a consequence of this same assumption: different modes of being also generate irreducibly different and incommensurable interpretations. The multiplicity of the elemental energies of life generates a variety of forms, which in turn produces a plurality of interpretations.[26]

It follows that this aspect of Simmel's hermeneutic—the possibility of a variety of equally legitimate immanent interpretations—is a consequence of his theory of forms: the postulate that reality is constituted by a multiplicity of autonomous and incommensurable forms. Furthermore, this postulate is a consequence of Simmel's philosophical anthropology: the doctrine that the process of life is constituted by a plurality of irreducibly different energies and motive forces. Therefore Simmel's theory of immanent interpretation may be explained as a consequence of assumptions to which his philosophical anthropology is committed. Readers familiar with Simmel's work will not be surprised to learn that he never makes the logic of this relationship between his hermeneutic, the theory of forms, and his philosophical anthropology explicit. However he employs this reasoning implicitly in a number of illuminating remarks on criteria for interpretation that are scattered throughout his essays. Three of these texts may be considered here.

In his essay "On the Philosophy of the Actor," Simmel criticizes two views of the nature of dramatic acting which he regards as completely mistaken (Simmel, 1967, pp. 229–65). One view is a version of aesthetic naturalism. On this view, the ultimate aim of the actor is to play a role—Hamlet, for example—in the way that a real Hamlet would have conducted himself if this particular prince of Denmark had actually existed. The other view Simmel regards as much more seductive and dangerous, possibly because he believes it is less vulgar and not so obviously defective as aesthetic naturalism. On this latter view, the ideal conception of a dramatic role is in some sense necessarily and unambiguously given in the role itself. It is as if the dramatic realization of the character of Hamlet could in some sense be derived from Shakespeare's text of the play. The first view entails that acting as a form is reducible to the form of reality. The second view entails that acting is reducible to the form of drama. Both theses entail that there is ultimately only one legitimate interpretation of a given dramatic role, one ideal and uniquely authentic conception which the actor may approximate more or less closely. This is, of course, one reason why Simmel thinks that these theories of acting are false: there is not one uniquely privileged and legitimate interpretation of a dramatic role. Simmel claims that this position is refuted by the following consideration. Three consummate actors may play the same role in three different ways. Consider the different interpretations of Hamlet realized by different Shakespearean actors. Or consider the different interpretations of this role which would be created by following the dramaturgic instructions of Goethe, Brecht, and Dürrenmatt. Simmel thinks that each of these conceptions of the role can be equally valid as an interpretation. It is not necessarily the case that one interpretation must be superior to all the others. This is because the criteria for dramatic interpretation cannot be subsumed under an axiom or universal norm which prescribes unequivocally how Hamlet must be played. On the contrary, there is a sense in which these interpretations are not only autonomous and irreducible, but also incommensurable. Simmel claims that a given dramatic passage or piece of action which is brilliantly executed in one interpretation sometimes cannot be incorporated into another without producing a jarring and repugnant inconsistency in the realization of the role. It is not difficult to appreciate the point Simmel has in mind here if we compare different interpretations of the same piece of music by different conductors. Compare, for example, the last movement of Beethoven's Ninth Symphony as performed by the Vienna Philharmonic under Karl Böhm with the same piece of music performed by the Berlin Philharmonic under Wilhelm Furtwängler. To transpose Furtwängler's furious and bombastic conception of the finale of this movement into Böhm's much more subtle and introspective reading of the same score would produce an incongruous result. A comparison of the Wagner interpretations by the same two conductors supports this same inference. These interpretations are not only different in the sense that divergent readings or realizations of the same text are produced. They are incommensurable in the sense that they are not constructed according to the same hermeneutic criteria.

From the perspective of this aspect of Simmel's theory of interpretation—the thesis that irreducibly different interpretations may be incomparable and incommensurable rather than mutually exclusive or inconsistent—it is enlightening to consider the different readings of Wagner's scores that conductors have presented at the Bayreuth festivals. At Bayreuth, complete records of the timings of all festival performances are maintained. The slowest *Parsifal,* for example, was Toscanni's 1931 performance: five hours and five minutes. Since Toscanni is conventionally regarded as a fast conductor, this is a surprising discovery. The shortest performance was by Clemens Kraus in 1953: three hours and fifty-six minutes. From Simmel's perspective, this discrepancy of more than an hour in length between the two performances is an index of the different criteria of interpretation that Toscanni and Kraus imposed on the score. Given the differences in their criteria, a specific passage as read by Toscanni could not be incorporated into Kraus's performance without fracturing its consistency and integrity. Even performances of the one-act *Das Rheingold* vary as much as a half hour in length. However the impression of tempo is not necessarily a consequence of metronomical time. It may be determined by subtleties in the conductor's interpretation of markings in the score; for example, the different ways of discriminating ritardando and accelerando and the sense of buoyancy or gravity that colors his reading. Thomas Beecham, who is also regarded as a fast conductor, presented *Die Meistersinger* for the first time at Covent Garden in 1913. He was criticized for taking the opera much faster than Hans Richter, who had not only studied the work with Wagner, but had actually lived with him during the period of composition and assisted in copying the score. Beecham, however, produced timings which proved that his performance was actually somewhat slower than Richter's. This impression of tempo was presumably a consequence of the relative vivacity and spring of Beecham's performance. According to Simmel, the coherence of Beecham's interpretation would be destroyed by the introduction of passages taken from a heavier or more profound reading, even though metronomically these two versions might have exactly the same length. This aspect of Simmel's theory of interpretation—the point that the imposition of different hermeneutic criteria results in irreducibly different and incommensurable interpretations—can be appreciated by auditing two commercially available recordings of Wagner's *Ring*. The celebrated version by Georg Solti sometimes sacrifices clarity of the libretto to orchestral pyrotechnics, which become especially deafening in passages that allow Solti to indulge his passion for overwhelming brass effects. In von Karajan's recording of the *Ring,* on the other hand, the range of dramatic and expressive possibilities of the music is limited in order to achieve a clear, pure, and—compared with Solti's version—undramatic sound. Solti sacrifices clarity to achieve spectactular dramatic effects. Von Karajan sacrifices dramatic expression to achieve sonic beauty and aesthetic clarity.[27]

According to Simmel, there is a certain ideal relationship between the text of the drama and the actor. This relationship is comparable to the relation between the empirical world and the intellect that interprets it. Simmel asks that we consider two different intellects constituted by two different sets of a priori categories. From the perspective of these two intellects, different pictures of the world would be "true." This difference in what constitutes truth is a consequence of the difference between their constitutive categories. For the same reason, Simmel claims, different interpretations of the role of Hamlet would qualify as "correct" or "authentic" for two actors whose gifts and temperament diverge significantly. Two different but equally legitimate interpretations of the same phenomenon are a consequence of two different modes of being. However Simmel warns that it would be mistaken to infer from these considerations that interpretation is purely subjective and capricious. Just to the contrary. As Simmel puts it, the individual interpreter himself is an objective factor constitutive of interpretation. In other words, the subjectivity of the actor—the unique constellation of his temperament and gifts—is a condition for the constitution of a certain object: an interpretation of a dramatic role. It follows that irreducible logical or conceptual differences in interpretation are grounded in irreducible ontological or existential differences between interpreters. Fundamentally different but equally legitimate modes of interpretation are ultimately a consequence of fundamentally different modes of being. For the same reason that it would be senseless to suppose that one mode of being or form of life could be refuted on the basis of another, it would also be senseless to suppose that a given interpretation could be refuted on the basis of a different and incommensurable interpretation.

Simmel considers these same issues in the essay on "Feminine

Culture." Minds which are differently constituted, Simmel claims, will produce different interpretations of the world. However each of these interpretations may be equally legitimate. Simmel acknowledges that different interpretations of the same phenomenon may be related in the same way that alternative hypotheses concerning the explanation of the same phenomenon are related: only one such hypothesis—and, therefore, only one such interpretation—can be true. However different interpretations of the same phenomenon are not invariably related in this way. On the contrary, the relations between them may be comparable to different portraits of the same model by different but equally competent painters. It cannot be said that only one of these portraits is true or correct. Simmel argues that a portrait is a self-contained totality, legitimated by its own intrinsic properties and its special relationship to the subject of the portrait. A given portrait expresses something that cannot be expressed by another portrait. However this does not mean that there is some sense in which one portrait contradicts another. On the basis of these considerations, Simmel asks that we consider the following four interpretations: (1) a male interpretation of a male interpretandum, (2) a female interpretation of a male interpretandum, (3) a male interpretation of a female interpretandum, and (4) a female interpretation of a female interpretandum. Simmel holds that there are fundamental differences between these interpretations. On this basis, he concludes that women can be expected to make original contributions to the sociocultural sciences, contributions which could not have been anticipated by men. This is because the feminine perspective on the interpretandum differs from the male perspective. This difference in perspective provides a new possibility of seeing and interpreting. Both the difference in perspective and the new hermeneutic possibilities are a consequence of the definitively feminine psychological structure. Presumably this uniquely feminine perspective includes both the possibility of seeing different, new, or unnoticed phenomena and also the possibility of seeing and interpreting differently: a novel, unnoticed, or undeveloped perspective. The definitively feminine interpretation of the world is a consequence of the a priori categories that constitute the feminine perspective. For this reason, women will interpret the world differently from men. However it does not follow that these interpretations must be regarded as mutually exclusive alternatives only one of which can be accepted as valid. On the contrary, feminine interpretations can reveal new or unnoticed aspects of the world. It follows that there may be specifically feminine hermeneutic functions in the sociocultural sciences, functions which are a consequence of the constitutive properties of the feminine mode of being.

On the basis of the reasoning employed here, Simmel would presumably be sympathetic to the suggestion that Jews—because of their peculiar predicament in the West, especially since the end of the eighteenth century—could create a social science which is in some sense definitively Jewish. It is, of course, notorious that this claim has been made about psychoanalysis and sociology. Simmel's view on this issue could be formulated in the following way: whenever a form of life produces a distinctive mode of being or a definitive existential type, a new perspective and new hermeneutic possibilities are created. In consequence, new kinds of social science also become possible for the same reason.[28]

Simmel returns to the same point concerning the ontological or existential bases of incommensurable interpretations in one of his last books, an extremely suggestive although allusive and enigmatical study of Rembrandt (Simmel, 1919). In this book, Simmel offers an interpretation of the significance of death in Rembrandt's portraits and compares this property of Rembrandt's work with the "timelessness" or "atemporality" of classical art. Simmel claims that this interpretation cannot be proven. It does not even have the status of an hypothesis which is verifiable in principle, even though in fact its truth or falsity may never be established. Verifiability cannot be ascribed to this sort of interpretation. On the contrary, its force and legitimacy are not grounded in the possibility of demonstration or proof, but rather in a certain "immediate plausibility" or "direct assent" that it can produce. An interpretation of a work of art can achieve this in the following way: in virtue of the coherence which the interpretation creates, a variety of fragmented and heterogeneous impressions is perceived as intimately related and harmoniously integrated. Simmel claims that when this impression of immediate plausibility is produced, it can only be acknowledged as an established fact. It cannot be verified, confirmed, or proven. The coherence which such an interpretation achieves cannot be derived as a logical consequence of premises. The interpretation itself is not grounded upon logical force and necessity, but rather upon existential conviction and persuasion. It follows that incommensurable interpretations of this sort are a consequence of the different criteria of coherence which different modes of being impose upon the world.

In his discussion of the difference between historical and immanent interpretation, Simmel takes up the criticism of a thesis that he calls historicism. Simmel's career antedates the massive scholarly debate in Germany over the status of historicism, a controversy which reached its peak shortly after World War I, above all in the works of Ernst Troeltsch and Friedrich Meinecke. Although Simmel never explains precisely what he means by historicism, the thesis that he criticizes seems to reduce to the claim that a given interpretandum can be understood only by reference to its origins. To understand a phenomenon is to identify the conditions for its genesis or production. It follows that all interpretation is historical interpretation. Therefore historicism, as Simmel conceives it, entails that no distinction between historical interpretation and immanent interpretation can be made. Put another way, historicism entails that there are no immanent interpretations. This is because historicism conceives the problem of understanding an artifact as exhausted by the problem of reconstructing the conditions of its genesis and development.

Problems concerning the objective and temporally independent attributes of being are reduced to questions concerning the process in which these qualities develop—questions of becoming (Simmel, 1957, p. 76).

Consider the translation that historicism proposes. Suppose that questions about the historically independent properties of the interpretandum are translated into questions about its temporally dependent properties. In other words, suppose that the problems of interpretation in general are regarded as exhausted by the problems of historical interpretation. As Simmel sees it, this translation is defeated by two radical defects. First and most obviously, it eliminates the autonomous status of immanent interpretation by conflating questions of immanent interpretation with questions of historical interpretation. Simmel describes the result as a "capricious foreshortening" of an entire dimension of the problem of interpretation, the immanent dimension. The satisfaction of immanent hermeneutic criteria is a sufficient condition for the legitimation of some interpretations. Therefore it is Simmel's position that historical interpretation is not a necessary condition for interpretation in general. Some interpretations—immanent or objective interpretations—are not historical. Second and less obviously, immanent interpretation also has a legitimate and essential place within history. Put another way, immanent interpretation is a necessary condition for historical interpretation.

It would be impossible for us to understand the what or the essence of things by reference to their historical development unless we already had some sort of independent understanding of this essence. Without this latter sort of understanding, historical understanding would obviously be a completely absurd undertaking (Simmel, 1957, p. 77).

In which case, it follows that historical interpretation is not a sufficient condition for interpretation either.

This critique of historicism leads Simmel to the third basic form of the relationship between interpretans and interpretandum. In this case, Simmel claims, the distinction between interpretans and interpretandum is not based on the distinction between mental process and observable event, the first form of this relationship, or the distinction between a specific mental process and a type of this same process, the second form of this relationship. It is based on the distinction between what Simmel calls a "mental content"—the import of the act or artifact that constitutes the interpretandum—and an "atemporal content"—a framework of logical relationships or conceptual structures that constitutes the interpretans. In explaining this distinction, Simmel employs illustrations from both the history of art and the history of philosophy.

Consider the development of western art from the collapse of the Roman Empire to the end of the sixteenth century. Simmel describes this development in the following way. The rigid forms of Byzantine and Gothic art are replaced by the individualistic plasticity and disorder of the fifteenth century, which are then synthesized in the unified harmonies of the High Renaissance. At the end of the sixteenth century, the strains on this synthesis lead to its collapse. This produces either an art in which style is determined by purely formal criteria or an art in which there are no settled or definitive criteria for style, a chaos of styles. Under what conditions is an historical interpretation of this development possible? As Simmel puts it, under what conditions is it possible to form these aesthetic constructs—the Byzantine, the Gothic, the quattrocento, the High Renaissance—into an actual historical sequence? Simmel claims that the following is a necessary condition for this historical interpretation: it is essential to understand the intrinsic relationships between these aesthetic concepts "in terms of their purely substantive significance and from the standpoint of the logic of art" (Simmel, 1977, p. 205). These relationships constitute "an atemporal structure of *meaning,* a structure that is independent of all considerations of antecedence and consequence" (Simmel, 1977, p. 205). Consider, for example, the relationship between Gothic sculpture and early Renaissance sculpture. According to Simmel, the artifacts that make up this development can be interpreted as constituting an historical sequence only if the logical relationships between the aesthetic concepts of the Gothic and the early Renaissance first become objects of immanent interpretation. Suppose that this condition is not satisfied. In other words, suppose that an immanent interpretation of the aesthetic import of Gothic and early Renaissance art has not been produced. In that case, the artifacts in question would only constitute "an incoherent succession of phenomena." These considerations entail that immanent interpretation is an indispensable condition for historical interpretation. And if this is the case, then it obviously follows that the historicist position is mistaken.

Simmel's illustration from the history of philosophy is also intended to support this thesis. Under what conditions is it possible to understand the philosophy of Kant? Historicism leads us to believe that Kant is to be understood by deriving him from history. The philosophical positions of the pre-Kantian era— Cartesian rationalism and British empiricism—are conceived as steps or stages which lead to the philosophy of Kant. According to Simmel, this view is mistaken. An historical interpretation of the philosophy of Kant is only possible on the basis of an immanent interpretation. An historical interpretation "would not be possible unless the logical content of all these philosophical theories— completely independent of any considerations of their historical genesis—constituted an intelligible sequence" (Simmel, 1957, pp. 77–78). Consider the relationship between rationalism, empiricism, and the Kantian critique. Simmel reconstructs the conceptual relationships between these philosophical theories in the following way. Rationalism rejects experience as a source of knowledge. The evidence of the senses is regarded as radically deceptive and fallacious. The clear and distinct ideas of reason itself constitute the exclusive source or criterion of truth. Empiricism, on the other hand, repudiates reason as a source of knowledge. Knowledge of matters of fact is based exclusively upon experience. According to the Kantian critique, the empiricists are correct in their belief that experience provides the only basis for knowledge of matters of fact. However they fail to see that experience itself is an a priori category constituted by the faculty of reason. Therefore the rationalists are also correct in their belief that knowledge is unconditionally valid, for it is constituted by the principles of the faculty of reason itself. However they fail to see that knowledge is only valid for possible objects of experience, a domain which knowledge can never transcend. Suppose that we did not understand the "purely immanent significance" of the logical relationships between these theories. Simmel claims that these logical relationships constitute a conceptual structure that is independent of its historical realization in rationalism, empiricism, and the Kantian critique. Without an immanent understanding of these theories, Simmel argues, their historical interpretation would be impossible. They would remain nothing more than a discontinuous sequence of brute facts. To the historicist thesis that the understanding of Kant is a function of his historical derivation or interpretation, Simmel claims, we can juxtapose the thesis that an historical interpretation of Kant is dependent upon an immanent interpretation of his philosophy. In other words, it follows that immanent or objective interpretation is a necessary condition for historical interpretation.[29]

There are several reasons why Simmel's views on interpretation resist any formulation into a coherent hermeneutic or theory of interpretation. These views were developed in a number of different works, published over a period of more than twenty-five years, and written for a variety of purposes. During this period—roughly 1892 to 1918—Simmel's thinking on the basic issues of the theory of knowledge and the methodological problems of the sociocultural sciences remained in transition. As a result, his publications often give the impression of intermediate stages situated between one conceptual scheme that is in the process of being abandoned—even though Simmel apparently remains committed to some of its basic elements—and another conceptual scheme the vague outlines of which are only emerging. In Simmel's work, this process of transition is never consummated. The shift from positivism through neo-Kantianism to a *Lebensphilosophie* remains incomplete. As a result, the project of providing a coherent and systematic summary of Simmel's position on any basis issue becomes a problematical undertaking.

In a memorial article published shortly after Simmel's death, Georg Lukács, who had studied with Simmel in Berlin, offers a number of trenchant and perceptive observations concerning this property of Simmel's work. Lukács suggests that Simmel qualifies as the most significant and interesting transitional phenomenon in all of modern philosophy. In developing a conception of impressionism as a general philosophy or world view, Lukács is led to compare Simmel with Monet, Rodin, Richard Strauss, and Rilke. Impressionism, as Lukács conceives it, may be understood as a form which is inherently or essentially transitional. Impressionism rejects all conclusive forms and complete systems in principle. From the perspective of impressionism, systematic thought distorts and violates the kaleidoscopic character of life, its profusion, heterogeneity, and "polyphony." Impressionism, therefore, may be conceived as a protest of life itself against the imposition of rigid, unequivocal, and permanent forms. Given this conception of impressionism, Lukács judges, Simmel can be called the greatest transitional thinker of our era. He is a Monet of philosophy, the authentic theoretician of impressionism (Gassen and Landmann, 1958, pp. 171–73).

In fact, Simmel explicitly rejects any mode of thought in the sociocultural sciences that lends itself to neat categorizations and clear and distinct ideas. In Simmel's view, much of Western sociocultural thought since the seventeenth century commits what could be called the fallacy of misplaced clarity and precision. Categories which are fundamentally and ineradicably obscure are analyzed as if their import were clear. Distinctions which are inherently vague or ambiguous are analyzed as if they were precise. The entire project of "Western intellectuality"—which Simmel sees as attaining its most sublime expression in the work of Kant—falsifies the complexities and obscurities of sociocultural reality by employing a method of investigation that inevitably oversimplifies and conceals the irreducible heterogeneity of life.[30]

Simmel's writings on interpretation exhibit this view of the radical obscurity of life and its recalcitrance to systematic analysis. There are not enough categories, Simmel is once alleged to have said, just as there are not enough sexes. Given his repeated stress upon the resistance of interpretation to analysis, it is not difficult to see why Simmel's views on interpretation resist formulation into a coherent theory. Consider an attempt to systematize Simmel's account of interpretation by classifying the different kinds of interpretation that are allegedly identifiable in his writings. Kinds of interpretation might be identified by employing as the distinguishing criterion the different relationships between interpretans and interpretandum. This distinction could be established by considering what kind of knowledge is essential to a specific kind of interpretation. Given differences in the kind of knowledge required, different relationships between interpretans and interpretandum could be identified. This would provide a principle for distinguishing different kinds of interpretation.[31]

In view of Simmel's explicit views on the essential properties of interpretation, it seems that such an analytical project is doomed to failure from the outset. For example, suppose that the analysis identified two different kinds of interpretation in Simmel's hermeneutic: genetic and immanent. This classification is not satisfactory because historical interpretation is both genetic and immanent. Nor will a dichotomy of psychological and logical interpretation serve, for historical understanding requires an interpretation of mental processes in terms of the logical and conceptual relationships that constitute their objective import. Nor is it even possible to establish a rigorous distinction between historical and nonhistorical interpretation in Simmel's writings, for an immanent and nonhistorical interpretation is a necessary condition for historical interpretation. In Simmel's work, the properties of different kinds or types of interpretation—psychological, immanent, and historical—overlap and intersect. For this reason, an analysis which introduces rigorous distinctions between them is self-defeating: in effect, it substitutes for Simmel's theory of interpretation views he would reject. In the attempt to understand Simmel's hermeneutic, it is important to recognize the following source of complexity: differences between interpretations are differences of nuance and stress, not differences of category. Put another way, differences between interpretations approximate subtle psychological and rhetorical differences rather than absolute logical and epistemological distinctions.

In the essays translated in this volume, Simmel develops and illustrates three of the crucial concepts on which his intellectual project depends: form, threshold, and interpretation. Although the principal works translated here are among the latest of Simmel's writings, the position which he takes in them cannot be described as final or definitive. No conclusive results are established. Nor did Simmel regard such conclusions as the real purpose of his work. He repeatedly emphasizes the importance of the process of the investigation over the significance of its results or findings. There is a sense in which the definitive purpose of the investigation does not lie in the conclusions it reaches, but rather in the activity or process of the inquiry itself. Simmel's theory of forms entails that any given conceptual scheme can only have an incomplete, fragmentary, and transitional status. It follows that these properties must also be ascribed to Simmel's own conceptual apparatus. Under these conditions, it is not surprising that Simmel was sometimes inclined to describe his enterprise in language which suggests a journey that has no end. In a letter to Marianne Weber which touches upon exactly this point, the metaphorical relationship between an investigation and a journey is the subject of the following observation.

And so I set sail in search of an undiscovered land. Of course the journey will probably end *before* I reach the unknown shore. However I will at least not share the fate of so many of my colleagues: they make themselves so comfortable on the ship that, in the final analysis, they mistate the ship itself for the new land (Gassen and Landmann, 1958, p. 132).[32]

Notes

1. See Simmel, 1977, p. ix and Simmel's letter to Heinrich Rickert dated November 11, 1904 in Gassen and Landmann, 1958, p. 101.

2. See the letter to Rickert dated June 3, 1913 in Gassen and Landmann, 1958, p. 111.

3. Concentration on the epistemological problems of the sociocultural sciences became increasingly difficult for Simmel because he was preoccupied with Germany's deteriorating economic and military predicament and the uncertain fate of German culture in the new sociocultural world which would be a product of the war. Some of Simmel's reflections on this subject are summarized in *Der Krieg und die geistigen Entscheidungen. Reden und Aufsätze* (1917).

4. "The Problem of Historical Time" was first published as "Das Problem der historischen Zeit," Berlin: Reuther, 1916, the twelfth in a series of philosophical lectures sponsored by the Kant Society. Simmel delivered the original lecture on March 3, 1916 at a meeting of the Berlin section of the Kant Society. The lecture is reprinted in two posthumously published collections of Simmel's essays: *Zur Philosophie der Kunst* (ed. Gertrud Simmel), Potsdam: Kiepenheuer, 1922, and *Brücke und Tür* (ed. Michael Landmann in collaboration with Margarete Susman), Stuttgart: K. F. Koehler, 1957. "The Constitutive Concepts of History" was first published as "Die historische Formung" in the journal *Logos*, 7, 1917-18, pp. 113-152, and was reprinted in the collection of essays *Fragmente und Aufsätze aus dem Nachlass und Veröffentlichungen der letzten Jahre* (ed. Gertrud Kantorowicz), Munich: Drei Masken-Verlag. This same collection was reprinted by Georg Olms, Hildesheim, in 1967. "On the Nature of Historical Understanding" was first published as "Vom Wesen des historischen Verstehens," Berlin: Mittler, 1918, and was reprinted in the volume *Brücke und Tür*. "On the History of Philosophy" originally appeared as "Über die Geschichte der Philosophie" in the Viennese journal *Die Zeit*, no. 31, May 28, 1904, and was also reprinted in *Brücke und Tür*. Research on these translations was supported by a grant from Monmouth College. Prof. Kurt H. Wolff provided detailed criticisms of the translations and helpful suggestions concerning a number of points in this essay. In addition, preliminary drafts of Wolff's own unpublished translations of "The Problem of Historical Time" and "On the Nature of Historical Understanding" were available to the translator during the final revision of the manuscript. Study of Wolff's translations proved to be a valuable aid in the last stages of the preparation of this volume.

5. Discussions of Simmel's theory of forms in English include Weingartner, 1960 and the translator's Introduction to Simmel, 1977.

6. Simmel's most sustained defense of the immanence of forms is presented in various criticisms of a thesis that he usually calls realism or naturalism. He represents realism as the claim that any form is, in principle, nothing more than a copy or reproduction of reality. In that case, the properties of knowledge as a form

could be derived from reality: epistemological realism. The properties of history as a form could be derived from human experience: historial realism. The properties of art as a form could be derived from the properties of the phenomena that art represents: aesthetic realism. For Simmel's most systematic attempt to refute historical realism, see Simmel, 1977, chapter one. See also his essay "On the History of Philosophy," translated in this volume. Here Simmel argues that the properties of the history of philosophy as a form cannot be derived from the properties of its subject matter, philosophy itself.

7. A translation of this essay is published in Wolff, 1959 and is reprinted in Simmel, 1971.

8. In his essay on "Feminine Culture," Simmel extends this thesis to cover other forms which do not seem to be so comprehensive as the forms he mentions here: for example, the state and the bourgeois household (Simmel, 1911b, pp. 278-319).

9. The thesis that philosophy is irrefutable on both empirical and logical grounds and the view of philosophy as the expression of a typical intellectual attitude toward the world are also defended in the essay "Henri Bergson" in Simmel, 1922b. Simmel's theory of forms as irreducibly different and incommensurable worlds may have its source in the influence of Stefan George, which seems to have begun around 1900. See Simmel's essay "Stefan George" in Simmel, 1922b.

10. In his essay "On Caricature," Simmel describes man's capacity for the self-transcendence of his own self-defined limits as an essential aspect of his nature. See Simmel, 1922b, pp. 87-95. Stefan George may have been an important source of Simmel's ideas on the objectification of the subject and the de-subjectification of the individual. See "The Seventh Ring" in Simmel, 1922b, an essay on George's volume of poetry which bears the same title. On p. 76, Simmel refers to the "monumentalization" of the subject or psyche in the work of George. In George's lyrics, the "solipsism of the psyche" is expressed in a "monumental form."

11. Simmel's most sustained and systematic analysis of the process of objectification is offered in *The Philosophy of Money*. See Simmel, 1978, pp. 295-303, 311-14, 318-19, 448-50, 462-63, 476-79. In his analysis of objectification, the influence of Simmel's thinking on Lukács, Benjamin, Horkheimer, and Adorno is clear. Their disposition to understress this influence on a variety of grounds—metaphysical, epistemological, moral, and political—is well known is perhaps best expressed in Lukács's judgment, presumably offered in complete seriousness, that Simmel's socioeconomic status as a *rentier* intellectual made him "the ideologist of *rentier* parasitism" (Lukács, 1974, p. 400). In other words, Simmel's intellectual work may be represented as an ideology for the decadent capitalism of the Wilhelminian period.

12. See Simmel, 1978, pp. 230-32, 236-38, 360-65, 481-84. In *The Philosophy of Money*, Simmel argues that the role of money in the process of instrumentalization is intimately related to the intellectualization of modern culture and its disposition to reduce qualitative relations to quantitative relations. See, for example, Simmel, 1978, pp. 150-52, 172, 277-80, 311, 314-15, 431-36, 440-46, 476-79.

13. On the inevitability of the tragedy of culture, see Simmel's 1909 essay "The Future of our Culture": "No politics of culture can eliminate the tragic discrepany between the unlimited advance of objective culture and the slow progress of subjective culture" (Simmel, 1957, p. 96).

14. Simmel, 1967, pp. 26-27. For the same points, see also the essay "On Love,"

Simmel 1967, pp. 72-74, 83-84, 114-15, and the essay on "The Philosophy of Landscape," Simmel, 1957, p. 143. This same analysis of tragedy is presented in several other essays. See the essay "Michelangelo" in Simmel, 1911b, pp. 171, 181; the essay "The Relative and the Absolute in the Problematic of Sexuality" in Simmel, 1911b, p. 82; and the essay "Ruins" in Simmel, 1911b, p. 142.

15. Simmel also identifies a species of sociological tragedy that exhibits these same two essential features of the tragedy of culture. See Simmel, 1964, pp. 31-32, 124-25, and Simmel, 1968b, p. 429. Simmel's view of the tragedy of culture and the sociological tragedy is discussed briefly by Levine on pp. xl-xli of Simmel, 1971. As Levine notes, Simmel reserves the term "tragic" "primarily to qualify two types of conflict, both of which involve some lesion of the boundaries of individuality" (p. xl). In the sociological tragedy, an inverse relationship between individuality and sociality develops. As the dimensions of sociality become more comprehensive, the bases of social interaction must be reduced to the lowest common denominators: properties which all the associated individuals share. This results in the isolation of the individual and the trivialization of his social relations. In the tragedy of culture, the conflict between subjective and objective culture results in the estrangement of the individual from the artifacts that he creates. However it seems that these two species of tragedy have rather different consequences. In *The Philosophy of Money* and *Soziologie,* Simmel argues that the interaction between life and social forms which is responsible for the sociological tragedy actually contributes to the conditions under which an expansion of freedom and individuality is possible. Social relations become more trivial and superficial. Every person becomes more dependent upon a larger number of anonymous and functionally interchangeable perons and a smaller number of specific or uniquely qualified individuals. As a result, the possibility that his individuality could be exhausted by any of his social relations is diminished. Therefore the intensification of his dependence upon the performances of an indefinite number of interchangeable individuals and the progressive elimination of his dependence upon specific persons extends the limits of his freedom. Especially in *The Philosophy of Money,* Simmel attempts to establish a relationship between the universalization of the money economy, the sociological tragedy, and the extension of individual freedom. See Simmel, 1978, pp. 284-89, 295-303, 332-36, 342-51, 354. In his essays on the sociology of culture and in the sections of *The Philosophy of Money* which bear upon the sociology of culture, however, Simmel argues that the interaction between life and cultural forms—the ultimate cause of the tragedy of culture—impoverishes individuality by confining the individual within the limits of increasingly ossified cultural forms. For a monograph devoted exclusively to Simmel's concept of tragedy, see Bauer, 1962. Curiously, this book does not identify Simmel's view of the definitive features of the tragic: the fact that an entity is threatened or destroyed by precisely the same immanent tendencies that produced it. Also there is no mention of the sociological tragedy and the tragedy of culture, nor is the distinction between subjective and objective culture identified.

16. In his posthumously published diary, Simmel asks: "What does our culture really represent for the most part? Only this: that we create instruments in order to mitigate the suffering that we inflict upon ourselves, in order to diminish the needs that we ourselves have created, and in order to resolve—quite incompletely—the contradictions that we have generated. For if these resolutions were complete and conclusive, it would not be necessary to change them

continually" (Simmel, 1967, pp. 44-45). See also Simmel, 1978, pp. 255-57, 468-69.

17. Hesse himself recognized these same properties in Castalia. The novel is the story of Joseph Knecht—musician, Glass Bead Game player, and eventually Master of the Glass Bead Game—and his apparently paradoxical attempt to escape both the sterility of the Castalian world and the confusion of the quotidian world. If the quotidian world is the domain of vulgarity, brutality, and irrationality, Castalia is the domain of passivity, resignation, and impotence, a world in which it is impossible to be free, to take "leaps," to imitate the fallen angel Lucifer: in other words, to create new values, even though novelty may be forbidden, rebellious, and dangerous. The novel, which ends with the death of Knecht, leaves some doubt about whether Hesse thinks it is possible to escape this dilemma. In Simmel's view, however, there is no doubt at all. Culture is inherently and inevitably tragic. Therefore Castalia, like any other culture, will end in sterility or chaos.

18. In *The Philosophy of Money*, Simmel also considers other threshold phenomena. On p. 263, he considers the thresholds of economic consciousness, philosophical consciousness, and the threshold of the tragic. On pp. 265-71, he discusses the relationship between monetary value and the threshold of the ascription of economic value. For Simmel's illustrations of various sociological thresholds, see Simmel, 1964, pp. 87, 97-98, 111-13, 193-95, and 1968b, pp. 362-64.

19. See also Simmel's analysis of the "threshold of reduction" in the same essay. The dimensions of any putative historical phenomenon, Simmel claims, must remain large enough to permit the ascription of meaning to this phenomenon. Phenomena which lie beneath this threshold do not fall within the domain of history because the interest in significance cannot be attributed to them.

20. Simmel recognized that the ontology of the irrationality of reality to which he was committed made it necessary for him to develop a theory of meaning and value. Ultimately, this theory is grounded on an axiology that establishes how certain values and meanings can be differentially ascribed to finite domains within the infinite profusion of reality. However Simmel realized that his theory of value also led to difficulties. For intimations of these difficulties, see Simmel's letters to Heinrich Rickert dated May 10, 1898, July 19, 1898, August 15, 1898, April 3, 1916, and April 15, 1917 in Gassen and Landmann, 1958, pp. 94-97, 115-119.

21. For Simmel's account of this a priori presupposition of history, see Simmel, 1977, pp. 39, 42, 44, 64, 87, 202-203.

22. Dilthey was born in 1833, twenty-five years before Simmel. He first established his reputation as an intellectual historian and Scheiermacher scholar. Dilthey began to concentrate on the philosophy of history only in the 1870's, and his *Einleitung in die Geisteswissenschaften* published in 1883 became one of the major events in generating the controversy over the status of the sociocultural sciences. In 1882, Dilthey was called to Berlin as Lotze's successor. He remained there until his death in 1911. Simmel was a student at Berlin during the period 1876-1884 and a junior faculty member from 1885 to 1914.

23. Notice that the psychological reproduction of the noematic properties of an act is logically impossible. This is because these properties are independent of any conception of the act as a psychological process. The supposition that psychological recreation of the noematic properties of a mental act is possible commits a category error: it mistakenly supposes that the noematic, logical, or conceptual

properties of mental acts can be subsumed under their noetic or psychological properties. In the ensuing, it will be established that Simmel attacks "historicism" because it commits precisely this category mistake. Simmel's later cultural hermeneutic, therefore, may be represented as a critique of both a psychologistic hermeneutic and an historicist hermeneutic.

24. Simmel, therefore, rejects the reductionist analysis of interpretation to which positivism is committed, an analysis which is based on the assumption that interpretation as a form of knowledge has no distinctive properties and can be derived from a deductive-nomological, causal explanation.

25. Simmel's early psychologistic phase is most clearly exhibited in his first three books: *Über soziale Differenzierung*, his first sociological publication, the first edition of *The Problems of the Philosophy of History*, and his two-volume work on moral philosophy, *Einleitung in die Moralwissenschaft* (Simmel, 1890, 1892, 1892-93).

26. This aspect of Simmel's thought is closely related to Max Weber's theory of the polytheism of values that is characteristic of modernity. However there seem to be two crucial differences between Simmel's view of the multiplicity of human energies, forms, and interpretations and Weber's view of the polytheism of values. (1) Weber locates the polytheism of values historically and sociologically. It is not a characteristic of all cultures. On the contrary, it is the product of a specifically modern culture. Simmel, on the other hand, bases the multiplicity of forms on ontological considerations. It is a consequence of the nature of man as a cultural being. Therefore it is an essential aspect of every culture. (2) According to Weber, modern culture is axiologically irrational in a specific sense. The different provinces of value are mutualy inconsistent: the gods or demons of modern culture are locked in an inexorable conflict. Simmel also argues that modern culture is axiologically irrational, but in a different sense. The forms of modern culture are not antagonistic or mutually inconsistent. On the contrary, they are autonomous, irreducibly different, and incommensurable. These premises, therefore, lead Weber and Simmel to develop intimately related, but nevertheless distinctively different, theories of modernity.

27. Most of these points concerning the interpretation of Wagner's music by different conductors are discussed in Magee, 1969, an uncommonly brief and lucid exposition of Wagner's music. For his discussion of differences in tempo, see, pp. 107-109. Solti and von Karajan as Wagner interpreters are considered on pp. 116-17.

28. In fact, the subjects that Simmel chose to investigate and the manner in which he approached them have been interpreted as expressing the peculiar predicament of the modern Jewish intellectual. The most ambitious defense of this interpretation is presented in Liebeschütz, 1970. Liebeschütz argues that the special qualities of the Western Jewish heritage are exhibited most clearly when their transformation into the modern mode of thought remains inadequate and the Jewish thinker himself remains incompletely assimilated into the Gentile intellectual world. Liebeschütz claims that the circumstances of Simmel's social world produced the following result: although Simmel himself was not always aware of this, the aims of his research and the objects of his interests were selected in such a way that they reflected his Jewish origins. Simmel, therefore, became a crypto-Jewish intellectual, the covert Jewish philosopher without explicit Jewish commitments. Simmel's work in sociology gave him an opportunity to investigate themes that Liebeschütz regards as characteristic of the Jewish predicament. The

conceptual language of sociology enabled Simmel to adopt an attitude of reserve or distance in dealing with these issues. Liebeschütz also connects—although obscurely and without any explanation—Simmel's turn to philosophical and sociological aesthetics with this type of Jewish existence. On this view, Simmel, his Jewish readers, and the Jewish members of his Berlin lecture audience represent products of an advanced stage of the cultural and social assimilation of the German Jew, a process that began with Moses Mendelssohn. According to Liebeschütz, it is not possible to prove that Simmel's predicament as a Jew and the problematic that this predicament entailed were in some sense necessary conditions for Simmel's turn to sociology. In other words, it is not possible to prove that Simmel would not have become a sociologist had he not been Jewish. However Liebeschütz does not doubt that Simmel's sociology is structured on the basis of his own immediate social surroundings: the experience of the highly educated, urbanized Jew.

A similar conception of the relationship between Simmel's intellectual project and his own peculiar sociocultural predicament is sketched much more briefly in Cuddihy, 1974. Cuddihy describes Simmel as the "father" of the "phenomenological family" of Jewish intellectuals who attempted to embrace the standards of Gentile civility that are constitutive of the bourgeois culture of the modern West. Cuddihy also attempts to explain Simmel's predicament as the consequence of a tragic conflict between the ritual requirements of modern Western civility that he embraced—especially its requirements of taste and etiquette, which Cuddihy calls "the Protestant esthetic and etiquette"—and the *Yiddishkeit* of the shtetl culture from which Simmel came. Simmel's problem, therefore, was the typical difficulty encountered by the modern Jew: the problem of ritual competence and the consequences of its lapses. See Cuddihy, p. 76. Cuddihy does not consider the fact that Simmel—whose family had been in Germany at least four generations—was not a product of the shtetl culture of the *Ostjuden*. The theory that explains the intellectual innovations of modern Jews by reference to their marginal cultural status in the West—the theory that both Liebeschütz and Cuddihy apply to Simmel—was sketched much earlier by Veblen in his remarkable essay on "The Intellectual Pre-eminence of Jews in Modern Europe," first published in 1919 and reprinted in Veblen, 1970.

29. See Simmel, 1957, pp. 78-79 and 1977, pp. 204-205. This critique of historicism is also sketched in the essay "On the History of Philosophy." Simmel also analyzes the relationship between immanent and historical interpretation in "The Problem of Historical Time," focusing especially upon the problematical relationship between the criteria for unique temporalization in historical interpretation and the criteria for immanent interpretation.

30. For an attempt to explain Simmel's fragmentary and antisystematic mode of thought and literary style as a consequence of these metaphysical commitments, see Axelrod, 1977. For a very different attempt to explain Simmel's idiosyncratic style as a consequence of his ambivalent status in academia—Simmel as "the stranger in the academy"—see Coser, 1965, 1971.

31. For a carefully executed attempt to undertake such an analysis of Simmel's theory of interpretation, see Weingartner, 1960.

32. A translation of this letter, the German text, and a facsimile of the original are available in Wolff, 1959, pp. 239-42.

References

Axelrod, Charles D.
  1977 "Toward an Appreciation of Simmel's Fragmentary Style," *The Sociological Quarterly*, vol. 18, no. 2, pp. 185-96.

Bauer, Isadora
  1962 *Die Tragik in der Existenz des modernen Menschen bei G. Simmel*, Berlin

Coser, Lewis A.
  1965 *Georg Simmel*, Englewood Cliffs, N.J.
  1971 *Masters of Sociological Thought*, New York

Cuddihy, John Murray
  1974 *The Ordeal of Civility*, New York

Gassen, Kurt and Michael Landmann (eds.)
  1958 *Buch des Dankes an Georg Simmel*, Berlin

Hesse, Hermann
  1970 *The Glass Bead Game*, New York

Liebeschütz, Hans
  1970 *Von Georg Simmel zu Franz Rosenzweig*, Tübingen

Lukács, Georg
  1974 *Die Zerstörung der Vernunft*, Darmstadt and Neuwied

Magee, Bryan
  1969 *Aspects of Wagner*, New York

Oesterreich, Traugott Konstantin
  1923 *Friedrich Ueberwegs Grundriss der Geschichte der Philosophie: Die Deutsche Philosophie des XIX Jahrhunderts und der Gegenwart*, 12th edition, Berlin

Simmel, Georg
  1890 *Über soziale Differenzierung*, Leipzig
  1892 *Die Probleme der Geschichtsphilosophie*, Leipzig
  1892–93 *Einleitung in die Moralwissenschaft*, 2 volumes, Berlin
  1911a *Hauptprobleme der Philosophie*, second edition, Leipzig
  1911b *Philosophische Kultur*, Leipzig
  1917 *Der Krieg und die geistigen Entscheidungen. Reden und Aufsätze*, Munich and Leipzig

1919 *Rembrandt: ein kunstphilosophischer Versuch,* second edition, Leipzig

1921 *Kant. Sechzehn Vorlesungen gehalten an der Berliner Universität,* fifth edition, Berlin and Leipzig

1922a *Lebensanschauung. Vier metaphysische Kapitel,* second edition, Munich and Leipzig

1922b *Philosophie der Kunst,* Berlin

1923 *Schopenhauer und Nietzsche,* third edition, Munich and Leipzig

1957 *Brücke und Tür,* Stuttgart

1964 *The Sociology of Georg Simmel* (translated, edited and with an introduction by Kurt H. Wolff), New York

1967 *Fragmente und Aufsätze,* Hildesheim

1968a *Das Individuelle Gesetz: Philosophische Excurse* (edited by Michael Landmann), Frankfurt am Main

1968b *Soziologie,* 5th edition, Berlin

1968c *The Conflict in Modern Culture and Other Essays* (translated with an introduction by K. Peter Etzkorn), New York

1971 *On Individuality and Social Forms* (edited with an introduction by Donald N. Levine), Chicago

1977 *The Problems of the Philosophy of History* (translated and edited, with an introduction, by Guy Oakes), New York

1978 *The Philosophy of Money* (translated by Tom Bottomore and David Frisby), London

Veblen, Thorstein
1970 *The Portable Veblen* (edited by Max Lerner), New York

Weber, Max
1975 *Roscher and Knies: The Logical Problems of Historical Economics* (translated with an introductory essay by Guy Oakes), New York

Weingartner, Rudolph H.
1960 *Experience and Culture, The Philosophy of Georg Simmel,* Middletown, Conn.

Wolff, Kurt H. (ed.)
1959 *Georg Simmel, 1858-1918,* Columbus, Ohio

Wolff, Kurt H.
1974 *Trying Sociology,* New York

Essays on Interpretation in Social Science

On the Nature of Historical Understanding

The relationship between one mind and another that we call understanding is a fundamental process of human life. The manner in which this process fuses the receptivity and the characteristic and spontaneous activity of human life can only be experienced. It is not susceptible to further analysis. The kind of understanding which is peculiar to history is embedded in our view of understanding in general. In the forms and procedures which the mind develops in order to satisfy the practical demands and further the purposes of life, there are fragmentary, proto typical traces of our intellectual, purely mental activities. For this same reason, prototypical forms of history as a science are significantly prefigured in the structures and methods with which praxis pieces together the images of the past. These images of the past are conditions for the continuation of life itself. Every step of our lives rests upon consciousness of the past. Without some measure of this awareness, life would be utterly inconceivable. But this is not a consciousness of the past as the vast, formless chaos of the totality of the material of life that is contained in memory or tradition. On the contrary, the practical purposes served by the consciousness of the past depend upon an analysis and synthesis of the material of life, its classification under concepts and into sequences, the emphasis and de-emphasis, interpretation and supplementation of this material. In this case, many different theoretical categories serve a nontheoretical interest. These theoretical categories are as continuously integrated into the purposive structures of life as any coordinations of movements, drives, or reflexes.

Consider the categories which form the raw material of life into an intellectually perspicuous, logically meaningful—and, therefore, above all, practically useful—system. Suppose that these categories are detached from this utilitarian function and acquire

97

an intrinsic and autonomous theoretical interest in which the images of the past are structured with a new completeness and with reference to their own definitive values. This is the source of history as a science. There is a sense in which each of us is always his own autobiographer in embryo. Seen from the inverse perspective, this is why, as scientific historians, we systematize and complete the attitudes and forms of prescientific life. On the basis of this completely general reciprocal relationship, insight into historical understanding is dependent upon insight into this other kind of understanding: how it happens that one man understands another. Although the premises and the methods, the interest and the subject matter may be very different, ultimately our understanding of the Apostle Paul and Louis XIV is essentially the same as our understanding of a personal acquaintance.

All understanding has the structure of an integral synthesis of two elements. Prior to the synthesis, these elements are discrete or independent. There is a given empirical phenomenon which, as such, has not yet been understood. The person for whom this phenomenon is a datum supplies the second element. This is the interpretive conception. This interpretive conception may be his own idea, or he may take it from some other source and assimilate it. The interpretive conception—as we might put it—penetrates the given phenomenon and constitutes it as an element that is understood. In some cases, this second mental element—the interpretive idea—is an autonomous object of consciousness. In other cases, it is perceptible only by reference to its results: the interpretation of the given phenomenon. There are three typical forms of the fundamental relationship between these two elements. All three forms are translated from their more or less extensive prescientific employment into the methodology of the historical sciences.

I

In the first form of this relationship, the observable activities and expressions of an individual are understood insofar as they are motivated. Put another way, the mental processes of this

individual are understood by reference to the observable manifestations which are ascribed to them. On the basis of initial
appearances, another person is a collection of observable impressions. We see, hear, and touch him. But consider the following propositions. An animate mind lies "behind" all these appearances. They all have a mental status, an inner aspect that is not
exhausted by their observable properties. In short, the other
individual is not a marionette, but rather a person who can be
understood from within. These propositions presumably do not
have the status of given facts, at least not in the same sense that the
observable impressions of the individual constitute given data.
On the contrary, they inevitably retain the character of
presumptions which can never be conclusively verified. That the
other person is animated or has a mind is a fact that we are obliged
to communicate to him. We do not experience this as a fact which
has the compelling vivacity of a sense impression. Obviously the
same point also holds for individual mental entities or contents.
On this view, we cannot determine what a person wants, thinks,
and feels by observing him. On the contrary, the observable is
only a bridge and a symbol. It provides ideas and suggestions that
we can use to produce a hypothetical reconstruction of what may
have transpired in the mind of the other person. This has a
further consequence. All our knowledge and understanding of
the mental processes of another person represents a projection of
mental events which we have experienced into his mind. Consider
any feeling, the appearance of one idea on the basis of a past idea,
and the force and dominance of impulses throughout the entire
domain of ideas. On this view, I can impute all these phenomena
to another person only if I have experienced them myself.
Consider the material on which my knowledge and understanding of his mind are based. Since the mind of the other person
cannot be read like a book that lies open before me, is there not
only one possible source of this material: namely, my own mind?

It is obvious that this is also the source of the fundamental
problem of historical understanding. Suppose that the man
accessible to my eyes and ears can be understood only if I impute
to him—in addition to all that I can see and hear—the contents of
my own mind. In that case, consider a person from the distant
past. My evidence of his existence only comprises matter-of-fact
actions, fragmentary expressions, and the objective traces of past
events. Suppose that I cannot identify mental states and activities

behind all this, mental phenomena the meaning and coherence of which can have only one source: my own mental life. Then this person will remain nothing more than a complex of apparently unintelligible brute facts. The historical person may be very different from me. But consider his properties that are intelligible to me. On this view, the understanding of these properties presupposes that there is an essential identity between us, a sense in which we have the same nature.

Certain observations may be adduced in support of this apparently necessary condition for historical interpretation. Experience seems to show that a person who has never loved or hated cannot understand the lover or the person filled with hatred. The sober pragmatist cannot understand the conduct of the idealistic dreamer, nor can the latter understand the former. Anyone with a phlegmatic disposition will fail to understand the thought processes of a person with a sanguine character, and vice versa. It follows that the historian who is a pedantic philistine and accustomed to the life of the petit bourgeois will not be able to understand the expressions of the lives of Mirabeau or Napoleon, Goethe or Nietzsche—no matter how profuse and perspicuous these manifestations may be. The hopelessness with which the European understanding confronts the oriental mind is acknowledged by orientalists. Indeed, it is confirmed even more decisively by orientalists whose knowledge is profound and extensive. Can the modern man understand in their real inner nature the Athenian of the Persian Wars, the medieval monk, or even the courtly life depicted in the paintings of Watteau? Although skepticism in these cases may be less authoritative, it seems to me that it is no less well grounded. The issue here does not turn on the lack of sources or their ambiguity. On the contrary, it concerns a breakdown of understanding which no amount or quality of documentation can repair. This breakdown is a consequence of the character or nature of the subject, the historian: he fails to produce the response to the object which qualifies as understanding.

Nevertheless, the conclusion that understanding rests upon an identity between the subject and the object would be premature. If these facts are examined more closely, it can be established that their force is purely negative. In other words, a certain degree of disparity or dissimilarity between the nature of the historian and the nature of historical persons makes understanding impossible.

But it certainly does not follow that understanding is a product of this sort of identity. The error involved here would be the same as the following. From the fact that damage to a certain part of the brain results in mental disturbance, it is inferred that the normal mental process must have its source in this particular part of the cerebral cortex. Consider both the immediate and the remote complex conditions for the functioning of organic processes. Suppose that there is an alteration or a deficiency in only one of these conditions. This is often sufficient to produce a complete disruption of the process itself. This point holds true especially for mental processes. However it does not follow that this single condition is the cause of the normal functioning of the process. In view of the foregoing, we are only justified in making the following claim. Given certain dimensions of psychic *difference* or *dissimilarity* in nature, the understanding of the expressions and manifestations of the latter is obstructed. Suppose, on the other hand, that two persons have exactly *the same* nature. It does not follow that this constitutes a sufficient condition for understanding. The following consideration excludes this possibility. There are innumerable cases in which the most vexacious misunderstandings arise between men of the same disposition.

The logical presupposition for the alleged dependence of understanding upon an essential identity of this sort is the following. We are obliged to *infer* the mental states of another person from the appearance of certain external symbols and signs. This proposition has a certain prima facie plausibility. The child supposedly hears itself cry when it is in pain. On this ground—and only on this ground—the child could infer that another person whom it hears crying must also be in pain. The same inference would be made in analogous cases. Against the generalization of this hypothesis, however, I shall only adduce a single empirical counterinstance. One of the observations which reveals the frame of mind of another person most forcefully and unambiguously is the look in his eye. But such an observation is not based on any analogy derived from self-observation. Suppose that I am not an actor and have not rehearsed the visual expressions of anger and affection, lassitude and ecstacy, terror and desire before a mirror. Then I have practically no opportunity to observe these expressions in my own case. Consider, therefore, the association between my own inner experience and my observation of its expression, the association on which the inference from the observed behavior of another person to the interpretation of his mental states is allegedly grounded. In this case, there can be no such association. This fact alone, it seems to me, proves conclusively that the relationship between my mental life and its observable expression cannot provide the key to the relationship between the observable behavior of another person and his mental life.

But why is such a key necessary? Only because of the unfortunate split of the human being produced by the mind-body dichotomy. On this view, the body is identifiable by reference to a form of observation that is alleged to be purely physical, public, and concrete. The identification of the mind, on the other hand, requires a projection of my mental states into another person, a transposition mediated by the process of association discussed above. This act of projection is complex, even mystical. And even if this act satisfies the conditions required of it, this is still not sufficient to identify the mind of another person. I am convinced, contrary to this view, that we observe *the whole person*. The isolation of his corporeality is a product of subsequent abstraction. For the same reason, it is not the observer's anatomically isolated eye which sees. It is the total person, whose entire life is concentrated upon this single organ of perception. This sort of perception of total existence may be obscure and fragmentary. It may be open to correction as a result of reflection and personal experience, and it may be susceptible to stimulation or suggestion. It may vary with differences in endowment or ability. And, thus far, it may not be possible to situate this sort of perception in one particular organ. Nevertheless, it is the fundamental and uniform mode in which one person affects another. It is a total impression which cannot really be analyzed in a rational fashion. Although open to considerable revisions and corrections, it is the first piece of knowledge—and usually the decisive piece of knowledge—which we have concerning another human being.

Historical understanding is only a variant of our *contemporaneous,* thoroughly quotidian understanding. In principle, therefore, the transmitted artifact or speech, the action or effect of an historical person really constitutes the man himself. It makes him accessible to our capacity for receptivity, a capacity which is no more divisible than he is. All the individual aspects of a person are *pars pro toto*. In history, of course, the available evidence is more modest, the way which leads to the production of a complete picture is more extended and laborious, and the result is less complete and more problematical. But suppose that it is possible to produce such a picture. In the final analysis, the image of the historical personality and his conduct has the same status as our image of a personal acquaintance. In both cases, the sense in which specific features and their causal relationship are accessible and intelligible to us is the same. And in neither case does the image of the person constitute a reproduction of our own characteristics and experiences.

Let us suppose that in order to *identify* or *define* the mental states of another person it were necessary to project our own mental states into his mind. Even so, there is no sense in which this would qualify as an *understanding* of these mental facts. Consider how frequently our own past remains completely unintelligible to us, how often the mature man finds the actions and emotions of his youth incomprehensible. Even many of the current objects of our feelings and desires must simply be accepted as brute facts of our existence. We cannot understand the conditions which were responsible for them, nor can we comprehend how they were generated by our character. We are not even able to understand what their real meaning signifies. In cases of this sort, however, the putative object of understanding is clearly given in our own experience. This is the most conclusive demonstration that the alleged projection of the contents of inner experience is not the method of understanding an historical personality. It may be true that we can only comprehend a mind that resembles our own in some way or other. The conduct of beings on a distant star like Sirius, for example, may remain unintelligible to us. From the fact that my mind has essentially the same nature as the mind of another person, however, it does not follow that I understand this person.

Consider the Greek mode of thought: its commitment to enduring substances, its belief in the plastic certainty of forms and their immediate power of conviction. The idea that the knower and the known must have the same properties—that knowledge is a relationship of identity—is a consequence of this mode of thought. From our perspective, however, this dogma is naively mechanistic. It is as if the interpretive concept and its object were merely two quantities which must be placed in a relationship of congruence or two variables which must have the same value. Such a dogma violates the facts in an astonishing fashion. For it is undeniable that everyone can grasp feelings that he has never felt, understand the entanglements of an inner fate that he has never experienced, and imagine volitional impulses that are totally alien to his own desires.

Consider the following response to this difficulty encountered by the thesis that first-person experience is a putative condition for understanding. Obviously, the mental process which I experience is not exactly the same as the mental process that I understand. Understanding rests upon some sort of transformation or modulation, some change in the quantity and quality of the contents of my experience. This is not a satisfactory response to the difficulty. Suppose that the difference between one mental process and another is regarded as insignificant or purely formal. It does not follow that this disparity is any easier to resolve. And what is the criterion which can be employed to establish whether a difference is objectively more or less significant?

The principle that we can understand the qualities of another person only insofar as we have experienced these qualities for ourselves is either valid or it is not. Consider some process in the mind of another person that is utterly trivial and insignificant. Suppose that we have knowledge of this mental process without experiencing it ourselves. This sort of knowledge refutes the principle just as conclusively as knowledge of the most significant or comprehensive mental process.

The dubious consequences of this entire theory of interpretation have their origin in realism—the thesis according to which knowledge produces things "as they really are." According to this concept of knowledge, my own experience consitutes immediate reality. Only if the experience of the other person can be represented as identical to my own, so this naive theory would have us believe, can I be certain in identifying his mental processes on the basis of his observable behavior. It is obvious that I must indeed be able to represent the experience of the other person. From this it is fallaciously inferred that I must be able to represent it as my own experience. This fallacy is comparable to the error committed by the doctrine of ethical egoism: from the fact that I am the subject of my volition it is inferred that I must also be its object. This inference is based on the assumption that genuine reality is limited to my own experience. Suppose that I cannot project my experience into the mind of the other person or represent his experience as my own. In that case, I cannot be certain that his experience also qualifies as real. Notice that this theory of the "empathetic" projection of my own mental processes into the mind of another person requires the following: before the process of projection takes place, I must know *which* part of my experiences is to be delegated for this purpose. It follows that the perception of the mental process of another person which is to be achieved by employing this method presupposes what it is intended to produce: namely, knowledge of the mental processes of the other person.

According to this theory, my own mind must be transposed into the other person. Otherwise he cannot be experienced as having a mind at all. I believe that this theory represents a completely illegitimate translation of the properties of other sorts of experience into the domain of the incomparable phenomenon of the person. In opposition to this theory, I hold that the other person or the Thou—like the ego or self—is an ultimate, irreducible entity. The projection theory of knowledge is no more valid for the domain of the Thou than it is for the world of external objects. Objects are not completely fabricated in our minds and then—by some mysterious process—projected into a space that lies prepared for them. This would be comparable to the manner in which furniture is moved into an empty apartment. It should be noted in passing that, on this view, the very consciousness of space as a whole would pose a difficulty no less serious than the problem posed by the assumption that we have an original awareness of objects as spatial. Contrary to this theory—assuming that we approach the question from the standpoint of the subject—space is an original mode or form of perception. In this case, perception simply means spatial or three-dimensional perception. The duplication of the object—as if it existed first in our minds and then in the external world—is utterly superfluous.

According to the theory of projection, we have knowledge of the mind as a result of our own experience. Then we project this mind into a body that is suited for it. Only by means of this curious process can we acquire knowledge of another person, the Thou. This theory is mistaken. At this point also we base our argument on the standpoint of idealism. Our mind contains certain ideas which, from the outset, are constitutive for the concept of the other person. They are apperceived as its mental contents. Consider the linguistic expression according to which the mind lies "behind" the visible and the tangible. This spatial metaphor, superficial as it is, has obviously contributed a great deal to the view of the mind as an mysterious, incomprehensible medium of another world, to be distinguished epistemologically from the directly accesible world of "external" objects. If we begin by splitting the other person into mind and body, then it is obvious that we are then obliged to construct a bridge between them. This is necessary in order to repair the a priori unity of the whole person. We consign the body exclusively to the domain of the visually perceptible world. And the mind becomes the exclusive domain of our own mind. By a process of transposition, translation, or projection—the act itself can never be identified with precision—this mind finds its way into the body. This reductive analysis, however, is an outrage perpetrated by the atomistic mode of thought.

Consider the praxis of everyday life and the formation of historical constructs on the basis of material that is invariably random and fragmentary and often utterly superficial. They seem to legitimate this dichotomy between the mental and the physical and the distance between them which thought is obliged to span. However this dichotomy—a product of the problematical and discontinuous character of the material of life—presupposes both as its point of departure and as its ultimate goal the fundamental fact that could be called the identity of the other person or the Thou as a unified entity: the other person who is immediately intelligible as an animate mind. Suppose that the path from an utterly superficial external symbol to its mental comprehension is the most tortuous and protracted imaginable. Even in a case of this sort, the category of the Thou remains fundamental. It reappears, fully developed, at the end of this path.

The category of the Thou has roughly the same crucial status in the world of praxis and history that the category of substance or causality occupies in the world of natural science. The category itself is incommensurable. The concept of the Thou does not have the same status as all the other objects of my ideas. I am obliged to ascribe a being-for-itself to the Thou. It is the same integrity that I experience exclusively in my own ego—the self, which must be distinguished from everything that is properly an object. Here is the explanation of the fact that we experience the other person, the Thou, both as the most alien and impenetrable creature imaginable, and also as the most intimate and familiar. On the one hand, the ensouled Thou is our only peer or counterpart in the universe. It is the only being with whom we can come to a mutual understanding and feel as "one." If, for example, we feel ourselves in harmony with the natural world, this is because it is comprehended under the category of the Thou. Consider Saint Francis, who spoke to both animals and inanimate nature as his brothers. On the other hand, the Thou also has an incomparable autonomy and sovereignty. It resists any decomposition or analysis into the subjective representation of the ego. It has that absoluteness of reality which the ego ascribes to itself.

The concept of the Thou or the other person and the concept of understanding express the same ultimate, irreducible phenomenon of the human mind. The Thou, as we might put it, is its substance, and understanding is its function. In this respect, they are like seeing and hearing, thinking and feeling, objectivity in general, space and time, or the ego. The Thou, or understanding, is the transcendental presupposition of the fact that man is by nature a political animal. The following points concerning this phenomenon are obvious. It only appears in the later or more advanced stages of our development. Most often, it lacks the precision of its content. Further, its appearance presupposes the satisfaction of extremely complex psychological conditions. However acts of consciousness that present themselves as primary also require the satisfaction of earlier, more primitive conditions. They require a period of development too. The issue here only concerns a difference of degree. Consider the view that mental phenomena like the concepts of the Thou or understanding cannot be intrinsically simple and primary because they only appear imperfectly, in advanced states of our development, and only given the satisfaction of many different conditions. This view is completely mistaken. Suppose that the *conditions* under which an image or a form of understanding arises are inadequate. This may constitute an obstacle to its complete expression. However there is no sense in which this proves that the image or form of understanding is produced exclusively by the associative interaction of these conditions.

It is obvious that distinctions can be made within this original, irreducible phenomenon. Chief among them are the differences between the understanding of an everyday, current event or a contemporary person and the understanding of an historical object. In the case of historical understanding, the available data are in general more meagre and random. Historical data are more dependent upon discursive reasoning or inference than upon direct observation. And there is no shared temporal atmosphere which embraces both the interpreter and the object of interpretation. In specific cases, these differences can rule out the possibility of understanding, either partially or completely. From the perspective of understanding, however, there is in principle no logical or conceptual difference between the present and the past. It is obvious that only the present can be an object of our own actual experience. However both the present and the past can be an object of historical understanding, for the past of every person is an object of his own historical understanding. In the remote past, it is clear that there is often a more significant discrepancy between our grasp of the external event and the mental process than is the case in immediate observation. And in history it is necessary to make inferences from the external to the internal process more often. However these differences only identify *more protracted and laborious methods* which ultimately lead to the sort of understanding in which one entity grasps another. Or, at least, they constitute the fragmentary expressions of this sort of understanding.

As a result of practical or random deficiencies, of course, the conditions for understanding are often dichotomized. From the perspective of conceptual analysis, therefore, understanding has the appearance of an interpretation of autonomous observable symptoms or symbols by reference to the mental processes which lie behind them. Although the concept of intuition is not unobjectionable, "intuition" is an appropriate description of this process. This concept creates the suspicion that the process itself is mystical and illegitimate. However this suspicion vanishes when the following point is clearly established: intuition as it occurs in historical understanding is only a form of the intuition which is inevitably employed in each moment of everyday life.

II

The second form of understanding betrays a more complex structure. In this case, an act which has been identified as a mental process is understood by reference to another act on the same psychological plane. Suppose that after 1866, a Hanoverian Legitimist tells us that he despised Bismarck. In the first place, we have an immediate understanding of this feeling. We understand it simply insofar as it is a feeling. Hatred is an emotion that we can identify at once. Within ourselves, we have knowledge of the subjective meaning of this emotion, a meaning that requires no further analysis. Our knowledge on this point is independent of both the circumstances under which the emotion appears and the person whom it affects. This sort of understanding of a given mental entity is transhistorical. It could also be called objective: Brunhilde's feeling toward Kriemhilde, the Hanoverian's feelings about Bismarck, the tenant's feeling about the chicaneries of his landlord—all involve the same basic psychological process. In the immediate understanding of a mental phenomenon, the duality of elements on which every form of understanding rests is the following: an individual case of a mental phenomenon is understood by reference to a more general form of the same process. This more general form is present in the mind of the interpreter prior to the appearance of the individual case. Historically, however, I understand the Hanoverian's hate for Bismarck if I am acquainted with the war of 1866 and the Prussian Annexation. Put another way, I understand this emotion by identifying it as an element of a complete temporal network.

Consider, however, the links which constitute the structure of this network. Each of these links must also be understood in the first sense, the psychological sense of interpretation. In the same way that I understand hate, I must also understand dynastic loyalty and the meaning of political autonomy. The first kind of understanding seems to be concerned with what might be called a timeless or superindividual content. The second, however, seems to be concerned with the real structure of a multi-dimensional process. In fact, however, this latter form of understanding is also constituted by a sequence of specific interpretive items each member of which must be understood transhistorically and psychologically.

The moments of such a sequence are discontinuous. They are also discontinuously and—at this might be expressed—atemporally understood. Therefore it is evident that genuine historical understanding is possible only if, from the perspective of the historian, these moments are engulfed in the perpetual stream of life. The stream of life connects these discontinuous moments and opens the gate which leads from one moment to another. Then it is possible to experience these moments as the pulse beats of one temporal process of life. Therefore we can see that the first sort of isolated or autonomous understanding of these moments rests on a certain abstraction. Within the ineluctable ebb and flow of life, atemporal interpretation places a certain wave in relief as an independent entity that can be understood on its own terms. In actuality, however, this wave flows continuously into all the past and future currents of the ebb and flow of life.

The construction of this continuous network is the definitive function of the form of history, the seal which it imprints upon the record of mere events. Suppose it is established that a certain event took place during a certain year. And suppose that this year lies isolated in an otherwise empty time-frame. This would not be sufficient to identify the event as historical. The intrinsic meaning of the event—its characteristic properties which are temporally independent—could still be understood. In every case, of course, atemporal understanding is a necessary condition for historical interpretation. Atemporal understanding, however, only provides the raw material in which historical becoming is realized as a specific formative process. History is not the same as the past. In the strict sense, the past is directly given only as a collection of discontinuous fragments. History, on the other hand, is a certain form or a collection of forms with which the reflective, synthesizing mind penetrates and masters the record of events, the phenomena that constitute the raw material of history. The historical interpretation of a sequence of events adds nothing new to its content. Historical interpretation only establishes or discovers a functional relationship within such a sequence, a relationship that is produced by a perception of the mind.

The historical mode of thought detaches a specific aspect of reality from the conception which circumscribes it. It represents this aspect as a component—a cause and an effect—of an immense structure. Interpretation functions in the same way when the given contents of psychological reality are comprehended as historical. First, the given phenomena must be understood on their own terms as—in some sense—autonomous psychological entities. Unless this condition is satisfied, they cannot be historicized. They become historicized under the following conditions. In a certain sense, they become fused or condensed. They appear as the concrete configurations of a dynamic of life, a dynamic which links each of these phenomena to all of the others. Therefore the concept of the historical interpretation of a specific mental fact may be more profoundly and precisely defined as follows. It constitutes the understanding of the single fact by reference to the totality of life in which it is implicated or embedded.

Consider the idea of a sequence of psychological data each member of which is identifiable only by reference to its own restricted, conceptually definable content. The belief that one such datum is sufficient to constitute an interpretation of any subsequent datum in the sequence—the belief that the succession itself constitutes an interpretation of subsequent data—is a common error. It is a consequence of the atomistic-mechanistic principle. According to this principle, the logically expressible contents of mental life are analyzed as isolated "ideas." Mental life is to be understood as the product of the motions of its parts, these juxtaposed ideas. Employing what could be called the logic of psychology—although, in reality, it is an obscure mix of logic and psychology—the interpretation should proceed directly from one mental fact to another. If this principle is employed, however, the dynamic relationship between mental phenomena, their interaction and interpenetration, and the manner in which diverse phenomena are integrated disappear from the interpretation. In consequence it is also impossible to understand one psychological datum by reference to another. This is because understanding requires an inner vision of a constant dynamic of life. The positions within this dynamic are constituted by the discrete psychological moments of life, each with its own given content. Subsequent mental phenomena can be understood by reference to previous mental phenomena only if the whole man—conceived not as a fixed substance, but rather as an animated, kinetic process of development—is perceptible in each of these moments. The earlier phenomenon exhibits the direction which the subsequent phenomenon will take only if this condition is satisfied. However, as just noted, this process of development cannot be understood as a leap from one mental content to another. On the contrary, it is intelligible only by reference to a representation of life, contemporary or historical, in which each independently identifiable moment is understood as a manifestation of life as a whole. This point is not confined to the understanding of the individual. The same principle applies when we attempt to understand a number of individuals implicated in the same current of life, a current in which one wave brings forth another. The irreducible phenomenon of understanding, therefore, is realized in the sequence of life itself. Although it is an extended process that transcends every individual, it also impels and embraces every individual.

In the foregoing account, two modes of understanding can be identified. Historicism, with its superficial grasp of these matters, has committed the most vexacious errors concerning these two modes of understanding. Therefore it is important to be clear about the relationship between them, their distinctive features as well as the respects in which they overlap. Suppose that I understand the import and the poetic significance of Goethe's poem "*Warum gabst du uns die tiefen Blicke.*" This form of understanding is completely ahistorical. On the other hand, suppose that I understand the import and mood of this poem by reference to the relationship between Goethe and Frau von Stein. Suppose I understand that this poem marks a definite epoch in the development of this relationship. This latter form of understanding is historical. The history of art provides an excellent illustration of the relationship between these two forms of interpretation. With the last stroke of the painter's brush, the meaning of the painting lies beyond history. There are various respects in which it can become an historical factor again: through the vicissitudes of fate, through changes in aesthetic conception and evaluation, or by virtue of its influence on subsequent art. Consider, however, the meaning of the picture in the following sense: the laws of its form and color, the relationship between the subject matter of the painting and its definitive style, the passion or the serenity of the composition, the differential emphasis upon drawing or painting. All of these properties—the constitutive or definitive existential features of the painting—remain unaffected by historical changes. In this sense, the meaning of the painting is *the consummation of an immanent process.* It is to be understood by reference to purely immanent factors which remain independent of historical changes.

The distinction at stake here between an objective and an historical interpretation of a mental entity is grounded in one of the most profound problematics of knowledge. This point holds true from the perspective of both the certainty and the clarity of knowledge. A creation of the human spirit which constitutes a putative object of interpretation may be compared to a riddle of a certain type: its creator has constructed the riddle around a specific word that will provide the solution. But suppose we discover a second possible solution to the riddle. And suppose that, objectively, this solution fits as well as the first: by reference to both logic and aesthetics, it is equally successful. In that case, this second solution is just as "correct" as the solution intended by the author of the riddle. There is no sense in which his solution is superior to this one. Nor is it superior to any of the other possible solutions that might be discovered. In principle, these possible solutions are unlimited. Suppose that a creative process has assumed the form of objectified mind. Consider all the extremely diverse forms in which this process can be understood. Each form of understanding is equally legitimate or justifiable to the extent that it satisfies the criteria of precision, logical coherence, and material sufficiency. The identification of the real intention which lies behind the creative process in the mind of the creator is not a necessary condition for this sort of understanding.

Consider, for example, the immanent interpretation of a work of art. Such an interpretation is infinitely variable, as variable as the emotions that it awakens. There is no sense in which these emotions are dependent upon the feelings which the artist himself invested in his work. Consider the feelings and values with which the modern individual responds to the Strassburg cathedral or the Moonlight sonata. This complex of feelings and values is the most profound and fundamental basis of his understanding. It is not possible to claim that this response is groundless or false just because it does not conform to the feelings and values of Erwin von Steinbach or Beethoven. And there is no sense in which this point only holds for the higher or ideal products of creativity. A technician who is a mere empiric may invent a mechanical device which is fully intelligible to him as a consequence of the relationship between the construction of the apparatus and the purpose for which he intended it. Suppose that a more reflective investigator considers the general laws of nature according to which this apparatus functions. He may discover that the same machine has uses which its inventor did not consider. In order to provide a genuine understanding of the invention itself, it would be necessary to completely exhaust the possibilities suggested here. In other words, it would be necessary to work out all these objectively immanent possibilities of under-standing. The same point holds for political constitutions or specific laws. Often the architects of laws and constitutions have an utterly inadequate knowledge—or no knowledge at all—of their real logical or practical significance. Quite often, the pos-sibilities that constitute their real efficacy are only revealed by other persons, the process of legal casuistry, or subsequent developments. However these possibilities should not be re-garded as errors or distortions simply because they cannot be identified among the intentions of the legislators.

The relationship between the creator and his work invariably betrays this rather curious property. The autonomous artifact contains elements that cannot be explained by reference to the intentions of the artisan: additions, deletions, something of greater value, or something of more modest value. In this sense, creation or creativity is never anything more than a modal expression of the creator's intentions and—in the strict sense—his capabilities. It is never more than one element of the actual artifact. An understanding of the real significance and import of the artifact itself depends upon a comprehension of the unlimited possibilities which lie beyond the element of creation. Implicated in every artifact that we create, there is—in addition to what *we* really create—another meaning and a system of laws, a source of creativity which transcends our own powers and intentions.

On the other hand, there is no doubt that we created the artifact as a whole. Creation is certainly not a matter of collecting extraneous elements which develop their own distinctive qualities and potentialities within the artifacts that we create. This problem concerns the definitive meaning and power of our own creations, a meaning and power that become possible and actual only in the process by which we create. Perhaps this sense of the relationship between our creative acts and their artifacts is the source of a recurrent and somewhat mystical idea. It is as if everything that we make is already ideally preformed. There is a sense in which we are only midwives who assist in the existential birth of a metaphysical entity. In any case, the basic substance of this idea would provide some sort of explanation for the following phenomenon. An artifact apparently produced by only one artisan has an unlimited number and variety of meanings that transcend all of the creative intentions and powers of the artisan himself. This idea, therefore, would also explain why the question of the intellectual understanding of such an artifact cannot, in principle, be regarded as a problem which has only one possible solution.

Here we see further proof of the distinction between the two senses of "understanding" discussed above. Consider, for example, an aesthetic and theoretical interpretation of *Faust*. As noted in the foregoing, such an interpretation is completely independent of any account of the genesis of *Faust* in the mental processes of the author. Suppose that different kinds of interpretation of *Faust* satisfy the following criteria equally well: logical and aesthetic coherence, a systematic clarification of obscurities, and an intuitively satisfying development of the interrelationship between the parts of the drama. In that case, each of these interpretations is, in the same measure, correct. Consider, on the other hand, an historical-psychological interpretation of *Faust*, an account which interprets the genesis of the drama by reference to the mental acts and processes which gradually evolved in Goethe's consciousness. In this case, the same sort of systematic ambiguity in interpretation is logically impossible. In fact, the creative process of the composition of *Faust* transpired in a specific way. Either we know how the process developed or we do not. However the process cannot be the object of several different but equally legitimate descriptions. A variety of equally legitimate objective interpretations of *Faust* is possible. However a variety of equally legitimate historical interpretations of the origins of *Faust* in the mental processes of Goethe is an absurdity. Obviously there may be several different hypotheses concerning the historical interpretation of some phenomenon. In the final analysis, however, one of these hypotheses is true, and the others are false. An interpretation of the objective content of the phenomenon does not require this alternative. On the contrary, in objective interpretation, this requirement is replaced by other axiological criteria. It is possible, for example, to provide a completely definitive historical interpretation of a given phenomenon. But an objective interpretation of all the possible meanings implicated in this phenomenon can never be complete or definitive.

This is the source of a profound paradox. Suppose that historical interpretation is a species of psychological interpretation. Psychological interpretation can never be completely unequivocal. In this sort of interpretation, we can never conclusively resolve the following problem: in a collection of different—or even mutually inconsistent—explanatory principles, which hypothesis is sound? The profusion and the dynamics of psychological associations are immense. There is no "psychological law" of any sort which can necessarily determine the subsequent evolution of a specific constellation of mental processes. On the contrary, it quite often happens that one such development does not seem to be any more plausible than its extreme polar antithesis. We can understand gratitude as a response to charity. But we can understand the responses of humiliation and rancor just as well. We can understand love as a response to a declaration of love. But we can understand the responses of rejection and indifference equally well. There are numerous other cases of this sort. In other words, suppose that genetic sequences are constituted by psychological interpolation. Explicitly or implicitly, this is always the case. In an interpretation of this sort, the perspicuous necessity required by an account that is unambiguously scientific is out of the question. Nevertheless, the assumption that there is only one true description of psychological processes is correct and corresponds to reality. Every alternative description is false, even though it may not be possible to prove conclusively which description is correct and which is mistaken. In any case, this account establishes the fundamental difference between historical interpretation and the interpretation of objective content.

III

Radical historicism proposes to resolve the entire problem of understanding a human artifact by reconstructing the conditions and stages of its temporal development. Problems concerning the objective and temporally independent attributes of being are reduced to questions concerning the process in which these qualities develop—questions of becoming. What were the origins and the preconditions, the developments, the necessary conditions and the obstacles that led to the production of the artifact? From the perspective of historicism, the answer to this question constitutes a satisfactory interpretation of the existing objective fact.

Suppose that the problem of the interpretation of an object insofar as its properties are atemporal is replaced by a different kind of question: what are the conditions responsible for the real temporal existence of the object? This translation is no more intelligent than the suggestion that the prospect from a mountain peak is the same as the path which leads to it, the trail which the hiker takes step by step until he reaches the top. It is obvious that this translation amounts to a capricious foreshortening of an entire dimension of the problem of interpretation. However the problem which is apparently eliminated in this translation is not only a valid question outside the domain of history. It also has a legitimate place within the province of historical interpretation. This is because the sort of interpretation that seems to be purely historical regularly employs a form of trans-historical or super-historical interpretation. However no methodological justification of this procedure is offered. It would be impossible for us to understand the what or the essence of things by reference to their historical development unless we already had some sort of independent understanding of this essence. Without this latter sort of understanding historical interpretation would obviously be a completely absurd undertaking.

This is the source of a third type of interpretive process. In this case, the fundamental duality of elements does not lie in the dichotomy of the observable and the mental or the distinction between one mental process and another. On the contrary, it is based upon the distinction between a mental content and an atemporal content. The reciprocal relationships between these two elements are quite singular. On the one hand, the transhistorical interpretation of objective content is concerned with specific items which acquire a systematic order and a reciprocal frame of reference only if they are embraced by the flow of historical development. On the other hand, the ideal existence of these items also exhibits relationships and points of reference. It could be said that they are atemporal symbols of their own temporal and psychological realization. In other words, the two components of this sort of interpretation are mutually interdependent in the most profound and fundamental sense.

Suppose that a historian of philosophy makes the following claim: to understand Kant means to derive him from history. From the perspective of this historian, the theories of pre-Kantian philosophy appear as steps or stages which lead to the philosophy of Kant. In this way, the content and the temporal existence of Kant's philosophy are determined in an intelligible fashion. The following, however, is the decisive point. This sort of interpretation would not be possible unless the logical content of all these philosophical theories—completely independent of any consideration of their historical genesis—constituted an intelligible sequence.

The same point holds for any piece of reasoning. We have a complete understanding of the dynamics of the following reasoning. Given the proposition that all men are mortal and the proposition that Caius is a man, there is a sense in which our mind organically makes the inference that Caius is mortal. However we understand this reasoning only because the logic of the inference is valid. Our comprehension of this reasoning, therefore, is atemporal and independent of the fact that we can only represent the contents of the inference in the form of a temporal sequence. The truth of the proposition that all men are mortal is independent of our own thought. We experience its truth neither as an antecedent nor as a consequent of the proposition that Caius is a man and the proposition that Caius is mortal. The domain of the validity of this inference is an absolutely atemporal system of coordinates. The death of Caius does not follow as a temporal consequence of the other two facts. The logic according to which this proposition follows from the first two is *not* the diachronic logic of *temporal sequence*. Therefore it is not the logic of our conception and expression of these propositions. On the contrary, it is a purely immanent logic in which these propositions are correlated in an ideally *synchronic* fashion. If this were not the case, then we would not recognize the force and the legitimacy of the mental process according to which the subject matter of this inference can be represented in terms of a temporal sequence.

The same point holds for the historical interpretation of Kant. Rationalism rejects the experience of the senses and situates unconditional truth exclusively in the a priori faculty of reason. Empiricism repudiates this faculty as a source of truth: experience is the only basis of valid knowledge. Kant's resolution of this problem runs as follows. The empiricists are correct in their belief that experience is the only foundation of objective knowledge. However experience itself is already constituted as such by the principles of reason. It follows that knowledge is unconditionally valid. But it is only valid for objects of experience. Knowledge can never transcend the domain of experience. These principles—rationalism, empiricism, and the philosophy of Kant—exhibit an ideal order which is defined exclusively by reference to their atemporal, objective import. Suppose that we were unable to understand the purely immanent significance of this order, independent of the conditions of its historical realization in rationalism, empiricism, and the philosophy of Kant. In that case, we would never be able to understand the temporal disposition of these philosophical theories. From our perspective, they would remain a discontinuous sequence of brute facts. Consider the rationality in this sequence of philosophical theories. By means of it, we grasp the direction of the stream of life of the philosophers who produce these theories, the subjects who realize themselves in these theories. This rationality is only possible as a temporally confused reflection of this purely objective order. To the proposition that the understanding of Kant is a function of his historical derivation, we can juxtapose the proposition that the historical derivation of Kant is a function of the understanding of his work. Suppose that we are able to grasp the unity that embraces the events in the stream of life. We see this stream of life as determined by earlier events which lead to later events. In other words, we understand the later events on the basis of our understanding of the earlier events. The force and the legitimacy of this process of understanding are dependent upon the objective understanding of the import of these events: an understanding of their logical relationships, which are completely independent of their organic and temporal relations.

At this point, it is necessary to consider a methodological presupposition which establishes a much more intimate—one might even say an unconditionally necessary—connection between historical interpretation and objective interpretation. In this discussion, I shall also employ the illustration of the development of Kant's perspective: from dogmatism through sensationalistic skepticism to critical philosophy. The question of whether the factual details of this example are sound or require revision is irrelevant for our present purposes. On what grounds are we justified in claiming that one of these philosophical positions or concepts "evolves" intelligibly into another? It is quite clear that each of these doctrines has its own definitive and completely self-contained content. To say that one of these doctrines "leads to another" is only a symbolic expression. It is naively committed to the assumption the very possibility of which is at stake here. The sequentially related concepts which constitute these philosophical positions are mutually juxtaposed. The attempt to derive a process of development from these concepts which would make it possible to understand one of these doctrines on the basis of another is utterly hopeless.

In fact, however, we see these philosophical doctrines from the perspective of such a process of development. The sequence of these philosophical positions is purely objective. There is no concrete individual life which has experienced this sequence, the movement from one philosophical position to another. Therefore how is this perspective possible? Only because we introduce a hypothetical or fictitious subject. Its mental life experiences these transitions and thereby establishes a coherent relationship between them. This hypothetical subject breaks down the boundaries which define the self-contained, immanent meaning that is peculiar to each doctrine. Only in this way is it possible for them to become links in a chain of development. This hypothetical subject could be called a technical heuristic device. We use it constantly and without any particular awareness. By employing this imaginary atemporal life, we establish a coherent relationship between phenomena which exist in what could be described as an atemporal time.

The same issues are at stake when the works within an extended period of the history of art are conceived as constituting a process of development. Paintings, for example, exist discontinously and independently of one another. They are insular, self-contained entities. Each painting is defined within the space of its own frame, which no other painting can penetrate. Within such a collection of paintings, the historian of art constructs a gradual process of development from rigidity to dynamism, from poverty to profusion, from uncertainty to the sovereign mastery of technique, from an arbitrariness of composition to a balanced structure in which each element is meaningfully and harmoniously arranged. It obviously cannot be supposed that the creator of the most sublime work of art has experienced all these previous stages in his own personal development. This consideration is also completely irrelevant to the present issue, which concerns the possibility of immanent criteria for constructing this "developmental" sequence on the basis of the objective existence of the works themselves, as if each work of art had appeared out of the blue. However precisely this possibility rests upon what might be called the methodological subject. It is an ideal structure that experiences all these creations—their preliminary beginnings, rise, and decline—in a psychologically comprehensible process of evolution. In this way, the objective order of these juxtaposed works of art is transposed into an organic sequence that is conceived temporally. The continuity of this sequence transcends the frame of each individual painting.

Ordinary language seems to legitimate this interpretation. We say that there are developments in art, law, and chemistry. However it is quite obvious that art, law, and chemistry as such are not real entities. On the contrary, they represent abstract conceptual syntheses of individual phenomena. Although these phenomena are interrelated in many different ways, they remain independent, discrete entities. Consider art in the historical sense that is at stake here. If art is the collection of works of art, then the word "art" does not refer to a concrete entity. Or, even if it did, this could not be an organic entity which "experiences" a process of evolution. If this were the case, it would be necessary for "art" to paint pictures. But in fact they are painted by artists. If, on the other hand, we employ this expression, then it is because we have hypostatized an heuristic concept and created a totally new subject. This subject has the capacity for self-development which can only be ascribed to living things. Individual works of art are the manifestations or stages of the life of this subject. A process of temporal development is imputed to this subject. For this reason, moreover, the moments of this process of development exhibit that supra-temporal and purely objective developmental relationship.

We even require this idea of a methodological subject in order to account for more disparate phenomena. Suppose that we understand love or hate in a quite general fashion, without any necessary connection to the real existence of an individual. In this case, we ascribe these emotions to an ideal subject, a life as such. With these emotions, it responds as a whole to a certain variety of stimuli. There is a sense in which these emotions are the ephemeral forms in which this life is embodied. Conceived as rigidly circumscribed concepts torn from the fabric of life, they would hardly be more than mere empty words which await the process that would make them intelligible. This point can be made even more clearly in a case in which one event makes it possible for us to understand another event. Consider an act of revenge, conceived either historically or in a purely abstract fashion. Suppose that we "understand" this act by reference to some injustice previously suffered. This understanding is not a consequence of some correlation that may be established between these two processes, no matter how intimate it may be. On the contrary, it is a consequence of the fact that we can imagine a homogeneous stream of life. These processes are two of its waves or currents, engulfed in the stream itself.

In other words, the rhythm and the constant dynamic of life is the formal agent of understanding. This holds true even for logical relationships that constitute a necessary condition for the intelligibility of the *real, vital* occurrence of the entities that they interrelate. However the actual, effective vitality of this ideal subject is the result of a tranposition or objectification of a kind of animation which we feel in ourselves. It could be said that we see ourselves as examples of this super-individual form of animation. Within the perpetual interplay of events and fluctuations that transpire within us, we perceive, more or less certainly, an end or purpose that is at least formal: a realization of predispositions, a blossoming of buds which lie within us—or, more accurately, which we are. A partial realization of this phenomenon or a concentrated instance of its appearance is the following. In the mind, items are ordered in a certain sequence: in relation to the earlier members of this sequence, we conceive its later members as representing an enrichment, a confirmed promise, an intensification and extension of our own state of being. I draw a conclusion on the basis of certain premises. I examine the philosophical theories of the eighteenth century until the critical philosophy of Kant appears as its result. I observe Italian art, from the Byzantine rigidity and the manifold uncouthness of the trecento to the individualistic disorder of the quattrocento and its result, the harmonious and comprehensive unity of High Renaissance composition. In each of these cases, I feel my spirit—insofar as it experiences these fulfillments as its own—gradually expand. Its powers of perception are increasingly actualized. As my mind experiences these sequences of contents and traverses them, it is aware of itself as being not merely moved, but rather endowed with a specific value: a process of development.

From this perspective, development may be an original and irreducible concept which is not accessible to further analysis. Nor is it dependent upon some pre-existing end or purpose. On the contrary, it is only a rhythm of the movement of mental life itself, a specific form of inner growth. Suppose that I ascribe a process of development to an historical or ideal order of things. It is obvious that there is no sense in which this description is arbitrary or capricious. However this shading of value is, in the strictest sense, a result of the feeling of the self-development of the spirit, a value which my mind experiences in the products of this process whenever they become its own contents.

Suppose that these contents are conceived in abstraction from the mind, by reference to the category of a conceptually definable form of objectivity. In that case, they constitute an objective sequence of evolution. These contents are permeated by the mind's vital feelings of aspiration and development. But suppose that they are abstracted from this stream of mental life. In that case, only an inner connection and structure remain evident in this sequence. As a result of this inner connection and structure, the later members of the sequence are conditioned by the earlier members. In consequence, the location of the later elements within the sequence becomes intelligible. According to the view represented here, the "understanding" of a single item is, in principle, simply its interpretation as an expression or manifestation of a total living entity. "Understanding" is only an abbreviated expression of this process. The same point holds true for the understanding of contents which may be presented as purely objective or as the products of different agents, understood either as the contents of the subject of ideal experience or as the contents of the subject of real observation.

The result is a fusion of the psychological-historical moment and the substantive-objective moment within the total process of understanding. Consider the real psychological development of a sequence the members of which are temporally related. Such a sequence can be understood only on the basis of the objective, transvital relationship of its contents. Without an insight into this perceptible process of ascent and descent, without the light which the members of this sequence shed on one another—one member grounds or conditions another independent of any consideration of their temporal realization—it would also be impossible to understand this sequence as an actual, temporal, psychological process. On the other hand, the ideal order of this sequence is possible as a process of development only insofar as it is structured by a continuous psychological dynamic. The objective development of the members of the sequence requires as its constitutive a priori a certain process of consciousness. It is manifested as a specific feeling that is not further definable. This process of consciousness is necessary in order to penetrate the self-contained and isolated autonomy in which all contents are locked and to transpose them into the continuity that is essential for any process of development.

It follows that the psychological development is a function of the objective process. The former is intelligible by reference to the latter. But it also follows that the objective process is a function of the psychological process. The psychological process is a condition for the intelligibility of the objective process. In other words, these two processes are only methodologically independent aspects of a single entity: the event insofar as it is an object of historical understanding. Understanding is an irreducible, primitive phenomenon in which a universal relationship between man and the world is expressed. Therefore the elements in which this relationship is realized—the one-dimensional aspects in which reflection conceives this relationship—can be inextricably related. They may be conceived autonomously. But they structure one another in a correlative fashion. Viewed from the other perspective, however, this circle is inevitable. This is because life is the ultimate authority of the spirit, its court of last resort. Therefore the form of life ultimately determines the forms in which life itself can be intelligible. Life can only be understood by life. Life is structured in strata in such a way that one stratum makes it possible to understand another. The interdependence of these strata exhibits the unity of life.

Consider the reasoning I employed in order to explain why certain prima facie plausible interpretations of the problem of understanding should be rejected. Now it is evident that this vitalistic aspect of the problem was already implicit in my argument. For if we examine them more carefully, these interpretations are all revealed as legitimate descendants of the *mechanistic* world view. On this view, only the physical aspects of one person are accessible to another. A mind and specific mental process can be located behind this exterior only by virtue of an intellectual act that is mediated by association. This is because mechanism cannot comprehend the unity and totality of life. On the mechanistic view, life can only be pieced together from its fragments. But these parts, from the standpoint of an organic conception, are only the products of an *ex post facto* analysis of the unity of life. Mechanism, therefore, cannot comprehend understanding as a primitive, irreducible phenomenon, a process that transpires between one whole person and another whole person. From the standpoint of mechanism, this process is only a derivative synthesis of separate factors.

For the same reasons, the mechanistic view cannot grasp what could be called the creative aspect of the process of understanding, the aspect which makes it possible for one person to produce the image of another mind within his own experience from alien and remote phenomena which he has not experienced. The ultimate purpose of mechanism is to reduce every relationship to a functional equivalence. From the standpoint of mechanism, therefore, understanding can only be based upon or reduced to an equivalence between the subject of understanding and its object. An object of interpretation is possible only as a mechanistic reproduction of a process which has already taken place in the mind of the interpreter. But this supposition is obviously inconsistent with the facts. In consequence the most desperate means are employed to construct the mental processes of the historical person on the basis of individual fragments which may be imputed to the inner experience of the historian. However this project simply cannot be taken seriously. Even the following consideration demonstrates its total invalidity: the understanding of mental life is concerned with the continuous *connection* and the sources of *unity* within independently identifiable mental contents. The definitive property of life and individuality is their integrity. However this property certainly *cannot* be achieved merely by piecing together a collection of analogous fragments just as they are. It follows from the mechanistic conception that historical interpretation is a mere copy or impression of the event "as it actually happened." But actually historical understanding is an activity of the subject, the historian. It is dependent upon the categories and forms which are employed to represent the object of interpretation (among these categories and forms, for example, the methodological subject discussed above is an a priori necessity). Historical interpretation is a distinctive mental construct. The truth of an interpretation is a vital and functional relationship between the interpretation and its object. It is the result of an active process, not a mechanical reproduction of a photographic plate. Perhaps this is sufficient to show that the problem of historical interpretation is much more difficult and profound than it seems from the following simple—but, actually, much more bizarre—perspective: understanding takes place when one mind exactly reproduces the contents of another, which is possible only if the experience of the interpreter is projected onto the mind which he interprets.

In these divergent interpretations of the process of understanding, the entire antithesis between a mechanistic and an organic or vitalistic perspective becomes clear. Like every intellectual controversy which is pursued to its ultimate source, the conclusions which we reach concerning this antithesis are dependent upon the most profound and comprehensive commitments of our world view.

The Problem of Historical Time

The subject matter of history as a theoretical structure is the past. It is to be distinguished from both the present and the future. It follows that time is one of the crucial components in the concept of history. Consider the following questions. What is the relationship between time and the other components of history? And what is the special import of the concept of time that is germane to history? It seems to me that these two questions have not yet been answered with the clarity that is desirable, nor even with the clarity that is possible.

I

A given aspect of reality qualifies as historical when we know how to fix it at a certain position within our temporal system. The precise determination of this location may be subject to many different degrees of precision. This observation is self-evident. In comparison with more formal definitions of the historical that seem to be more profound and comprehensive, however, it will prove to be more crucial and definitive.

First of all, this definition rules out the following possibility: an aspect of reality falls within the domain of history simply in virtue of the fact that it occurred at some time or other. Suppose that the archeological rubble of an urban settlement filled with all sorts of interesting things is discovered somewhere in Asia. Suppose that there is no data of any sort concerning the antiquity of this settlement, neither through its style nor through any direct or indirect evidence. In that case, these ruins may perhaps be of value and significance from many perspectives. However they do not constitute an historical artifact or document. As long as their temporal existence is only general, as long as they cannot be located within a determinate time-frame, then they exist in an historical vacuum. Suppose that it could even be established that this settlement was a relic of a people with which we are already familiar. Although there is, of course, no concrete example of this phenomenon available, such a discovery would not be sufficient to locate this settlement within a specific time-frame in the development of that people. Therefore it follows that this site would still fail to qualify as an historical document.

Nor does the *interpretation* or *understanding* of an aspect of reality entail that it is included within the domain of history. The fact that interpretation or understanding is not a sufficient condition for historicity is a consequence of rather peculiar structural relations. It is indubitable that understanding is the *conditio sine qua non* for the identification of a given item as historical. Suppose, for example, that we receive a report of the alleged conduct of a person with whose character we are otherwise familiar. And suppose that this report of his conduct, although logically possible, is utterly "unintelligible" in view of what we know about his character. In that case, we would hesitate to accept this report as an historical fact. Even the mere identification of an entity or an event—the identification of its potential historicity—depends upon a certain degree of understanding. In the absence of this measure of understanding, the item would remain an unqualified and undifferentiated variable, a complete unknown. Suppose that we describe an event as a battle or as the construction of a canal; suppose that we describe an action as an act of government or production; let us even suppose that we describe an action as unintelligible: in principle, each of these descriptions is grounded upon some form of understanding.

Prima facie, however, this relationship between interpretation and history seems to be completely paradoxical. Interpretation as such is completely irrelevant to historical reality as such. Understanding or interpretation is completely atemporal. The act in which I "understand" the character of the Apostle Paul or Moritz of Saxony is in principle exactly the same as the act in which I understand Othello or Wilhelm Meister. Understanding—that is, the ability to empathize or to project oneself into a structure of elements—is exclusively concerned with ideal contents. Understanding is a consequence of the coherence and the association of these ideal contents. From the perspective of understanding, therefore, the question of whether these contents fall under the categories of reality or fantasy, the present or the past, is of no consequence. I do not understand the Apostle Paul as a consequence of his historical reality. On the contrary, there is a sense in which the inverse of this proposition holds true. Consider the historical reality of the Apostle Paul. I only understand the ideal aspects of this reality which can be abstracted from historical reality itself. The existence of an historical phenomenon, its reality as such, is a brute fact which can never be understood. But historical time is exclusively the form of reality. It follows that understanding is also completely independent of historical time. Suppose that we infer from one of these ideal relationships of contents that a certain ideal content is real. This deduction is only a consequence of an inference from one real content—the reality of which is established by some method that is independent of understanding—to another.

Quite often, understanding comprehends temporal relationships. For example, the causal production of one phenomenon as a consequence of another may be an object of understanding. However this fact does not contradict the foregoing thesis. In this case, the group of these phenomena constitutes the interpretive complex. The temporal relationship, conceived as having a necessary order and duration, now becomes an autonomous content and the putative object of understanding. However this sort of understanding, which is based on the relationship between specific elements, is obviously quite independent of the following question: at what point in our system of temporal coordinates is the entire group situated? This collection of phenomena is understood not in virtue of the fact that they are situated in a certain location, but rather because of the functional relationship between their contents. This immanent time of such an interpretive complex of facts is not historical time. It is similar to the kind of time the measurement of which is important in a scientific experiment, a species of time which has nothing at all to do with the calendar date on which the experiment is performed.

It would represent a complete misunderstanding of the import of the foregoing thesis if the following objection were raised on purely empirical grounds. Certain phenomena can be understood only as a consequence of the fact that they occur within a quite specific time-frame. The diffusion of Christianity can be understood only as a result of its coincidence with certain mental structures of the ancient world, mental states which prevailed at that time, but neither before it nor after it. The appearance of the baroque style was only possible in the epoch in which the Renaissance had exhausted its characteristic energies. There are many other examples of the same sort.

All this is, of course, quite true. In these cases, the temporally given conditions of the fact which constitutes the object of interpretation is implicated within the interpretive complex itself. Suppose that we have already understood the phenomena of the baroque as a consequence of the interrelationship of the contents of this style. In other words, suppose that our understanding is independent of whatever temporal location may be ascribed to the complex of the baroque. Then the interpretive problem is extended to include the Renaissance. In this case, the interplay of understanding occurs not only between the elements of the baroque, but also between the baroque and the Renaissance. In this latter case, the Renaissance and the baroque constitute a single interpretive complex. A perspicuous representation of the immanent, objective structure of this complex is completely independent of the location of this complex within historical time. Suppose that the Renaissance only seems to be intelligible as a consequence of the antecedent conditions of the Middle Ages. In that case, the self-sufficient and self-contained collection of phenomena must be extended to include the Middle Ages. However this new and more comprehensive group would also be understood purely in terms of its contents. If its actual empirical realization had taken place a thousand years earlier, this would have absolutely no bearing upon its interpretation. Let us suppose that the interpretation could be either repaired or impaired by such a temporal shift. This would contradict the presupposition according to which it is precisely the objects of understanding —precisely these contents and no others—which should be temporally dislocated.

In principle, no explanation is ever ultimate or exhaustive. The understanding of a given moment inevitably requires the understanding of some antecedent moment. From a logical perspective, therefore, the interpretive complex acquires an infinite extension. From an empirical perspective, it extends to the content of the earliest event known to us. If we assume that the known events of history are exhaustively structured in causal sequences, then the totality of these events constitutes the only complex which makes possible the understanding of each individual event.

Suppose that such an interpretive complex is structured as a consequence of objectively immanent interpretation. In the moment in which such an interpretive complex exists—either as a real or as a hypothetical intellectual property—the temporal relationship between the interpretive entities discussed in the foregoing account is transformed. Consider a single item that is understood in a self-contained and autonomous fashion. It can be located at any position within a temporal sequence without producing any change in its character.

Suppose, on the other hand, that the interpretive complex embraces the totality of all known contents. Then this relationship between temporal location and interpretation is no longer possible. From our perspective, what exists both before and after this totality is only empty time, a vacuum in which no change of position is possible. This is because, within such a temporal vacuum, no position can be differentiated from any other position, just as no body can have a "location" in the vacuum of absolute space. The spatial location of bodies is only reciprocally determined as a consequence of their spatial interrelationships. The totality of the corporeal world, therefore, is nonspatial. For there is nothing which exists outside of this totality that could serve as a point of reference to "define" its location. For the same reason, time is only a reciprocal relationship between the contents of history. History as a whole, on the other hand, is atemporal.

Consider the heuristic construct which makes possible the temporal displacement of the single, self-contained historical complex, even though this apparently has no adverse effect on the comprehension of the relationship between the contents of this complex. It is only at this point that we can understand both the significance as well as the paradoxical character of this heuristic construct. As the foregoing account demonstrated, the reciprocal process of interpretation which forms this complex into a coherent whole is only preliminary and fragmentary. Such a process of interpretation qualifies as complete only if the complex is extended in both temporal directions—for our understanding of an event is complete only if we can identify its *consequences*—until the limits of the complex approximate the limits of our knowledge. Within this *total* sequence, the location of each content is definitively and, in principle, unambiguously determined. As a self-sufficient entity, there are no restrictions on the temporal displacement of the more limited complex. Only the elements of this complex are rigorously determined by their reciprocal interrelationships. In the total complex, this determinateness of temporal location is ascribed to the process as a *whole*.

It is, of course, true that atemporal contents—in other words, contents which could be realized in any arbitrary temporal location—are also objects of interpretation. However we can make no use of the arbitrariness of their temporal location. The reason is as follows. Consider the exact location which is ascribed to every content within its partial group. It is a logical consequence of this concept of location that the position of a content is determined only by its location within the *totality* of history. Within the totality of history, therefore, a displacement of such a content is impossible. The relative determination of the temporal location of contents is a consequence of their purely immanent and objective relationships. This definition of temporal location, therefore, is independent of the external and absolute frame of reference. However temporality in this relative sense is exhaustively defined only when it is identified as a relationship between the *totality* of potential objects of knowledge. It follows that the determination of temporal location on the basis of the pure content of an entity or an event becomes the determination of temporal location by reference to an absolute temporal point of reference. This latter definition requires the exhaustive determination of the sequence of events, from the earliest to the most recently known datum.

This resolves the antinomy with which the present discussion began. An item qualifies as historical only if it is temporally defined. In addition, however, an item qualifies as historical only if it constitutes part of an interpretive complex. Because understanding is exclusively a function of the immanent, atemporal logic of contents, it follows that such an interpretive complex can be located within any temporal frame without impairing its understanding in any respect. The contradiction which arises here is resolved by the following consideration. Understanding is complete only if it embraces the totality of real contents. Within such a total interpretive complex, however, each component has only *one* location. Under these conditions, arbitrary or imaginary displacements are no longer permissible. This is because each successive position is already occupied by another content which cannot be transposed to any other location. This conclusion could be stated in the following way: an event is historical if, on the basis of purely immanent and objective grounds which are completely irrelevant to its temporal location, it is unambiguously located within a specific temporal frame.

In summary: from the fact that an item has a temporal status, it does not follow that it is historical. And from the fact that this item is understood, it does not follow that it is historical. Suppose, however, that both of these conditions are satisfied. An item is historical when it is temporalized on the basis of an atemporal interpretation. In principle, this criterion for historicity can be satisfied only if interpretation embraces the totality of contents. This is because the single item can really be understood only in its relationship to the absolute totality. It follows that in this context temporalization can only mean location within a *specific* temporal frame. This logical consequence is based on the following two considerations. First, if temporalization is based on the *total* process, then every event can have only one unique location that cannot be exchanged with any other. Second, interpretation is possible only given the relatively precise determination of time. It is not possible to understand an item simply by ascribing a general temporal location to it. To ascribe a general temporal location to an item is simply a way of saying that the event in question really happened. And that is precisely what *cannot* be achieved by interpretation.

For quite some time, the character of individualization has been the criterion employed to distinguish historical knowledge from natural science. The individualization of an item can be properly understood and assessed only by means of the foregoing definition of historicity as location within a specific time-frame. The source of this individualization, we are always told, lies in the uniqueness of the content of the event. The natural sciences, on the other hand, conceive the content of the event from the perspective of the atemporal and general law. For such a law, the uniqueness of the event or the frequency of its repetition are completely irrelevant considerations. This distinction, however, does not seem to me to be conclusive. Consider a complex of events which can be understood as a relatively self-contained and self-sufficient entity. In that case, the temporal location of the complex can vary without jeopardizing its intelligibility. The content of this complex of events may be completely unique.

However we would not ascribe an historical status to this complex until its temporal variability is replaced by an unambiguously determined location within the total cosmic process.

The historical character of an event is certainly not an exclusive consequence of the uniqueness of its content. Perhaps this proposition only expresses a variant reading of the foregoing thesis. An historical status can be ascribed to events even though they may be repeated thousands of times with exactly the same qualitative properties. The thesis that the historicity of an event is defined by reference to the uniqueness of its content seems to be based on an illegitimate inference or extrapolation from the uniqueness of the cosmic process as a whole. This total process, of course, cannot be repeated. This is because every repetition— including the repetition of the eternal recurrence—is already included in the cosmic process itself. Any such repetition would be identifiable as some aspect of the total cosmic process. In principle, the occurrence of an unlimited number of events with exactly the same content is possible. Therefore I fail to understand the import of the uniqueness or the individuality of these events if the expressions 'uniqueness' and 'individuality' are meant to refer to the content of the events in question. The concept of the uniqueness or individuality of an event makes sense only if it refers to the time-*frame* in which a given content is located. The concept of time entails that such a time-frame is nonrepeatable.

Consider the temporal *point* which is situated at the location between everything that precedes the event and everything that follows it. This is the exclusive source of the unique individuality of historical contents. Only under this condition does the content of an historical event participate in the only absolute form of uniqueness known to us: namely, the uniqueness of the total cosmic process (the fact that our knowledge may be quite incomplete in comparison with the totality of this process is irrelevant here). This total process determines the location of the historical event. It follows that any historical event can have only one such temporal location. From a qualitative perspective, such an event may be individual or repeatable. However its temporal location is unique. Consider the thesis that an object of knowledge can be deprived of the individuality which qualifies it as historical only if an atemporal status is ascribed to it. This thesis is mistaken. Suppose that an event cannot be located at a "determinate" temporal point. This consideration alone is sufficient to establish that it does not fall within the domain of history. Historical uniqueness is exclusively grounded on the temporal determinateness of the event. The content of an event must be uniquely individual only insofar as this is necessary in order to provide an unambiguous definition of the temporal location of the event.

It follows that the mere temporality of a process is simply not sufficient to qualify that process as historical. This temporality must have the character of a determinate point in time. Temporal relations which have an objective basis also obtain within the domain of physical and chemical processes. Suppose that a laboratory measurement is taken of the duration of an oscillation, a chemical reaction, or a psycho-physical response. In that case, a beginning and an end—or the intermediate stages—are identified in terms of specific points in a temporal continuum. However the scientific experiment, which has the status of an objective, temporal entity, bears no relationship of any sort to the events that may precede or follow it. The entire problematic of this sort of scientific knowledge excludes the possibility of such a relationship. Consider the question: when did this event as a whole take place? When was this experiment preformed? This is a way of asking: what is the relationship between this experiment and the past and the future? From the perspective of the knowledge of time that is at stake in the scientific experiment, this question is totally irrelevant. It follows that the scientific experiment as an event is not an historical process. Suppose, on the other hand, that an experiment is the first of its kind. Suppose that this experiment had a revolutionary effect upon the further development of the science in question. In that case, it would obviously be of theoretical importance to establish its position in a more comprehensive temporal process. In other words, it would be important to determine its location in relation to the preceding and the succeeding stage of the development of the science. This is all a way of saying that *this* particular experimental natural process would qualify as historical. Depending upon the perspective from which the process is considered, either it would have an ahistorical temporality, or it would designate a specific temporal point which is the necessary condition for ascribing an historical status to it. The import or significance of this temporal point is determined by reference to the antecedents and consequences of the process—and, therefore, in principle by reference to the totality of the cosmic process in general.

This definition of temporality can be expressed in a fashion that seems to be quite self-evident. Therefore this expression was also employed in the foregoing account. In reality, however, this manner of formulating the definition of temporality helps us acquire a view of the categories of history that is not at all self-evident. This holds true especially for the concept of duration. Consider what, strictly speaking, can be understood by the duration of a state. This concept certainly cannot be analytically reduced to or derived from the logical or physical concept of continuity. Suppose that duration is understood in this latter sense. In that case, the extension of a given duration would be completely irrelevant. As paradoxical as this may sound, it would be of complete historical irrelevance whether a certain condition persisted for a year or for ten years. Consider what is entailed by the concept of continuity: within the duration of a certain state, no given moment of such an individual, societal, or cultural period of existence could be distinguished from any other moment. It follows that the qualitative difference between the beginning and the end of such an epoch would collapse completely. Therefore I do not see what interest could be ascribed to the brevity or length of such a period. Within such a period, the content of a given moment is the same as the content of all the other moments. Therefore no moment could be defined as earlier or later than any other by reference to its content. That is to say: no moment within a duration of this sort would qualify as historical.

Consider what we mean when we say that the duration of a government, the constitution of a state, or a form of the economy is important to us. Such a claim embraces a large number of individual events that are temporally differentiated from one another. At the very least, it means that by the end of the period the state of the group has altered in the following way. Consider the events which follow the period in question. These events are intelligible with reference to its end in a way that they would not have been intelligible with reference to the initial state of the period. Suppose that the only information we have about an otherwise obscure epoch is the fact that a certain king ruled thirty years. Historically, this fact tells us no more than we would learn from a report which claimed that he only ruled ten years. In other words, only the possibility of future discoveries would determine whether individual events could be differentiated as earlier and later in this purely abstract temporal period of duration. Suppose that the only fact we knew about the war which Frederick the

Great began in 1756 is that it lasted seven years. Suppose that we did not know that these years were filled with events the succession of which is mutually intelligible. Or suppose that we were not familiar with the *transformations* of European politics which this war produced. Then the number seven would tell us no more than a larger or a smaller number.

Consider the sort of event which qualifies as the ultimate element of historical knowledge. The aspects of such an event do not exhibit antecedents and consequences that are identifiable by reference to their content. Nor can past and future be determined by interrelating this event to other sequences of events that are external to it. The claim that any kind of temporal extension can be ascribed to such a process is completely irrelevant from the perspective of history. Consider a duration such that the question of its length is of no consequence. Practically speaking, this is no duration at all. An event of this sort has the status of an historical atom. It can acquire an historical significance only under the following condition: in the characteristic way, it is possible to identify it as earlier than one event and later than some third event. To say that an event falls within a certain *temporal moment* is a striking symbolic expression. Strictly speaking, the historical significance of duration may be reduced to the relationship between the earlier and the later. Consider, therefore, the episodic quality of the existential status of any event: the unique localization of its existence. This condition alone is sufficient to establish that the event is an element of history. It is necessary for us to understand—logically or intuitively, physically, physiologically, or psychologically—that one event is the cause or the effect of another, or that it is functionally interrelated or correlated with this other event in some way or other. This sort of understanding, however, is not sufficient to transpose the event into the objective flow of time and locate it within the domain of temporal extension. On the contrary, it only identifies the correlative position of one event by reference to another.

II

At this point, however, a paradoxical set of problems of the most difficult and perplexing sort arises. Consider any historical atom. Depending upon what we know or what we want to know, the administration of a government as well as a war, a battle as well as an episode within a battle can qualify as an historical atom. In fact, every such historical atom continuously fills a temporal space. Suppose that the administration of a government exists in an isolated fashion and produced no results of any sort that we are aware of. Nevertheless, an objective duration can be ascribed to this period. In this particular case, the period in question is of no historical significance. Such a period only defines and determines a temporal point within history, a point which can be identified either as earlier or as later than other points. The intrinsic, manifold differentiations of this point are, of course, based on other parallel synthetic concepts. This divergence extends throughout the whole of history. It is based on the fact that the contents of localized events are identified by reference to single concepts. However the event as an object of real experience does not have this form. On the contrary, it transpires in a continuous medium without any interruptions at all, a medium which is welded onto time itself without a break.

There is, perhaps, no other point which so clearly exhibits the depth and profundity of the distinction between the event and "history." The historical image that we *intend* by the "Seven Years' War" has no lapses or gaps. It extends precisely from August, 1756 until February, 1763. In reality, however, this continuity can only be ascribed to the *event* which transpires within these temporal limits and the geographical space in which the war was localized. There is no sense in which the "*history*" of this period is continuous. Consider the continuity with which a battle develops on the march or from an encampment of troops; the continuity of the movements of the soldiers from the preparations for battle to the battle itself; the continuity with which the battle itself proceeds from flight, to pursuit, and ultimately to cessation and peace. It is true that, in the abstract, we are convinced of this continuity of the real event. However the historical image which we actually *have* at our disposal on the basis of our research and the hypothetical constructions of our imagination consists of discontinuous, partial images like those just mentioned, images which, in a certain sense, revolve around a central concept. The mode of thought which is constitutive for history collects a number of discrete single events and processes around each of these points of crystallization. These events and processes in their entirety, conceived as the totality of this "single process," are thereby completely differentiated from adjacent or contiguous events.

Consider the following narrative. In 1758, Frederick won the Battle of Zorndorf. Then he intended to withdraw to Saxony in order to come to the aid of his brother Henry. On the way, he suffered horrible losses from a surprise attack near Hochkirch. Nevertheless, he was eventually able to join forces with Henry by means of a clever strategy. This account contains four moments, each of which constitutes a single conceptual unit. Although these moments follow one another in a certain sequence, the special conceptual synthesis of each moment exhibits a discontinuity. The elements of each synthesis are more intimately and continuously interrelated than the moments themselves. Everyone, of course, will admit that the event of 1758 described in this narrative was completely continuous. It is analyzed into parts only as a result of the conventional concepts which are superimposed upon it: the concepts of battle, victory, defeat, and the regrouping of the army. It is obvious that these retrospective syntheses do not lie in the same plane as the images of concrete experience. However these syntheses entail that the distinctions which they introduce cannot be erased.

The result of this process is quite curious. Consider the idea of the form of the event, certainly the only idea which conforms to the reality of the event. It is a continuous and abstract concept of reflection that is only remotely related to the concrete historical content of the event. However the structure which actually delineates the content of this event is situated in the form of the discontinuity of "events" that is remote from reality. The "Battle of Zorndorf" is a collective concept constituted in a special fashion from innumerable single processes. Suppose that military history attempts to discover all the details associated with this battle: every attack, each defensive maneuver, every episode, every specific engagement between different groups of troops, and so on. To the extent that this sort of knowledge is approached and a picture of the battle "as it really happened" is approximated, the concept of a battle becomes atomized. It loses the continuity which is expressed in all these atoms of knowledge, the continuity which constitutes the single event that we call "a battle." There is a sense in which this continuity is the consequence of an a priori form of knowledge that hovers over the event, as if it were traced by an ideal line: namely, the concept of a battle. Suppose that each of these atoms of knowledge is classified under a specific differential concept. Then each such atom will be isolated from the preceding atom and the succeeding atom. Increasingly diminished or abbreviated particles, therefore, become the objects of knowledge. An unfilled space arises between each of these successive particles. From the perspective of our historical knowledge and our conceptual scheme, such a space has the status of a mere cipher. Historical contents have the form of life, the form of experienced reality—namely, continuity—only to the extent that they are comprehended under a single concept which constitutes them as a coherent *unity* of some sort. Suppose that the single, temporally discrete and autonomous components of such a unity are identified and defined. In that case, the unity of the whole collapses, and unity can only be ascribed to the particles that have been conceptually identified and defined.

From the perspective of a perspicuous survey that embraces its beginning and its end, therefore, "the reign of Frederick the Great" is a coherent unity. But suppose that the historical consciousness attempts to grasp what is meant by this expression: the wars of Frederick the Great and his economic development of Prussia, his relationship to the spirit of France, and his establishment of the Prussian legal jurisdiction. Each of these aspects of the reign of Frederick the Great constitutes a coherent element in its own right. Each gravitates to its own center. A continuous relationship of interconnection is established between these elements only as the result of a kind of interpolation in which the idea of a vital and continuous event flows through the empty spaces which separate the elements. However the image of life which is developed in this fashion lies within an epistemological plane that is different from and more abstract than the plane of its single elements. These elements can be comprehended within this image of life only if they are detached from their circumscribed, concrete individuality and placed in relief.

This same process is susceptible to further analysis. Suppose that the Seven Years' War is conceived as an integral whole that is constituted by battles, troop movements, and negotiations. Each of these battles may be analyzed into its respective stages according to the method indicated above. It seems that the pursuit of this method would lead to an atomistic construct of the event. In the final analysis, it seems that we would have only purely episodic images of moments, each moment situated in such a way that a given moment closely approximates some other moment. However an interval which cannot be bridged would separate any two of these moments. If the intervals between these moments were continuously filled, then the integrity of these moments, their self-contained, pictorial framework which defines their status as single historical elements, would be destroyed. Under these conditions, therefore, it would be impossible to attain that vital continuity which exactly conforms to reality; just as there is no number of points—regardless of now large it may be—which can replace the continuity of a line.

The decisive point, therefore, is certainly not the following: we simply do not know "enough" in order to achieve an exhaustive comprehension of the total stream of living reality within the limits of historical knowledge. Just to the contrary. *In principle, historical knowledge simply does not have the form* which would make it possible to reproduce the continuity of experience. And the more we "know"—in other words, the more concrete and precisely defined constructs we establish as conceptually circumscribed entities—the less possible such a reproduction becomes. We experience the continuity of the event directly—but in an inexpressible fashion—as our own peculiar form of existence. For this reason, we are also able to ascribe the continuity of the event to historical processes. But suppose that each of these historical entities becomes the object of the increasingly specialized, precise, and perspicuous function of knowledge. In that case, they will collapse into purely discontinuous phenomena. Then each aspect of such a phenomenon acquires the status of a continuous period, until it is also analytically fragmented, and thereby de-animated, by the progressive movement of knowledge. Suppose that this mode of reductive analysis is pursued to the following limit: the synthesis of the cognitively distinctive episodic atoms into the total process which constitutes them as history is no longer possible. The quantum of the intrinsic meaning of each atom becomes too modest and insignificant. It is no longer possible to establish a coherent relationship between the content of a given episodic atom and all others.

Consider the individual battles of the Seven Years' War as isolated atoms which have no definitive temporal location. Suppose that the Seven Years' War itself is conceived as a continuous entity in which each of these battles has a specific location. Then these battles can acquire an historical status. In the same way, the war itself becomes part of history when it is comprehended within the politics of the eighteenth century. Suppose, on the other hand, that we reverse this process to the point at which we can identify a skirmish between a Prussian and an Austrian grenadier at Kunersdorf. This encounter no longer has the status of an historical phenomenon. This is because it could just as well have taken place at Leuthen or Liegnitz. Suppose that we had knowledge of every nuance of the mental processes and physical movements which took place among the Russians, the Austrians, and the Prussians on August 12, 1759. From the perspective of this knowledge, consider the concepts which identify this sequence of facts. None of these concepts would comprehend a measurable temporal span of the event itself, the battle. The aim of history cannot be realized by knowledge of this sort. The purpose of history is not knowledge of these details. On the contrary, its purpose is knowledge of the more comprehensive and abstract structure: the Battle of Kunersdorf.

That engagement between a Prussian and an Austrian grenadier is an authentic and essential part of the battle. Nevertheless, it does not lie within the province of the historical interest. Otherwise the sequences which are embraced by this interest would collapse into discontinuity. The Battle of Kunersdorf as an object of our cognitive interest is an entity which is necessarily continuously *extended* throughout an expanse of time. The form of this entity is such that it represents an image of reality. Reality is continuous. However it can never be filled with real content. The reason is as follows. Although the ultimate and elemental components of reality have the form of the earlier or the later, it follows that they also have the form of discontinuity. Consider a specific span of time, which is only a product of abstract intuition. These elemental components cannot fill such a span of time, no more than a number of points, regardless of how large, can fill a line, even though these points identify the direction of the line itself.

The result of the foregoing seems to be a general principle. Consider the analysis of a phenomenon into elements. The phenomenon itself is conceived as the sum or product of its elements. Given a certain level of reduction in this process of analysis, the individuality of the phenomenon is destroyed. Consider the character of another person. It is accessible to us in a vision or perception that is quite peculiar. Suppose that character is analyzed into its individual aspects. In such an analysis, we usually discover that each of these aspects is more or less general. The person in question shares his characteristics with many other men. As a total entity, the fate of an individual is incomparable and unique. Nevertheless, it can be analyzed as a sum of processes each of which is really an event of frequent occurrence. The more precisely and minutely the aspects of the character are discriminated, the more episodic these events become. The atomistic world view, for which the smallest elements and the properties of their motions constitute the exclusive realities cannot resolve the problem of individuality. From the perspective of this world view, it is not even possible to acknowledge the existence of the problem.

Because of the individual character of a given phenomenon, it can be temporally located, and therefore also historically defined. The analysis and the discrimination of the elements of this phenomenon represent an increase in precision and an approximation of knowledge of things "as they really are." Quite often, although naturally not always, this process of analysis and discrimination dissolves the individual character of the phenomenon.

In view of the foregoing, it is possible to speak of a *threshold of analytical reduction*. Knowledge of all the muscular movements of a soldier would destroy the coherent animation of the total process which correlates its beginning and its end into a temporal construct. The dimensions of the element of history must remain large enough so that individuality can still be ascribed to its content. The individuality of an historical element makes it possible to ascribe a definitive temporal position to this element. In consequence, it acquires a unique relationship to every other historical element.

Historical knowledge, therefore, is suspended in a perpetual compromise between the following two extremes: on the one hand, the construction of comprehensive unified entities, the continuity of which reproduces the form of the event even though it cannot be exhausted by the concrete phenomena of reality; on the other hand, the concrete phenomena of reality. From the perspective of ideal cognitive criteria, these concrete phenomena only identify a single chronological point. Precisely for this reason, the continuity of the real event cannot be ascribed to these ideal criteria.

This profound antimony of historiography exhibits the problem which I regard as the fundamental question of the theory of historical knowledge: how does an event become history? Life assumes the intellectual or mental form of the historical. From this perspective, consider historical realism, which holds that history reproduces the events themselves, and historical idealism, which holds the reality is the same as knowledge of reality. Both theses represent a one-dimensional distortion of the substance of this problem. While historical realism sacrifices the contents of the historical process, historical idealism sacrifices its continuity.

This problem has its origins in the space between life as an object of experience and the transformation of life that we call history. In response to this problem, I should like to venture the following hypothesis. Although the distance between life and history may remain an ultimate epistemological dichotomy, it is not an ultimate metaphysical postulate. This is because, in the final analysis, history is also an expression and an act of life, precisely the same life to which it is originally *juxtaposed*. The juxtaposition or contrast to life is also a form of life. The realism of history is not grounded in the *content* of life which history reproduces as it actually was. On the contrary, it lies in the following consideration: somehow the inevitable dichotomy between history and life must have its origins in the motive forces and the law of life itself.

The Constitutive Concepts of History

The premise of the Kantian critique according to which "all knowledge has its source in experience" is not entirely unambiguous. It would be roughly comparable to the claim that the "origins" of the art of painting lie in drawing. This may, perhaps, identify the initial link in the chain of artistic endeavor. But it does not identify the beginning of the entire mental process of development which leads to drawing and, transcending that, to painting. For the same reason, experience may be the earliest stage in cognitive development. However knowledge itself is not the first form of mental activity. It presupposes other forms. Therefore it can be said that the "origin of all knowledge"—and, in consequence, also the origin of the most abstract levels of knowledge—lies beneath experience. From this point, the path to knowledge leads through experience, as if through a wayside station. The process of development which leads exclusively and unambiguously to the totality of knowledge begins with experience. Considered as an intellectual function in general, however, this process presupposes an extended sequence that lies beyond experience. We can acquire a perspicuous view of the relationship between knowledge and experience if we consider an item which, at some point, is constituted as theoretical. Suppose that we can identify its pretheoretical state and observe its transition into the form of knowledge. This earlier state, which continues to exist along with the theoretical stage, could be called "experience." In this state we have, or so I believe, the most primitive mode in which a content of consciousness—objectively juxtaposed, in whatever way to consciousness itself—becomes accessible to us.

In the process of knowledge, certain differential aspects of our nature respond to things, or they mediate our relationship to the world. However we are probably justified in claiming that experience constitutes a response of our total existence to the existence of things, a response which arises from much more extensive and quite fundamental strata. Experience is *our* perspective of the relationship between an object and the totality or unity of our being. In "experience," life—the most intransitive of all concepts—is placed in an immediate, functional relationship with objectivity. The mode of this connection is unique. In it, the activity and passivity of the agent are linked in a fashion that is irrelevant or indifferent to the mutually exclusive logical relationship between them. Experience is the expression of our initial, primary relationship to the world. In an absolute sense, therefore, knowledge also begins in experience. In knowledge, this relationship is canalized by special organs or channels and is grounded in the integrated totality of the subject, a unified entity. Knowledge, however, produces a remarkable result. A phenomenon is assimilated and fashioned by life. Then this vital relationship of dependence is dissolved. As an object of knowledge, this phenomenon acquires the status of an autonomous representation. It comes to exist in an objectively ideal sphere. An experiment in physics which has been understood or a phonetic law remains completely indifferent to the fact that its objective contents were accessible—and remain accessible—to experience. Although they are grounded upon life, they have left it behind.

At this point, we can see the definitive characteristic of historical knowledge. Suppose that historical sequences are constructed on the basis of the strategic facts of a military campaign, the works of an artistic epoch, the alternating states of the economy, the decrees of ecclesiastical councils, or from some other source. These facts constitute a collection of objective facticities. The intrinsic properties of each datum and its logical consequences or technical results are potential objects of a purely objective knowledge. The objective status of this knowledge is categorically independent of the fact that these data are also objects of experience. Viewed from the perspective of this sort of knowledge, however, such a sequence does not yet have the status of history. It is merely systematic. Such a sequence lacks the real dynamic which embraces every member of the sequence and its necessary and ideal connection with every other member, a dynamic which permeates this necessary connection as if from within. It is the continuity of this dynamic which actually develops one given member of the sequence from another. Suppose that the characteristic dynamic form that we call life does not establish a relationship between one element of this sequence and another. Linguistically and logically, of course, this can only be expressed as a relationship between objective contents. However we *mean* or *intend* this relationship in a completely different way: immanently, dynamically, in such a way that the limits of the single phenomenon are open-textured. If this condition is not satisfied, then we cannot speak of history.

Recall Hegel's view that only the mind has a history. It seems to me that this definition of history needs to be revised by the following addition: only the living mind has a history. Consider the single datum of the past, the isolated concept, the independently intelligible objective structure in which mental activity is crystallized. They are all mental phenomena. But they do not yet qualify as history. They become history only if they fall under the form of life. Or, viewed from the perspective of the form of life, they become history only if they constitute an experience. Life can be ascribed to a concrete individual. In a more extended sense, however, it can also be ascribed to a societal group. And, as a symbolic, heuristic concept, it can also be employed to introduce order into the developmental stages of a science, an art, or a branch of technology. These individual phenomena must always acquire an order within the crests and troughs of the characteristic rhythm of life. Because they are objects of experience, the rhythm of life is the exclusive form in which these phenomena become structures of history.

Suppose that a phenomenon falls under the form of life and becomes an object of human experience. The satisfaction of this condition alone is not sufficient to constitute it as an historical phenomenon. It is true that an event which falls within the domain of history must be animated—it must fall under the form of life. However the event as such does not yet qualify as history. Here, it seems to me, is the source of the fundamental problem of every theory of historical knowledge: how does an event become history? History is a form in which the mind comprehends the event and its contents. However it is only one form among others which structure the same material. This material can be conceived from the timeless perspective of its purely logical content. It can be represented by the form of art. And the very same material can become part of a life and fall under the form of human experience. When contents transcend the form of experience and become history, they are subjected to certain novel transformations that are peculiar to the structure of history. In this way, they become detached from experience. Of course the same points hold for the definition of every science. Historical science, however, has the following peculiarity. The form of life also functions in this process of transplantation. The existential status of the material as an object of human experience is not eliminated. On the contrary, it is transformed. In the ensuing, I shall attempt to sketch some of these transformations. They are the essential differentia in virtue of which the events "as they really happened" become the intellectual structures of history.

I

First, it is obvious that history analyzes the continuous process of experienced reality into discrete sequences. These sequences are invariably grounded upon an objective concept. Universal history and world history are unfortunate expressions. First of all, consider the actual empirical extent of universal or world history. Compared with the dimensions of knowledge to which these concepts lay claim, this empirical domain only represents a minimal approximation. The following consideration, however, is much more important. These concepts explicitly entail that there is a unity of representation in which the images of specific facts cohere—or rather, from which these images follow. Precisely such a unified conception of this sort, however, is unattainable. These ideas imply that the universally procreative *life* of the species and of individuals can be formed into an image or representation. But this is *impossible*. Only the artifacts of this life which have become objective and which, for this reason, exist discontinuously are possible objects of a representation. There is some sense in which they transcend the immediate unity of life. However, as we shall see, a certain rhythm and symbolic representation of life itself enter into their historical constitution. In fact, there are only specialized provinces of history: the history of foreign policy and domestic politics, religion and fashion, medicine and art, world view and technology—in other words, all the phenomena that we classify in temporal sequences. However the criteria on the basis of which phenomena are classified in these sequences are trans-temporal. These criteria are based on logically defined concepts of the objective content of these phenomena. We do not construct the development of a total event that develops multi-dimensionally, in such a way that all of these dimensions seem to be aspects of a single perspective. On the contrary, we construct one-dimensional, independently identifiable lines of development that are juxtaposed to one another. At most, we can occasionally discover within these lines of development a diagonal cross-section which correlates abstract similarities in their characteristics. In the strict sense, universal history or world history is a superficial or extrinsic synopsis of fragments from these different lines of development within the space of a single literary work.

The definitive procedure of historical method begins with the distinction and discrimination of contents from the form of experience in which they are implicated and the classification of these contents in conceptually linear syntheses. Consider, by way of example, the political biography of a ruler. The politically important ideas and activities are distinguished within the continuity of a rich, multi-faceted, and expansive life. They make up his political career, the course of which is intrinsically continuous. However it is hardly the case that any moment of his political life transpires in the artificial isolation that this historical construct requires. On the contrary, there are invariably relationships between his political career and mental events that have other sources. Each moment in his political life is also dependent upon the general disposition of his character and transitory moods. His political life is completely intelligible only in relation to his life as a whole. Knowledge of his life as a whole, however, is impossible for any science. So the historian constructs a new synthetic concept: politics. In view of the abstract precision required by this synthetic concept, it is possible that politics in this sense never enters the consciousness of the ruler. Perhaps, in this sense, he never consciously performs a political act. Consider the following analogy. A single strand is extracted from the multi-threaded web of life. It is unraveled from all the other strands—with which, in reality, it is intertwined—and woven into an entirely new fabric. Even this analogy goes too far. It is a poor comparison because there is no continuity in the relationship between fragments of historical thread that are woven together. In history, we find fragments of a fabric that are only partially and discontinuously interwoven. They constitute a "history" only from the perspective of the historian. He imposes upon them the problematic which he regards as definitive, the only problematic that will produce a synthesis of these fragments.[1]

The issue here does not concern a partial representation of a complete process in a given time, place, or personality, a total event which is the real, putative object of knowledge. Just to the contrary. From the outset, the purpose of the investigation is to acquire knowledge of an aspect of the total process, as this aspect is defined by a certain concept. It is not our purpose to know what Richelieu or Wilhelm von Humboldt experienced from dawn to dusk, including an account of their head colds and their menus. On the contrary, our aim is only to acquire knowledge of the elements of their existence that fall under the concept of political activity—or under the concept of some other specific mental activity. Our purpose is to establish a relationship of coherence among these elements. In the real nexus of life, however, meals and physical or psychological sensations exist in a continuous relationship with the moments of life that are historically significant. The undifferentiated, continuous development of the contents of life from a productive centrifugal point which is its own ultimate cause is reserved exclusively for the domain of the reality of experience. The necessary path of history proceeds from a synthesis of the objective import of these contents and their significance.

Of course a mental fact of immediacy exists. There is even a sense in which life is essentially a function of this fact. It could be said that the immediacy of life is a proto-form or preliminary form of the historical and theoretical constitution of the sequence of events: the link between an actual content of consciousness and the contents of the past with which it is objectively correlated. Suppose, for example, that we interrupt the reading of a book and return to it after a lapse of days or weeks. In such a case, we link what we are reading now with what we read earlier. There are no gaps or breaks. This continuity, given in the objective content of the text itself, is grounded in the psychological moment. It is as if all the thoughts and experiences that separate the two periods of reading did not exist. It is obvious that the same point also

---

[1]Some of this material is taken from my book *The Problems of the Philosophy of History*.

holds for the scientific ideas of a scholar, the political projects of a ruler, the execution of all extremely complex plans, and the struggle to resolve a protracted relationship of antagonism. Suppose that, following a period of interruption, we return to the production of a work. Even the unaffected and spontaneous *mood* with which the work is associated reappears in this moment. Often it even happens that the same nuance of mood reappears, the feeling that is necessary in order to preserve the coherence and continuity of the work. Thoughts, moods, and volitional interests may lapse over astonishingly long periods of time that are filled with absolutely heterogeneous contents. However they transcend these long intervals and reappear exactly at the point where they began to lapse. It follows that human life is constructed from innumerable sequences. Because they are objectively coherent, they are also psychologically coherent. In the temporal process of mental life, however, fragments of these sequences are repeatedly disconnected and detached from one another.

This is the basic phenomenon the degrees and forms of which constitute the so-called split personality. Sometimes this phenomenon assumes a pathological character. The state of intoxication, for example, produces ideas and actions which disappear completely from the consciousness of the sober person. When he becomes drunk again, however, the same ideas and actions reappear and their consequences are consistently developed. This is similar to a phenomenon that occurs in dreams. During one night we dream. On the following day, we are completely unaware of the contents of the dream. In the following night, we continue the dream, beginning at the point at which we were awakened that morning. Exactly the same process of association and continuity appears in repeated episodes of hypnosis. In psychiatry, there is a verified case of a girl who was raped while in a state of somnambulism. Upon awaking, she had no recollection of this at all. With the onset of the next attack of somnambulism, however, she immediately told her mother the entire story. The least mysterious type of explanation for these phenomena is probably the following. A given mental event cannot be abstracted and isolated from the total mental state that prevails at the same time. The primary event is both a cause and an effect of a certain disposition and tendency of the mind as a whole. It is inextricably implicated within a sphere of characteristic feelings and impressions. Suppose that a state of drunkenness or somnambulism reappears. In that case, one becomes precisely the same sort of person that he was on the last occasion that he found himself in such a state. Therefore it is quite comprehensible that the given contents and sources of action characteristic of such a state are further developed in accordance with their own immanent logic. The normal person reverts to earlier ideas which establish associations that transcend all intervening lapses of time. He persistently forms conceptually and practically coherent sequences on the basis of temporally incoherent fragments. These normal mental phenomena probably have the same explanation: the reappearance of total mental states which still retain their own intentional essence and its characteristic possibilities of development.

The phases of our mental life that actually transpire in a logically and teleologically continuous fashion are, strictly speaking, astonishingly brief. This is astonishing for the following reason. The affinities which are actually established between the fragments of mental life make us practically oblivious of its discontinuity. We are not even disposed to notice this discrepancy between the temporal process and the objective or substantive process of our life. The appeal to "memory" will not work here. In any case, it would provide no explanation for this phenomenon. Essentially, there is no sense in which this issue is concerned with a mere process of association in which a present impression conjures up an earlier impression that is related to it. On the contrary, the issue concerns the *development* (and there is no sense in which this is necessarily a teleological process) of a stream of life which has an objective tendency. This stream flows through all of its temporally discrete elements. Within this stream, each element can have only one specific location. But there is no sense in which association entails a determinate temporal sequence. This issue concerns a dynamic teleological tendency, not merely an associative form of juxtaposition or coexistence which correlates the later element and the earlier.

This stream of life has a mysterious continuity. There is a sense in which this continuity is simply not interrupted by the intervals which the total current of life interposes between its waves. The mental process realizes its purely organic and vital continuity in the characteristic interpenetration of sequence. From the standpoint of their temporal relationship, the components of these sequences are completely dispersed and fragmented. Nevertheless, they form the links of a chain the cohesion of which is comparable to the coherence of meaning. However this form of coherence does not have a purely ideal existence that is only embodied in a synopsis. On the contrary, it represents the further development of a real psychological force. Elements which are discontinuous from the standpoint of their meaning are regularly re-integrated by this same meaning. On the one hand, it is the total, integral mental event—conceived purely as such—which is responsible for this discontinuity. Ultimately, on the other hand, it is this integral mental event which constitutes and comprehends the coherent sequence of these elements. It must be responsible for the force and direction of such a sequence. Consider those contents the sequences of which make up one human career. Viewed exclusively from the perspective of the process of life itself, they have the property which can only be described as unity or homogeneity. Seen from the perspective of objective or substantive concepts, however, they exhibit the most disordered and incoherent contingency imaginable. The logic of life is completely different from the logic of things, concepts, and ideas. But its necessity is no less rigorous. And the integral relationship which it establishes among elements is no less coherent.

Perhaps this difference is grounded in the forms of both sequences. The moments of life are interrelated in a real *continuity*. Every form of rational logic, however, establishes connections between elements that are relatively autonomous and independently identifiable. In the continuity of life, it could be said that the rigid definitions of individual contents are collapsed. The result is a possible form of coherence between contents that is much less restrictive and more comprehensive than would be the case in the conceptualization of contents. In the latter case, rigidity of form is more a consequence of a coherent relationship that is established between independently identifiable contents. It is not a result of the interpenetration of one content by another. Consider the following form of existence. Its vital logic produces the most uniform and homogeneous process of development imaginable. From the perspective of its objective logic, however, the contents of this process are diametrically juxtaposed in the most atrocious—and often totally incomprehensible—fashion. The most vivid and perspicuous example of such a form of existence is Goethe. In Goethe, all possible practical and poetic activities, scientific and purely personal enterprises, productive and receptive interests, moments of candor and moments of reserve are intertwined. In consequence, the accomplishments of one day are often absolutely alien to those of the previous day. In addition, consider the value of both his masterful creations and his completely unsuccessful productions, his deepest insights and also his astonishing blunders. They become so arbitrarily and incoherently related that it would never be possible to achieve an immanent understanding of their relationship.

But suppose that we are able to comprehend the rhythm and the total structure of this constantly changing life. Then we can perceive a most amazing unity and coherence in its inconsistencies and the illogic of its contents. Consider all the phases of Goethe's life, its pinnacles and its depths, and the affinities it creates between the most remote phenomena. They all represent the pulse beats of a single life, the immanent development of an inflexible law. Within all these phenomena, a "vital form has evolved and impressed itself upon them." Phenomena of this sort are interwoven through every human life. In the case of Goethe, however, the problematical relationship between these phenomena achieves both its most extreme degree of tension and its most complete form of release. These phenomena reveal intact the enigmatic character of the relationship between the process and the content of a mental event. They also make it clear that the validity of the apparently mutually exclusive distinction between continuity and discontinuity does not hold in the case of mental events. The same point holds for other dichotomies the validity of which is alleged to be logically necessary. Perhaps the process of life falls under a third form for which this distinction between continuity and discontinuity is not absolutely essential, a form which we are not yet able to grasp conceptually.

At this point, however, we are concerned with the following brute fact. The succession of experience is chaotic from the standpoint of its meaning and continuous from the standpoint of its temporality. Within the real process of life, nevertheless, there are relationships between its elements. Life is uncertain and incoherent—incoherent precisely because of its temporal coherence. By employing this meaningful link between mental sequences of development, there is a sense in which we correct the randomness with which life arbitrarily extracts fragments from logical sequences or other objective sequences of contents in order to form its own structure. At this point, there seems to be a certain symbolic relationship or a broad similarity between experience and history. History systematizes certain aspects of experience by employing synthetic concepts and represents these aspects in the form of a coherent, unified process of development. However there is no sense in which this similarity eliminates the difference between their juxtaposed aims and tendencies. In experience, mental sequences are formed in such a way that all gaps and lapses are transcended. This is a condition for the possibility of an intimate interrelationship between these sequences. Therefore it is also a condition for the structure and coherence of the compulsive, progressive tendency of life. History, on the other hand, isolates the individual sequence and reduces the unity of life as a whole in which each of these sequences is inextricably interrelated with the others. It could be said that history creates a fictitious, hypothetical life the contents of which are linked on the chain of *a single* concept. Real life, however, is a product of the innumerable interruptions and lapses in these sequences, breaks which necessitate a continuous process of retrospection and synthesis. If we keep in mind all the reservations which any metaphor requires, life as it is experienced may be compared to a tapestry. Only short strands of its many threads are visible. The rest of the fabric is woven beneath the surface, continuously weaving together the part of the fabric that can be seen. However this function is concealed by the surface fabric, which is interwoven in the same way. It follows that only a linear arrangement of the threads of the fabric will reveal the design that cannot be identified in any of its individual parts. History, on the other hand, extracts a single thread from the tapestry and represents this single strand as if its development were uninterrupted. In consequence, a form of continuity is created, but not a pattern.

Experience as an object of historical knowledge, however, exhibits some sort of symbolic relationship to life. Somehow life is projected in the form characteristic of a concept. In this case, the form of its reality, of course, has disappeared. However the most universal aspect of the nature of life—even if it has become somewhat diffuse—is retained in the conceptualized sequence of its contents. Consider a narration of the political biography of a ruler; the religious development of a reformer; the trials, blunders, and successes of an inventor; the legal history of a nation; or even the history of chemistry or architecture, for which the unity of a subject is quite unnecessary. In each of these cases, the sequence of contents that is extracted from the profusion of life is based on—or underpinned by—the principle of life itself. This establishes a difference between history and a systematic conception of these contents, a structure the purpose of which is knowledge of objective content as such.

It could be said that the structure of history—even though it is formed on the basis of the a priori of objective theory—remains vital and organic in its quality. It is true that history is completely alien to the reality of life, a form of reality that is neither constituted by reference to concepts or intelligible in terms of concepts. But the differences between history and theoretical, aesthetic, or metaphysical systems are just as great. In these systems, life does not even have a symbolic or supplementary status in the synthesis or understanding of its contents. Nor is it employed as a theme or motif of development. This is the definitive property of history as a form of knowledge. This property differentiates history from the experience of contents as well as from the kind of objective investigation and systematization of contents in which their status as objects of experience is irrelevant. History extracts contents from the interwoven fabric and the continuous dynamic of life and places these contents in relief. By the use of objective concepts, these contents are structured into novel and distinctive sequences. These sequences are formed in such a way that they satisfy our cognitive criteria. However these sequences remain perceptibly active products or offspring of *life,* documents of human experience. Unlike objectively systematic science, history does not cut the umbilical cord that connects it to the blood stream of human life as it is actually experienced. The inner dynamic that is derived from life itself also vibrates within the structure of history. It creates the relationship between one member of an historical sequence and another, a relationship that is only intelligible on psychological grounds. History is the only construction in which human experience—as a source of meaning, dynamism, animation, and development—does not disappear. However the form in which experience directly brings forth its contents is replaced by a completely different form, which has its source in the theoretical ideal of knowledge.

Consider every cell of an organism as a repository of the genetic inheritance of an entire species and the potentialities of its development into the indefinite future, an invariably essential component of an inevitable process of development. Each element of an historical sequence is a symbol of such a cell. An historical sequence is formed and constructed in such a way that a given link is historically comprehensible only on the basis of the previous link. This given link, furthermore, is a condition for the intelligibility of all subsequent links. Only sequences of this sort qualify as historical. Such a sequence is, of course, not a vital or organic structure, but rather a conceptualized intellectual structure. The relationship between its components is completely different from the sort of relationship in which the phenomena of human life are grounded. Nevertheless, only a sequence of this sort maintains that incomparable relationship to life which symbolically translates the continuous development of the process of life into the sequences of history in a thousand different ways. History, of course, is a form. The categories for the historical systematization of contents establish a rigorous dichotomy between history and the experience of these same contents. However the distinction between history and experience should not be confused with their a priori irrelevance. By means of analysis and the creation of novel syntheses, history transforms the object of experience into a completely new structure. Nevertheless, experience remains an unexpungable component of the forms and contents of history. It is true that the forms and contents of history transcend experience. However they remain the forms and contents of objects of experience.

II

If we examine the relationship discussed in the foregoing section more carefully—the relation between life as such and its contents, contents which form their own definitive totalities—then from the perspective of these totalities, it is clear that the individual aspects of life have a fragmentary status. Knowledge requires that even the most isolated entity must occupy a position in the total cosmic scheme. Every concept must have a place in the pyramidal structure of subordination and superordination. Consider creativity—in art or in any other domain. The idea of perfection hovers over it—always vaguely, in the form of a presentiment—like an astral satellite. Consider the domain of practical conduct, which always raises the claims of ethical validity and rectitude. All these considerations produce the picture of ideally complete worlds. Every single human life passes through these worlds, sometimes realizing one aspect of these worlds as its content, sometimes realizing another. If this content is situated within the objective frameworks of one of these worlds, harmoniously or continuously structured into its totality in such a way that its force and meaning are fully exhausted in it, then the content does not have the status of a fragment. Such a content becomes fragmentary only if it is detached from these ideal or real structures and situated within the unity and totality of a process of life. The unity and the totality of a process of life are grounded in completely different requirements. Under these conditions, the content seems to be constituted from fragments of possible items of knowledge, possible implications of sequences of action, and possible forms of consummation and perfection of the most diverse sorts. From the perspective of its own meaning and its own motive forces, there is no sense in which it follows that life itself must be a fragment. It does not even follow that the contents of the individual segments of life are fragments. This is because these segments are—as this might be expressed—suspended in the stream of life. The stream of life defines their form in an a priori fashion. Even from this perspective, however, it cannot be denied that life still retains its fragmentary character. From the standpoint of its transtemporal idea, the whole of life has this fragmentary character. Since this standpoint does not lead to an a priori of history, however, we are not concerned with it here. On the other hand, perhaps we can identify the fragmentary character of life on the basis of other aspects of the human phenomenon that may be characterized as fragmentary. Quite often the fact that life does indeed have this fragmentary character becomes obvious only when it is subject to correction or revision. Certain intellectual processes may be identified as forms of "complementation" or "supplementation." Suppose that we subtract—as this might be expressed—these processes from the core or nucleus to which they are added. Such a nucleus must be characterized as a fragment.

Within the structure of history, one such process of supplementation is taken from the praxis of everyday life. We constantly represent the individual in terms of general concepts. He is conceived as an instance of general categories. These categories may be logical-psychological or societal. As a result of instinctive impressions or more precise knowledge, one man considers another clever or stupid, generous or petty, moral or unprincipled. In other words, he regards this other person as a man of a certain qualitatively definable type. However it is quite obvious that an individual is not *exclusively* clever or stupid, and so on. On the contrary, this description fails to take into account the innumerable other qualities which he possesses. This description abbreviates or telescopes the man himself. Perhaps this is precisely the reason such a description heightens the special shade and nuance with which he is said to represent this quality. As a result, it constitutes a more comprehensive and general property. The proposition that a person is clever or stupid complements or supplements the concrete, individual properties of his intellectual character and transforms them into something that is super-individual. Suppose that there is a certain sense in which the single thoughts and actions that exemplify this quality supercede all his other thoughts and actions, in such a way that they cast a uniform shade on the entire person. Then the actual, discontinuous moments of his character and history—which, in fact, ground and exhibit this quality—are, in principle, complemented and supplemented in such a way that they acquire the status of invariable and universal properties.

Our everyday relationships with our contemporaries insure that this sort of supplementation of the partial aspects of an individual existence remains within certain limits and subject to mutual revision and correction. Above all, the impression made by the living personality is sufficient to remind us that a person cannot be reduced to a schema defined by reference to a general category. If the individual personality is viewed from the perspective of history, however, then only single qualities or expressions of his motives are directly accessible to observation. Under these conditions, extrapolation beyond the brute facts to a total phenomenon is essential and unavoidable. As a result, the infinite complexity and scintillating flux of individual life are veiled by a more or less general concept. Every one-dimensional quality placed in relief from the concrete individuality of life has a universal or general status. It is a property that can also be ascribed to many other individuals. Only the total circumference of life—with all its manifold qualities and contradictions—can be called individual. In historical knowledge, a personality falls under several of these general concepts, each of which has the function of complementing and supplementing the characteristics which experience presents in a fragmentary fashion. But this does not alter the foregoing fact. Either these categories are juxtaposed, or they are related in a hierarchical fashion. The individual falls under several general concepts. Each of these concepts extends a particular property of the individual in such a way that his entire personality is embued with it.

If we consider what we really know about the majority of historical personalities, then it should be clear that this knowledge is extremely modest and fragmentary in comparison with the unfathomable profusion of the career of a real human life. However, we are not satisfied with this sort of knowledge. On the contrary, these fragments—in most cases, only the projection of one dimension of the personality onto the plane of a larger superpersonal event—develop into the total character of the personality itself. One of the a priori functions by means of which one person acquires a conception of another is the following: he conceives this person as a living totality, regardless of the range of data available for this purpose. This process has one direction and tendency in the case of a living person. In the case of an historical person, it has a logically different direction and tendency.

Our image of a contemporary is formed on the basis of a characteristic and rather peculiar intuition. Such an intuition makes the total unity of his personality accessible to us, often on the basis of nothing more than an initial glance. Such an image may be accurate or mistaken, precisely defined or blurred, clearly self-conscious or vaguely instinctive. This image may be based upon some observed fact of his life. Usually, however, the contrary is the case: our image and interpretation of the individual expressions and manifestations of his nature are formed on the basis of our perspective of the essential nature of his personality.

This prospect, however, is not open to history. The perspective of history is obliged to adopt the polar antithesis of this point of view. Our knowledge of the concrete conduct of the historical person really "supplements" the quality of his character. In other words, our conception of his conduct acquires a more general or a more profound status until it constitutes his character as a whole, the self-contained unity of his personality. Naturally the rigorous distinction between these two directions or tendencies only has a conceptual status. The historical conception of the personality is always implicated in our actual empirical knowledge of a contemporary individual. It represents one of those attitudes in which—independent of any scientific or scholarly intentions—we are historians. Our intuitive knowledge of the organic totality of the individual—a form of knowledge that transcends all empirical facts—is also indispensable and active in historical knowledge. In the domain of historical knowledge, the synthesis of the given partial manifestations of the person to form the total character of the individual—a total character which is imbued with the colors of this synthesis—appears as one of the formal necessities that are produced by the relationship between mind and reality when mind attempts to constitute reality as history.

In the foregoing discussion, the general property on which the synthesis of the personality is based has a psychological character. In other cases, however, this general property is defined socially. In history also, this synthesis is only the extension of a process with which the praxis of everyday life regularly establishes its own immanent presuppositions. In history, however, these syntheses are detached from the structures of everyday life and the subordinate and utilitarian role which they play there. In everyday life, the representation which is produced by this process rarely has an unambiguous and self-sufficient status. Consider any cultural relationship in which individuals are implicated. In the vast majority of cases, it is inevitable that the image which one person has of another is a function of the social position of the latter. When we are speaking with a priest, an officer, a professor, or an artist, our conduct with respect to this person is—as we might put it—affected reflexively by our perception of him as an occupant of this status. Moreoever—and this is the relevant point here—the extent of this influence upon our conduct transcends the extent to which the profession and its accouterments become immanent components of the personality itself. The social class to which he belongs and the sphere of life which he shares with his professional colleagues hover over the individual like an ideal atmosphere. In one way or another, it defines the conduct of the person who enters it. We do not perceive a person in the guise of a pure individual. On the contrary, we see him as if through the haze of the generalities of his situation, a mist which, in a certain sense, dissolves the clear outlines of his individuality. Often it even obscures the extent to which we have no knowledge of the real personality. In thousands of variations and analogies, the abstract generalization of the individual penetrates the insubstantial manifestation of every contemporary life. In the conceptual scheme of history, however, it acquires a much more significant logical status.

In some sort of physical or psychological fashion, one of our contemporaries impinges upon our present. It is at least *possible* to represent him in an autonomous fashion, like a sculpted figure, detached from all the surroundings in which he is implicated, surroundings which are not a part of his personality. The historical person, on the other hand, is much more inextricably embedded in the structures of *his* present. Unlike a contemporary, he can never confront us incognito. On the contrary, if there is any sense in which he is identifiable, then it follows that we know—more or less, but nevertheless in some sense—*what* he was: a statesman or a soldier, a physician or a priest, an adventurer or a trader, and so on. It follows that he falls under a general category. He is accessible to us from one perspective only, the perspective of his career, his position, and his accomplishments: in short, from the perspective of his significance for the more general circumstances in which he is implicated.

There are innumerable cases in which the historical person becomes coherent to us only in the light of such a perspective. Quite often the figures of the past seem to have a characteristic bulk or magnitude that surpasses the dimensions of the person of our everyday, empirical experience. Moreover there is no sense in which this characteristic property is confined to the genuine heroes of history. At least a partial explanation for this phenomenon may lie in the following consideration. The historical person does not appear as a self-contained, unambiguously empirical and individual personality. On the contrary, he is primarily accessible to us from the perspective of a general societal concept. Here we see a conceptual contradiction in the historical configuration of the person. In comparison to the contemporary person, who is accessible to our immediate experience and implicated in the interplay of thousands of nuances and dynamic moments, the historical person is more precisely limited to his essential characteristics. On the other hand, it is also the case that the historical person can easily appear quite blurred. His contours may be very loosely defined. This is not only a consequence of the temporal distance which separates us from the historical person. The effects of this temporal perspective would be comparable to the optical effects of *spatial* distance, which renders the object more obscure. On the contrary, this phenomenon is also a consequence of the domain of general concepts that were discussed in the foregoing. These general concepts denude the identity of the person whom we do not directly experience, the person that is only an object of historical knowledge. His identity as a person is replaced or reconstituted. These general concepts may be the psychological concepts discussed above. Or they may be societal concepts: his profession or position, his accomplishments or his response to the intimate or the more remote and public circumstances of his life. These concepts define the historical individual. But they transcend the limits of his intrinsic, genuinely individual nature and identify him as an instance of some more general phenomenon.

Suppose that these configurations belong to the type of "supplementations"—for they extend the historical personality and simplify it in an abstract fashion which transcends the concept of the personality of the present. As such, the historical personality is possible only within the limits of these configurations. It follows that there is a sense in which they represent certain additions to the purely individual concept of the person that is formed in everyday experience, the more rigidly defined (although, *essentially,* much more fluctuating) concept of the person. These configurations are not interpolations. Nor are they hypotheses which imply the existence of intermediate entities. Nevertheless, interpolations, hypothetical constructs, and these configurations all fall under the same category. However there is a kind of supplementation which does not produce a totality by adding to what is given. On the contrary, the whole is produced by a more precise restriction to the limits of the given. In this context, "the given" refers to the sum of the direct and indirect documents of a period which make it accessible to the knowledge of a later period, the documents which constitute this period as a possible object of historical knowledge. Even if all of these documents were exhaustively collected and compared, it is obvious that this would still not constitute a history of the period. History is only possible on the basis of another function which has its source in the subject, the historian. If this point is clear, then the following question arises: as a result of this function, what forms are imposed on this raw material of history? What are the forms that constitute this material as history?

The concept of form only identifies the definitive or comprehensive aim of this function. However the function itself depends upon all sorts of material additions, ad hoc relationships, and an underpinning of basic mental processes—or other sorts of processes—which can never be conclusively proven to exist in the material itself. Strictly speaking, however, the satisfaction of these conditions is still not sufficient to constitute a totality. On the contrary, it only constitutes a form of matter in which the imputation of a form of totality no longer encounters any obstacles. However it is obvious that the difference between the original complex of raw material and the material as constituted in this fashion is only relative. In some sense, each aspect or fragment of this material is autonomous and conceptually self-contained. Such fragments, therefore, cannot possibly be inter-related in an absolutely continuous fashion.

In order for these fragments to be accessible to the function of totality, *how* small must the interval between them be? The answer to this question depends upon the criteria for completeness which the resulting structure must satisfy. It also depends upon every conceivable bias and habit. In material that is synthesized in some way or other, there is no form of incompleteness that fails to qualify as a totality of some sort; and there is no form of completeness which cannot be perceived as imperfect, as an obstacle to absolute totality. It is obvious that those structures the totality of which is an a priori consequence of numerical definition are not affected by this sort of relativity. Regardless of the circumstances, the game of chess is played with thirty-two figures, and twenty-six letters make up our entire alphabet. However an absolute totality of this sort is only possible under the following conditions. A unified idea defines a certain *criterion* for totality. It is only necessary for reality to satisfy this criterion in order to quality as a totality. This mechanically or analytically grounded criterion for totality, however, cannot be satisfied when the issue concerns questions of the following sort. What must we know about an epoch in order to produce a picture of the epoch as a whole? What characteristics define the nature of the whole man?

What collection of indices is sufficient to make us "completely" certain of a fact? In order to claim that we understand a nation-state as a whole, what branches of the political organization must we be acquainted with? There are numerous other questions of the same sort.

At this point, we can identify a disposition and an extraordinarily instinctive aptitude for arranging the given facts in such a way that the resulting picture seems to be a complete whole. The importance of this disposition is also quite obvious in the domain of nonhistorical issues. Consider a young man who is still unaware of the enormous force of the significance of sexual facts in human existence. Although the significance of these facts remains concealed from him, he will still suppose that he understands all the events that are occurring around him in toto. He will produce some sort of self-contained picture of human conduct without employing this factor. Once one acquires knowledge of this factor, however, such an understanding of the human world is invariably fragmentary and incomplete. During the era in which there was no knowledge of electricity, people still believed—on the basis of knowledge of the natural forces which had already been discovered—that they possessed an understanding of the universe that was, in principle, exhaustive. In quite the same way, the elements of the historical cosmos still seemed to present a gratifying picture of uniformity and completeness during the era in which there was no idea of the significance of economic forces and forms for the total structure of society.

Our world view seems to us to be exhaustive in principle. This is the case in spite of the fact that we are willing to acknowledge its incompleteness in innumerable points of detail. Only an intellectual chauvinism of the present can resist the conclusion that the apparent completeness of our world view is only a consequence of the remarkable plasticity of the elements of our knowledge. They seem to be mutually interrelated in a coherent and exhaustive fashion, in such a way that they satisfy our criteria for wholeness and totality. This point about the role of the plasticity of the elements of knowledge is quite obvious in the present case, in which the given raw material or data have an arbitrary status. It is less obvious in a case in which the data are made more amenable to this principle of completeness by interpolating hypothetical intermediate links within the raw material itself.

The completeness of reality is dependent upon the "idea."

From the perspective of the idea of a semi-circle, the semi-circle itself is a whole. From the perspective of the idea of a circle, however, it is not. By examining the intrinsic properties of any real entity, it is impossible to determine whether it is complete or incomplete. On the contrary, only the criterion which we employ for ideal completeness can resolve this question for a given material. Of course it follows from the manner in which our ideas are constituted that certain complexes of reality easily fall under categories of totality. Their wholeness seems to be an immanent consequence of the relationship between their components. The work of art seems to exhibit this property most clearly. Its essence consists in the a priori, concrete and graphic coherence of elements that—independent of the work of art—are arbitrarily and incoherently related. On the other hand, suppose that we consider the immense variation in the conditions that different epochs and individuals have stipulated for the coherence of a work of art. This consideration should be sufficient to show that even in this case it is not the material itself—the work of art—which determines what constitutes a whole. On the contrary, it is the idea which is imposed upon this material. From another perspective, the human personality illustrates the same point. On the one hand, it is perceived as a microcosm, a counterpart to the unique and absolute totality. On the other hand, it seems to be the most fragmentary phenomenon imaginable, a bundle of contingent mental events buffeted by all of the forces of nature and history. The radicalism of the criterion for totality as it applies to our own personality shows how little we constitute a whole—even to the point that we yearn for a post-existential form of "completeness" or "perfection."

If the propensity to constitute totalities is a general function of the intellect, then this disposition is expressed in the material of history with a special logical force and with reference to principles that are peculiar to history. Any given content that is either contemporary or atemporal is a logically possible object of a whole. The system of chemical elements could be complete. It is possible for statistics to comprehend the total structure of society. Lexicography could catalogue the entire vocabulary of a natural language. In these cases, our knowledge remains fragmentary only because of shortcomings that are not grounded in the nature of the material itself. This is the only reason why our aspirations for wholeness in these cases are relatively unsuccessful. However consider a complex the material of which was once vital and organic. If this material has disappeared and can only be reconstructed on the basis of the residue that is accessible to us, then it is logically impossible for us to have knowledge of this complex as a whole. Irrespective of whatever synthetic ideas might be employed to constitute this complex as a whole, it must remain a fragment from the standpoint of our knowledge.

Consider the arbitrariness and contingency of the documents of human life and the discontinuity of the fragments in which the contents of the experience of life are preserved or from which they are reconstructed on the basis of indices. It is quite impossible to surmount these obstacles. As a function which proceeds spontaneously from the material itself, the constitution of wholes in the domain of historical knowledge is much more intimately, immanently and necessarily related to the properties of this material than is the case in the province of nonhistorical knowledge. And perhaps the distinction at stake here is not only a difference of degree. Any entity that is contemporary, quotidian, and vibrantly alive has a certain sphere or atmosphere that transcends the conceptually definable content of the entity itself. We implicitly regard this atmosphere as a self-evident aspect of the entity. We feel that the atmosphere emanates from the entity that it surrounds. Suppose that we are in close physical proximity to another person.[2] Or suppose that we enter a social circle or

---

[2] I am convinced—although it is obviously impossible for me to prove this—that the human being cannot be defined within the limits of our senses of sight and touch. At least this is one way to state this thesis. On the contrary, the characteristic personal domain discussed above transcends the limits that are defined by what we can see and touch. This personal sphere may be conceived as a substance or as a kind of subtle emanation. Its extension cannot be defined by any hypothesis. However it is just as much a part of the person—it is just as constitutive for his identity—as the visible and tangible properties of his body. It is related to these properties in the same way that infrared and ultraviolet are related to the spectrum of colors. Although we cannot see these two colors, this does not call into question their force and efficacy. Consider the characteristic influence or susceptibility which we feel when we are in close physical proximity to another person. There are innumerable different indices of this sort of influence. However its cause does not lie in phenomena that are accesible to the "five senses." There seems to be only one possible explanation for this phenomenon: it is a result of being plunged into the ultra-material field of force which surrounds the person himself. There is nothing at all mystical about this phenomenon. On the contrary, in principle it lies within the limits of our possible experience and our generally

gathering of people. In each of these instances, we feel, more or less clearly, an atmosphere that is quite distinctive, an atmospheric chord of life the tone of which carries beyond the perceptible limits of the instruments which produce it. In a city—or even in a country, especially a foreign country—we feel this characteristic breath of life. It is obviously a composite of hundreds of minute impressions. However it cannot be reduced to a unified entity composed of discrete, concrete parts. Such an atmosphere, the compelling force of which is so indefinably comprehensive, only surrounds life insofar as its presence or contemporaneity is perceived. It is evident that this atmosphere establishes a kind of continuity between one life and another. It is instrumental in smoothing out the idiosyncracies, the contradictions, and the primary sources of incoherence in an individual. As a result, he produces the impression of a whole person.

Within the domain of history, however, this atmosphere disappears. We encounter both historical individuals and pluralities in the hard, bold outlines which are defined by the concrete facts

valid cognitive methodology. In order to identify this phenomenon, however, this methodology must be refined. This component of concrete, individual existence seems to me to be extraordinarily important for all real social life. Consider the mysterious phenomenon of prestige, the sympathies and antipathies between men that are not susceptible to rational explanation, the frequent feeling that we have of being gripped in a certain way by the mere existence of another person, and many other phenomena which are often the decisive processes within the province of history. They may be a consequence of this personal atmosphere. However it is obvious that this phenomenon is less accessible to empirical confirmation and reconstruction than the phenomena that are identifiable by reference to the "five senses." Therefore it is also more difficult to conceptualize this phenomenon as a set of qualities which characterize the person. Nevertheless, it is probably intimately related to the qualities of the person. Interrelated with these qualities, it constitutes the whole person. At this point, of course, no hypothesis concerning the content of this relationship can be ventured. As a result of this phenomenon, it sometimes happens that the surviving vestiges of human life—a person's speech, his actions, a description of his appearance—produce an impression of the luster of this more comprehensive ontological domain. The association between this domain and the world of visible phenomena is represented most successfully in the works of the great portrait painters. It is above all in the most sublime portraits of Rembrandt that we find ourselves captivated by the ontological sphere of the person, a sphere that is graphically and physically perceptible. The radius of this sphere does not extend to the pure, concrete perceptual properties of the person or to the intellectual or spiritual qualities which can be derived from these properties. Our only other access to this sphere is the living presense of the person himself.

that we know about them. That atmosphere which only emanates from life itself does not embrace historical phenomena. Therefore it cannot weave them into a unified totality. In history, such a totality can be constructed only on the basis of an exact composite of fragments. These fragments must be structured—or perhaps also imperceptibly restructured in their outlines—until they interlock perfectly, insofar as possible without any seams or gaps. Under these conditions, the category of totality itself can have a function within the domain of history.

Perhaps the classical example of the issues at stake here is provided by the fifth volume of Mommsen's *History of Rome*. In this book, a whole is actually constructed on the basis of mere scraps of evidence. Although certain interpolations are inserted into the evidence, the totality is usually achieved by a mere arrangement of parts. Of course Mommsen himself only calls this a substitute or makeshift whole—the sort of totality that can be produced within the imagination of the historian. Strictly speaking, however, *every* historical image is in this sense the surrogate for a whole. In this context, what Mommsen calls imagination or phantasy is essentially only the spontaneous constitution of totalities. It is indispensable to every province of theory, and it is most essential in the domain of history. What kind of evidence and what quantity of data are sufficient to constitute a whole? This is obviously a subjective question. The answer will vary from one case to another. In all candor, however, we should be obliged to acknowledge that it is a *feeling*—a kind of intuitive judgment, rather than an objective criterion—which determines when this condition is satisfied. Quite often, the criterion for what constitutes a total representation is a function of the level of knowledge that can be attained. This, of course, corresponds to the general human capacity for adaptation. However a criterion of this sort does not really conform to a methodologically justifiable idea. Under these conditions, perhaps we can understand the following move. An extremely cautious and circumspect scholar makes the following claim about the establishment of colonies under Philip of Macedonia: we only have "a few scattered memoranda, and they only allow us a very vague general idea about the precise intentions behind Philip's plans for colonization." Then, following three allegations which remain somewhat problematical, he adds that this evidence gives us "an insight into a grandiose policy of colonization."

There are many different forms of the constitution of historical totalities. At this point, I shall only consider two of the more characteristic forms. Among other things, the production of an historical totality is dependent upon a correct selection of the axis or perspective *from which* the material is synthesized to form a whole. For example, it is possible to construct a history of the development of Shakespeare's work which exhibits the progress or the rhythm of the evolution of style and the extension of technique, the mastery of language, and the increasing profundity of motive and theme. It is obvious that each of the dramas is a self-contained work of art. Each play is discontinuously juxtaposed to all the others. Nevertheless, their objective qualities make it possible to arrange the plays in an order that invariably gives the observer a sense that their progress or variation is continuous. We project these properties of our classification onto the playwright himself. There is a sense in which we see the unbroken line of a creative life. The direction of this creative life is determined by its creative works in the same way that the direction of a line is determined by discrete points. On the other hand, suppose that our intention is to produce a genuine biography of the history of Shakespeare's development as a product of the evolution and the phases of his total personality. Such an account would provide an understanding of the origin, the nature, and the gamut of the individual works on the basis of the total internal and external scope of Shakespeare's life. The material for the construction of such a biography is not available. Such an account would not qualify as a coherent whole in any sense.

The following point, it seems to me, is extremely important. By a purely formal examination of the immanent relationship between its parts, it is impossible to determine whether an historical complex qualifies as a whole. Perhaps it is only individual living organisms and individual works of art that constitute wholes in this sense. An organism is an entity which contains the definition of its own form. The criterion for its ontological status as a whole is implied in the self-sufficient, reciprocal relationship of its parts. This point holds true for the work of art insofar as it is considered exclusively from the standpoint of its purely aesthetic form. This conception of a work of art poses no problems in music, architecture, and the decorative arts. On the other hand, suppose that the work of art is considered from the perspective of the meanings and values that it creates. In that case, the work of art also depends upon an extrinsic idea that it is imposed upon it, the idea with reference to which the status of its wholeness or incompleteness is determined. From the outset, however, the historical tradition is only constituted by isolated fragments of data. In this case, such a superimposed idea is always necessary. Consider the contingency of the relationship between this essential idea and the raw material available to us and the available historical data. In what sense, if any, can the material of history be synthesized into a coherent whole? The contingency of this relationship entails that this question cannot be answered on the basis of an inspection of the data alone. It can only be answered after the superimposed synthetic concept has been chosen.

There are other paths which lead to the formation of historical totalities. A method which is diametrically opposed to the procedure just described lies along one of these paths: namely, the omission of certain elements of the historical material. In an account which does not simply reproduce the raw material of historical documents, the historian eliminates matters that are "unimportant." Apparently this concept of what is important only refers to the intrinsic significance of the historical data. If we examine this matter more carefully, however, we find that "the unimportant" often refers to pieces of evidence that would resist or upset the synthesis of the historical data into a coherent whole. On the one hand, the historian says more than he actually knows in the strict sense. The reason is as follows. By employing the synthetic concept of a whole, he is justified in filling in the gaps in the historical tradition by interpolating and refashioning the fragmentary documents until they fit together. On the other hand, the historian also says less than he knows when an established historical fact is of no significance and cannot be comprehended within the whole that the synthetic concept defines. If the fact in question is actually inconsistent with this concept, then it would be necessary to consider whether the concept should be given up or whether the fact should be repudiated.

In every case of this sort, the retention and justification of the totality is the primary or definitive consideration. Here we are concerned with cases in which a fragment of the historical tradition is omitted not on material or substantive grounds, but rather on formal grounds: because it does not fit consistently into the total structure as defined by the synthetic idea. Consider, for example, a description of the theories of Heraclitus in the history of philosophy. Such an account will be based on the perspective formed by the idea of the basic philosophical significance of the writings of Heraclitus. It will employ the fragments that are relevant for this purpose and synthesize them into a coherent whole. But suppose this account included some of the traditional sayings of Heraclitus: for example, the fragment concerning the stench of the souls in Hades, or the observation that swine wallow in filth while birds bathe in dust. The inclusion of these documents would only fracture the coherence of the account in a senseless fashion. It may be logically possible—although, in fact, it is surely very unlikely—that someday the theories of Heraclitus may be conceived from the standpoint of a different fundamental conception. From the perspective of this conception, it may be justifiable to include these fragments in the account as a symbolic addendum to the theory as a whole. In that case, perhaps some of the other fragments of Heraclitus that are now essential components of our philosophical understanding of his doctrines would be eliminated from the account.

In a case in which there are variations in the *scope* or *perspective* from which one and the same historical period is represented, the historical principle of omission in the interest of the form of wholeness and the importance of the modalities of this principle are most obvious. Compare a book of one hundred pages on the Seven Years' War to a book of one thousand pages. The former requires not only a more compressed and economical style of expression. In addition, it necessitates a radical elimination of many points of detail. This point is quite obvious. However it is important to see that the incorporation of assorted details into the shorter book would destroy its unity. Within the constitutive limits of a historical form, a given relationship between the total scope or perspective and the total event only permits the inclusion of events of certain dimensions. Any event which does not attain these dimensions has no place in this particular historical structure. Such an event creates a breach in the structure. If, on the other hand, the relationship between the total event and the total scope or perspective is altered, then such an event might even function as a link in this structure. In the former case, in which the inclusion of the event has the status of an anecdote, the effect which it achieves is diametrically opposed to the aim of the historical principle. The creation of a coherent *structure* of events is the essential feature of this principle. The events, of course, must be independent of the structure itself. Moreover the autonomous content of these events must have meaning or significance of a certain kind. Otherwise they would not be possible objects of the historical perspective. Does this sort of meaning or significance have its source in real or potential structures, in events of the past which concentrate at a certain point, or in future consequences which emanate from this point? Suppose that we leave this question aside and ascribe an intrinsic meaning and value to the moment of reality itself. Such a moment falls within the domain of history only if it is situated in a multi-linked chain of other moments of the same sort. They are joined by the perceptibility or tangibility of the stream of life which flows through them and links each moment with all of the others.

The anecdote, however, places one of the moments in relief and emphasizes it for its own sake. In the anecdote, the continuity between this stressed moment and all others becomes irrelevant. Even if an anecdote has an historical subject, it still stresses an interest in the amusing, characteristic, exceptional, or gripping features of the content of this subject. It is as if this subject constituted an autonomous and self-sufficient figure. This is the exclusive motive for narrating the anecdote. If a detail is discriminated as such within the representation of a totality, this individual fact is abstracted and isolated from the rhythm or the general dimensions of the totality. As a result, the totality itself is shattered. However the discrimination of the individual fact would not have this effect if it remained constant while a standard of larger dimensions and a more comprehensive scope were continuously applied. In this context, it is very instructive to observe how the genuinely great historians employ detailed facts of the historical tradition for anecdotal purposes. In the work of the great historians, the concrete fact never has the self-contained, epigrammatic status of an anecdote that is related for its own sake, the status which it acquires if this particular detail is not subordinated to the general standards of dimension and significance employed in the historical account. On the contrary, this particular fact is included in the account only in the interest and from the perspective of the whole, the style of which is determined by its dimensions.

If this fact does not fit into such a whole, if its only claim to inclusion is based on an autonomous and self-contained interest in its own content, then it has no legitimate place in the whole. At this point, the distinction between history and the mere event appears as an absolute dichotomy. The event as such is a totality. Objectively considered, every element of such a totality is essential. The continuity of the whole is such that each real element forms the indispensable bridge between the preceding elements and the succeeding elements. On the other hand, the totality that history produces, the whole in which it presents itself, is variable. Subject to the contingencies of historical documentation, such a whole can often be constructed from the data supplied by the historical tradition only if hypothetical fragments are interpolated into the account. Sometimes, on the other hand, it is necessary to excise some of the material of historical documentation from the account. It is the extension or the limits of the chosen form of representation which defines the extremely variable criterion according to which single facts either fall within the domain of history or lie beyond the limits of this domain, in the province of the anecdotal. The "wholeness" or "completeness" of an historical account is only a product of the variability of the criterion for the inclusion and exclusion of historical material. This provides further proof of the autonomy of history as a form and its independence from the form of the real event, the form of reality.

III

It is very curious that one of our most universally employed and practically and theoretically most indispensible concepts, the concept of the present, has an import that is obscure in a sense that is difficult to clarify. The exact logical import of this concept is quite indubitable. It is the temporal moment as such. Any temporal extension of this point—in other words, genuine time as such—represents either the past or the future. If the concept of the present is limited to this meaning, then it cannot be said that we possess or experience time. This is because we only *exist* in the present. Only the present qualifies as reality. The past lies within the domain of memory, and the future lies within the domain of fantasy or imagination. Our existence, like the existence of all things, is comparable to a point that is always moving or advancing. As reality, however, our existence cannot be temporal. This is because all time, as expansible or extendible, is the domain of the past or the future. Therefore it is unreal. It also follows that no object which qualifies as real can fall within the domain of the temporal. If this were not the case, then reality, which can only exist in the present, would exist in a stationary or permanent present. But this concept of a stationary or enduring present is self-contradictory. A "present" cannot be ascribed to an empty expansibility of purely abstract time. On the contrary, it can only be ascribed to an event which transpires within such a medium. The contents of such an event are in process. In other words, they change. Only these aspects of the event fall within the domain of reality. However, as a consequence of the import of the concept of time, they have no temporal status. This is because their existence in the present is only the point on which the extended past and the extended future impinge.

This is the source of the paradox that temporal reality is only an imaginary concept. In the same way, spatial reality would also be imaginary if the real were only constituted by points to which no spatial extension could be ascribed, even though these points were defined by reference to spatial coordinates. It should be obvious that these reflections have nothing to do with the ideality of time and its inapplicability within the domain of the absolute, the super-empirical side of existence. On the contrary, these reflections concern the manner in which logic penetrates the empirically given. If a phenomenon is considered from the perspective of the objective reality of its existence or occurrence, then a temporal status cannot be ascribed to it. On the contrary, it is only the mind which—in retrospection and projection—links that which no longer exists or that which does not yet exist in one temporal line.

The concept of the present is defined by reference to the point or the episodic moment. The mind, however, employs this ability to connect in order to extend the concept of the present beyond the strict logical limits of this definition. In practice, this more extended concept of the present is constructed from a fragment of the past and a fragment of the future. This extension of the concept beyond the centrifugal point of the present or the episodic is, of course, quite vague and extremely variable. Suppose that someone speaks of the present status of a relationship between friends, a momentary pain, or the pleasures of the moment. These expressions imply very different durations of the recollected past or the imagined future in which the present moment itself is implicated. In principle, the duration of these past and future moments is extended when a present is ascribed to super-individual subjects. The contemporary geological period, the present scientific level of medicine, or the present policy of a nation—these expressions cover a much more extended temporal duration than expressions which ascribe a present to some person. And even in these super-personal cases, what constitutes the present may be extremely variable. Is this only a result of a psychological process which blurs the distinction between the present and the temporal? Independent of this psychological process, in reality itself—including psychological reality—does the absolute dichotomy between the reality of the episodic present and the irreality of the past and the future still obtain? At this point, I shall not pursue this question in detail. Suppose, however, that we examine the ultimate and fundamental inner substance of this relationship.

Unless I am mistaken, we shall discover that the reality of our lives is never committed to this logically absolute, episodic definition of the present. In general, we cannot even experience the present within these limits. On the contrary, life and its contents extend beyond the limits of the momentary or the episodic. Yet life and its contents are immediately "present" to us. They constitute an actual, palpable reality. Perhaps life has its own rhythm and a possible mode of understanding the world and itself that cannot be derived from the logical categories of the past, the present, and the future. In any case, it is *as if* experience had broken through the self-contained conceptual exclusiveness of the present and incorporated within the concept of the present a dimension of continuous time. As a result of its continuity, this dimension—without reaching any perceptible threshold—is lost in the distinctive reaches of the past and the future. The past contains some moment that extends to the present. In this sense, therefore, it is not past. And the future includes a phase that is linked to this same moment. Therefore the future is not a pure antedate. On the contrary, it is really filled with our life. The practically decisive point is this progressive tendency to be directed to the future. Perhaps it is impossible for us to conceptualize this progressive tendency. This may remain one of the ultimate, immediately perceptible facts of life; we perceive it in the same way that we perceive the distinction between right and left. Contents which logically fall within the domain of the past, but which still lie within the consciousness of our present experience, are also oriented to the future. At least in a practical sense, their value or significance for life lies in what they contribute to the future. In short, life is an irreversible stream in which each moment flows into the next. If we describe its direction as progressive, then perhaps the progressive is not an independently definable concept, a concept that is only synthetically filled with the dynamism of life in which it is exhibited. On the contrary, the progressive may simply be the name for the direction of this dynamic. We might even say that this is the name of its quality. If this is the case, then, in the strict sense, the "progressive" can only be ascribed to the phenomenon of human life.

In order to gain a clear perspective on the question of how these matters bear upon the constitution of history, further elaboration is necessary. At this point, consciousness performs a radical operation of rotation or reversal on the direction of the stream of life that flows through it in one direction. Now the conscious interest is to "re-present" the past insofar as it is past, to constitute the past as a content or object. The past as such acquires the status of an autonomous value. It is true that the contents of the individual phases of the past collectively share the progressively oriented direction. However a given phase is detached from this tendency and placed in relief. Its historical significance lies in the fact that it falls under the total form of the past. A relationship can be established between an historical fact and some subsequent fact. A relationship can even be established between an historical fact and the entire future. This organic interrelationship between the past and the future is the exclusive source of the significance of the past for life. History, however, dissolves this relationship. As we can see—and we shall have occasion to repeat this observation—it is certainly not the case that all of past life falls within the province of history. On the contrary, the conditions under which any event qualifies as historical are dependent upon further conditions and requirements. However the fact that contents lie in the past is the indispensable condition for their historicity. The past status of an item and the fact that it is completely detached from the progressive stream of life must be interrelated with all the other variable conditions in order to constitute this item as history.

Our interest in objects to which a timeless or atemporal status is ascribed—concepts and ideas, works of art and laws of nature, pure forms and religious configurations—may be quite abstract and remote from the immediate impulses of life itself. However the posture of life is not so positively and definitively juxtaposed to these atemporal objects as it is to every historical object. The atemporal is—as this might be expressed—indifferent or neutral to all temporal distinctions. An atemporal quality can be temporally realized in any object, regardless of the time span in which it is situated. History, however, remains anchored in its locus. It directs our perspective in a retrospective fashion, in opposition to the vital stream of life which points us in a forward, progressive direction. Or, more accurately, the retrospective gaze constitutes history.

This is probably the source of the most profound difference between the form of history and the form of life. Its most subtle—and, at the same time, most vivid—expression lies in the autobiographical perspective of personal life. Every practical step that we take presupposes some sort of recollection of our past. Particular or general, more or less clear images of the past define the import and force of every move we make, an import and force that are infused by the dynamics of the will, which is impressed in the direction of our life. However we can make a rigorous distinction between these practically oriented recollections and memories which bring the past—purely as past—before our inner vision. Although these two kinds of recollection may have exactly the same content, there is a sense in which they lie on different levels. In their intentionality, these two kinds of recollection are diametrically opposed. This opposition creates the effect of an abyss. It excludes the possibility of establishing an intimate relationship between these recollections or classifying them under *the same* direction or tendency. As noted above, this is the ultimate foundation of the definitive qualitative distinction between life and history. It does not lie in the difference between the contents of life and history and their complexion. It is obvious that this distinction can be blurred by many different considerations. Within a period of time that is viewed from the perspective of history, the structure which is oriented to the future is, of course, predominant. The empirical facticity of this historical period is correlated with the empirical facticity of immediate experience. The former is temporally and objectively continuous with the latter. As a mental and historical fact, this period as a whole is created or comprehended by phenomena within the steam of life that are of historical interest. Nevertheless, the historical interest suspends the progressive rhythm which inheres in every idea that is ancillary to life. The autonomous and self-contained import of this interest lies in an ultimate and axiomatic a priori form of the mind: the significance of the past as such.

The foregoing thesis that the inner structure of an historical complex is a function of the temporal form of life might lead one to the mistaken idea that the historical understanding of a fact consists in understanding it as a consequence of preceding facts. In reality, however, the historical understanding of human conduct is logically dependent upon an understanding of its *consequences*. On the other hand, consider a fact not from the perspective of history, but rather as an object of immediate experience, our own experience or the experience of another person. Our comprehension of such a fact is much more satisfactory if we understand it as a consequence of its physical and psychological antecedents. In this context, it is important to consider a point that is essential to any comprehension of human conduct.

By an "act," we almost never mean the precise content of an action defined in its self-contained, autonomous concreteness. On the contrary, we have an a priori concept of the act as the sum of the consequences that it produces. It could be said that the act is simply the potentiality of this composite of consequences. Suppose we claim that someone has undertaken, attempted, or produced something, anything from the most ordinary performance to the most bizarre. If we examine the matter carefully, this description does not refer to the act itself, precisely defined and exhaustively constituted by its own inner forces. On the contrary, our description transcends the limits of this definition of action. It refers directly to certain consequences for which this action is casually responsible. This concept of the consequences of the action is directly imposed upon the concept of the action as a performance of the agent. The two concepts become so intimately related that it is really no longer possible to identify the act itself independent of its consequences. On the contrary, the act is represented by reference to the events, conditions and values—the immanent constitutive forces and the destruction—for which it is responsible. Given this conception of action, every act is seen only as an inherently insignificant germ or seed. From the outset, only the fruits which grow from this seed qualify as the substance of the action itself. This conception is so obvious and unproblematical to us that we are hardly ever inclined to acquire a clear view of its status. Within the domain of sense perception, it is impossible for us to distinguish with certainty what we really observe from what we impose upon our observations. The problematical designation of "unconscious inferences or deductions," for example, refers to the latter process of supplementation. In the same way, what we call an action is a fusion of the concretely definable action itself and the consequences which are only expected to follow from it. It often happens that the definition of the action itself is really only a husk or pod which envelopes the real essence of the action—the consequences that follow from it. The *intended* results of the action form one part of these consequences. They constitute the subjective meaning of the action. From the perspective of this subjective meaning, the action itself is only an incidental or irrelevant means for producing the intended result. However it is obvious that the intended results only represent one extremely variable dimension within the totality of the consequences of the action. It is the empirical facticity of the totality of these consequences which exhibits—or, more precisely, defines—the full meaning of the action.

This fundamental relationship according to which an action is not understood by reference to its antecedents, but rather by reference to its consequences, exhibits many different variations within the domain of historical knowledge. First of all, in history the relationship between an action and its consequences is exhibited in a much more radical fashion than is the case in the actual experience of the present. In history, the consequences of the action have already transpired. They constitute a perspicuous collection of empirical facts. Each action and the consequences it produces lie in *the same* plane. They are both implicated in the definition of the event itself. If, on the other hand, an action is more contemporary, then we have the impression that an understanding of this action is more dependent upon its *terminus a quo* or motive, the antecedent conditions of the action. In the final analysis—and this is the crucial point—it is dependent upon the psychological impulses and the mental constitution of the actor, the motives in which these antecedent conditions are implicated. This mode of understanding action—which is actually psychological—seems to be most unconditionally indispensable to the agent when he attempts to understand *his own* conduct. The same point holds, although in a more conditional fashion, for the understanding of personal acquaintances, contemporaries, and phenomena which we perceive as implicated in the present, as if they were suspended in *one* vital stream. If the temporal distance which separates us from events increases, then the satisfaction of our criteria for understanding by a causal explanation in terms of psychological antecedents becomes increasingly inadequate. From our perspective, the action is increasingly defined in terms of its consequences, its objective meaning insofar as this meaning is exhibited in these consequences.

If the perspective from which we view the action becomes increasingly remote and more purely historical, if, in other words, our perspective increasingly embraces the total scope and continuity of the movement of an event, then the understanding of an action by reference to its consequences acquires an even more decisive predominance in comparison with an explanation of the action by reference to its antecedent subjective forces and causes. Prior to the action itself, its consequences—or at least a part of its consequences—assume the form of purposes which motivate the agent. If the action is an accomplished matter of historical fact, then its consequences are plainly observable. The purposes which are not realized, those purposes which do not fall within the form of reality, even though they are among the antecedent intentions of the agent, are nullified. With the exception of special instances of these purposes which require an explanation, they have no place in history.

It follows that there is a sense in which history exhibits a radical revolution or reversal in the direction or tendency that is characteristic of life. From the perspective of life, all moments which are prior to the present have only one significance: they constitute the antecedents from which the future proceeds. The mental structures of history, on the other hand, are grounded upon the autonomous value and significance of the past. In history, the past is not subservient to life. In a certain sense, therefore, life becomes retrogressive. This concept of the past may be explained by reference to another concept, which is related to life in a peculiar fashion. It is a continuation of life, and yet it is also antithetical to life. Consider life as it is actually experienced and the understanding of life, including the sort of understanding that directly defines life and is mutually defined and constituted by it. From this perspective, the antecedent conditions of any given moment have a preeminent significance. We understand this moment as a consequence of psychologically causal antecedents. From the standpoint of such a moment, the future is quite precarious. It is only present and operative in the form of a motive or purpose, a hope or a fear. However we see the historical moment in a continuous relationship with the realities that follow from it.

Significance can be ascribed to the energies collected in this moment only if they are implicated in this relationship. Any phenomenon which only qualifies as an antecedent of this moment is—*cum grano salis*—historically insignificant. A radical statement of this distinction may be formulated as follows: although it could be said that we understand the moment of actual experience as a consequence of its past, we understand the historical moment with reference to its future. This is the principal obstacle to a historical understanding of the present. If understanding meant derivation from antecedent conditions, then in principle, this sort of understanding would always be possible. However the consequences of the present have not yet developed in an identifiable fashion. *That is* why we cannot understand the present historically. The fact that these complexities of the relationship between life and history appear to be quite subtle and hypercritical should not mislead us. If we inquire how extremely complex mental constructs may be characterized in terms of quite simple elements like temporal directions, then it should be quite obvious that the answer may present astonishing—perhaps even mutually inconsistent—syntheses of these elements. The idea that "simplicity" is the criterion for truth naively presupposes a mystical relationship between the objectively intellectual theoretical structure of things and our extremely variable ideal of simplicity. On the one hand, it is obvious that the elements from which knowledge derives phenomena can be described as relatively simple. On the other hand, the combinations in which these elements are implicated and the processes of development through which they must be conducted can be extremely intricate and complex. Therefore the dogma which represents simplicity as the criterion for truth seems to be based on the confusion between the substance or material of the ultimate explanation of these phenomena and the formal functions by means of which this explanation is produced.

At this point, I shall only mention one other permutation in which the form of temporality transforms life into history. Suppose that we posit certain momentously consequential events, persons, or epochs as fixed points and identify historical events as occurring either before or after these points. In that case, the unambiguously progressive direction of time as a mode of actual experience is either blocked or reversed. The foundation of Rome, the birth of Christ, the Renaissance, the French Revolution, the foundation of the new German empire, or in the history of philosophy Socrates and Kant, all have this status. There is a sense in which we construct indices within the progressive stream of life. We define and distinguish a certain temporal moment by reference to its content. The moment is identified in such a way that we can reckon from its temporal location both prospectively and retrospectively. Sometimes we even symbolize the importance of this moment in a system of chronology. The interesting aspect of this phenomenon is the following. The purely qualitative significance of a date moves us to transpose or reverse the form of time for the historical sequence. Years are numbered, for example, from the birth of Christ on. Before the birth of Christ, however, the number of the year is subtracted from the date of Christ's birth, which is completely inconsistent with the unequivocal nature of the temporal process. In consequence, we create a kind of axis of rotation in time. We position ourselves on this prospect in order to gain a vantage point from which we may view *both* directions.

Our position in relation to any conceivable process or occurrence reproduces this same perspective, albeit in a less explicit and pronounced fashion. In every such process, we accentuate a certain point of culmination on which our perspective is firmly grounded. This perspective structures the formless totality of the flow of time. The events within the temporal stream which have elapsed before this point of culmination are reckoned in terms of a retrospective, inverted view of their consequences. The events which transpire after this point are reckoned in terms of the normal, prospective view. Perhaps everyone feels somehow moved by his external fate and his inner development to reach such an axial point in his life, the moment which establishes a permanent distinction between "before" and "after." From that point to the beginning of life, it might be said that memory swims against the stream of time. Only between this point and the present can it be said that memory swims in the direction of this stream. This phenomenon is most vivid and dramatic in instances of inner psychological revolutions, especially cases of religious "conversion." Such an event occurs in a blinding flash of light. It is not dependent upon any process of development. The occurrence of such an event is curiously disproportionate to its determination of all of one's subsequent life. Consider, for example, the conversions of Buddha, Paul, Rancé, and Tolstoy. In each of these cases, the moment of illumination appears as the apex of life, the pinnacle from which life as a whole is seen. In consequence, only the part of life which follows this moment of illumination conforms to the direction of time. There is a sense in which the events which occurred before this moment are represented as flowing in the opposite direction.

IV

In the formation of history from everyday life, therefore, there is a sense in which decisive moments constitute points at which the progressive movement of time is concentrated. There is another form of the crystallization of the dynamic forces of life which has its source in more extended stretches of time. I have in mind the concept of a "state." It is true that this concept is also implicated in everyday life. Within the images of history, however, it has a much more specific import. In addition, within the domain of history it represents one of those categories which makes us into fragmentary historians of our own lives and our contemporary surroundings.

Consider an enduring power relationship between social variables, the purity or the corruption of morals, the mode of production which prevails at any given point, the legal system, the division of labor, the content or discontent of classes. We describe all these phenomena as states. In reality, however, these phenomena are never purely static. On the contrary, they invariably seem to be formed by sequences of events, each of which continually experiences its own changes and fluctuating qualities.[3] The privileged status of one social stratum in relation to another rests on the fact that the proceeds which the latter stratum receives from its labor are only sufficient to produce the bare necessities of life. The remainder of these proceeds are employed to the advantage of the members of the first stratum, who do not work for them at all. Consider violations of rules, which in every class only reach a certain frequency. In the class with higher status, punishment of these violations is quite moderate. In the other class, it is severe. Legal regulations, which also only regulate a specific number of the actions that are actually performed, are instituted by the members of the privileged class. The members of the other class have no influence upon them. The same point could be made by means of other examples. In short, a sequence of specific events takes place. Each of these events and the sequence as a whole have the fluid form of life. In the totality of life itself, they frequently intermingle within limits that are quite indefinite. Yet we describe this totality as a "state" of the social group. It is as if these extremely heterogeneous events and processes constituted a totality with stable qualities. It is even as if the condition of privileged status extended throughout this totality like a continuous existential entity which closes all the temporal gaps that lie between the concrete individual facts. Within these gaps, no "privileged" status of any sort can be explicitly identified. There may not even be an intuitive sense that such a state exists. The same point holds within the domain of individual existence. Someone who is chronically ill or unhappily married is in a miserable "state." However this state is composed of a sequence of individual moments of suffering and

[3] Here, therefore, we see the reverse side of the position which Bergson regards as the absolute truth. In many cases, actually, the form of temporality is a source of error and falsification. In organisms, works of art, logical relations—in other words, cases in which we can identify reciprocal interrelations and the coherent unity of heterogeneous properties—our conception of a necessary connection which identifies one element as antecedent, another as consequent, and establishes a reciprocal relationship between the two elements is only a very supplementary and symbolic mode of representing the real substance and import of what is at stake here. In these cases, time destroys the source of coherent unity. Moreover, the reversal in the order of the sequence of their contents only re-establishes this unity in a very incomplete fashion.

pain. It is not a static existential condition the temporal moments of which are homogeneous or indistinguishable. On the contrary, it is a physical and psychological process constituted by acts the single components of which are dynamically and heterogeneously juxtaposed to one another and interrupted by pauses. Under these conditions, what is the status of the concept of a state? How must the individual processes of experience be transformed so that a state develops from them, or at least develops concomitant to them in a parallel and continuous fashion?

In view of the foregoing remarks, one might be inclined to draw the following conclusion at this point. In the events themselves, a state has no concrete existence of any sort. It is only an abstraction which an observer deduces from these events as their least common denominator. This conclusion would be completely inconsistent with the import of the concept of a state. Actually the concept of a state designates a reality which exists in the subjects. Of course this reality falls under a category which is different from the category of the single events that constitute the directly identifiable agents or documents of the constant "state," agents or documents which are singular and which vary and fluctuate in an irregular fashion. At this point we can see that the structure of human existence reveals a dual form of stratification. This appears most clearly within the domain of individual existence. Within the periods of our life—which may be of very different durations—we perceive a pervasive and continuous shade or hue. On the one hand, this is a precipitate of the single contents of life which appear and disappear. On the other hand, it defines the mode, significance, and force of these contents. In other words, there is a sense in which these contents become symbols of the constant state of determinateness or stability that prevails within or above their variability. Objectively, however, this constant state of determinateness can only be identified in the contents themselves. We can identify this state directly and from within only in the case of our own person. And, in fact, we perceive it not only in concrete individual facts, but also in data that are completely irrelevant to it. Such a state is a tone which sounds unceasingly within us. However we do not always hear it at a uniform and constant level. This is perhaps the purest case of a "state" as an existential continuity: an entity that is defined as relatively chronic or recurrent. It is perceptibly differentiated from the discontinuity of acute and pressing events. At the same time, however, it exhibits reciprocal relationships with these events.

In practice, naturally, the limits of the definition of the concept of a state are quite flexible. However I believe that all states which are identifiable by reference to public observation are modeled on this case. When we speak of the states of the political or religious, moral or artistic life of an epoch, there is a sense in which we see the epoch as grounded upon a unitary subect. The experiences of this subject are constituted by the individual facts of the epoch— facts which, in reality, are experienced by very different individuals. Parallel to the feeling of the epochs of personal life, the meaning of these experiences is comprehended in a trans-episodic state which remains unaffected by the fluctuations in the here and now of these experiences. The state can also be a symbol which expresses and intensifies its determinateness and its temporal preponderance and superiority in relation to every individual event. A state acquires the status of such a symbol when it is conceived within the atemporality of the objective mind. This is the case, for example, when the state of a certain period in relation to the distribution of power, property, and moral ideas is formulated as a binding law, or when the religious state of a period assumes the form of ecclesiastical dogma. We may employ the concept of a state in a naive, free and easy fashion. As one of the categories which we employ in order to provide an intellectually perspicuous representation of reality, however, the concept of a state is certainly not easy to analyze. A state is comparable to a continuous medium that extends throughout the qualitative discontinuity of the facts of life. Naturally its shade and coloring can only be identified in these facts. From an epistemological perspective, the state appears to be an abstraction. From the standpoint of its existence, however, we recognize the state as an objective reality. Intrinsically, we do not consider it an abstraction, no more than we regard the trans-singular feeling of life which is pervasive within our own lives as an abstraction. Within the form of immediate existence, the state occupies a position which corresponds to the abstraction within the domain of retrospective reflection.

Perhaps it is possible to formulate these points by employing a more general intellectual procedure. If history, in principle, is a form of classification and comprehension of everything that falls within the domain of human reality, then a discussion of these most general categories seems to be appropriate in this context. Such a discussion should identify the specifically historical concepts as certain modifications of these general categories. The reductive analysis of the heterogeneity of actual events under the general concept of a state, a state which comprehends these events—or is interrelated with them—as their co-existent cause or effect is animated by a curious and characteristic necessity of intellectual praxis: the need to regard phenomena that are different from one another as if they were the same. It seems that the modes with which we respond—both mentally and physically—to the impressions and demands of things and events do not have the same degree of differentiation and graduation that can be ascribed to the things and events themselves, the degree of differentiation and graduation which make their immediate impression or their mediated reconstruction possible for us. We regard both ourselves and others as if we were the same person today that we were yesterday. The same motives, the same happiness and suffering, the same desires seem to be just as possible tomorrow as they were today—even though the purely organic changes which take place from yesterday through today to tomorrow exclude the possibility of a genuine identity. From the domain of the crudest brute physical facts to the domain of the most subtle and refined intellectual and spiritual phenomena, there are innumerable cases in which the diversity of existence is concealed by means of the fiction of identity. This is because we are simply not able to adapt our mental processes to the full individuality of these forms of heterogeneity.

In general, this process of concealment occurs in a completely unmistakable and obvious fashion only within the domain of theoretical knowledge: by means, namely, of abstract concepts. From the perspective of abstract concepts, an unlimited number of single existential entities that are individually extremely different from one another appear as the same. Of course they only appear to be the same from this perspective. However we conceive phenomena, both mentally and physically, in terms of such an identity. Moreover, this identity is valid for *the phenomena as a whole*. The cross-section between the homogeneous and the heterogeneous which we establish in every single phenomenon is superimposed on the phenomenon. It is an act of the observer and is not prefigured in the objective unity of the phenomenon itself. The concept of a tree entails that the palm and the beech are identical as trees. However this essence of treeness does not inhere in the palm as a definitive characteristic which transcends all of the properties that differentiate it from the beech. On the contrary, in virtue of this essence, the palm is a tree. In this respect, therefore, it is the same as the beech. A small lead ball and a large wooden ball are both the same insofar as they are spherical figures. There are many purposes—including, for example, the demonstration of the geometric form of the sphere—for which they may be regarded as equivalent. They are complexes of quite different properties, including even the difference in the dimensions of their spherical form. From this perspective of sphericity, however, they qualify as "the same" total entity. In practice, it is necessary for us to treat heterogeneous phenomena as homogeneous. This necessity is a consequence of the relationship between our energies and the raw material of the cosmos. The formation of general concepts is the means by which this procedure is intellectually clarified, defined, and logically justified. However this process is never more than an incidental clarification of a function of approximation and comparison that is continually exercised. Moreover, this process only apprehends the real empirical efficacy of this function by degrees. It is never exhaustive.

It seems to me that the idea of a state represents one of the structural forms of this process. When we speak of the state of moral corruption, the single events of immediate experience which are comprehended under this concept are extremely heterogeneous. Often the phenomena in question may not even be compatible with one another. The concept of moral corruption draws an ideal line through these phenomena. As a result, they seem to be interrelated—in spite of and including their differences—in one homogeneous state. The concept of a state—and, in a certain respect, the general concept—has the following structural peculiarity: in different real phenomena, its content is *juxtaposed* to all of their properties which make them incomparable. Nevertheless, the concept of a state comprehends these realities as a whole. It represents them as a totality—or as constituting a totality. *Within* this totality, all of these realities qualify as "the same." Perhaps the characteristic manner in which the concept of the "state" represents phenomena that are different as if they were the same has its prototype in the form of immediate personal life. Consider the manifold events and experiences of our lives, the complete, variegated, qualitative, and immensely heterogenous sequence of the contents of our lives. We feel that this sequence is linked to a completely continuous ego. The oak and the pine, the beech and the palm are all trees. Each is an instance of the same concept which comprehends them all. Pusilanimity and extravagance, materialistic avarice and indolence all represent instances of the state of moral corruption when they coincide in the same period. Although they may constitute very different kinds of facts, in this sense they are the same.

From this perspective, consider the identity which comprehends the material fragments of an individual life in such a way that they all constitute contents of a life that is unmistakably the same. This identity must resolve tensions that are both more concrete and at the same time much more extensive. Suppose that the completely immanent development of this life independent of its substance even traverses the enormous spaces that separate strength and weakness, expansion and concentration, need and satisfaction. Nevertheless, these manifold states of the pure ego all have a similar status as instances or bearers of its life. The most heterogeneous states imaginable invariably appear—from a physical as well as from a psychological perspective—under the same aspect: from the perspective of my life. It follows that a personal or characterological identity can be ascribed to my life, even though there is no sense in which this personal identity obliterates any of these differences. Perhaps this is the most profound and fundamental source of the schema (not in the literal sense, obviously) of the typical mode of treating the heterogeneous as if it were homogeneous. There is a sense in which the concept of a state is a conceptual mean, an intermediate concept which falls between the external and superficial instances of this process and the instance discussed above, the version of this process which has its source in the form that constitutes the nucleus of life itself. This aspect of the matter may be supported by the following consideration. Insofar as our discussion of the concept of a state is dependent upon the distinction between a state and an event, we feel that everything which falls under the concept of a state is more intimately related to the ego than the phenomena which fall under the concept of an event. Even in a case in which the state has an external or extraneous source and is intimately related to the sequence of events, our knowledge of the state approximates a response of the ego or a modification of its characteristic complexion in a more definitive measure than we usually claim for experience of an immediate event.

The principal point to be made here is the following. In our intuition, the complete unity of existence is analyzed into the flux of heterogeneous events and the relatively stable and homogeneous state. Or these events are compressed into such a state. This process reveals a category that is particularly important for the historical development of the contents of life. Experience—the immediacy of life itself—transpires within the ebb and flow of the stream of single events that are qualitatively distinguished from one another. Although the "state" of this life does indeed qualify as reality, life itself becomes increasingly remote from us when it is represented by means of this concept.

Perhaps the foregoing discussion of the relationship between the event or process and the state can be summarized in the following fashion. Life may be conceived as the variable succession of singular phenomena. Or—in its single periods—it may be conceived as a relatively stable state of some sort. Life appears under this latter aspect when the distance between life itself and the perspective of the observer increases. This holds true even if the life in question is the observer's own life. This latter perspective does not entail that the differences between the individual facts of life are merely obliterated. It does not constitute the pure fabrication of an inherently homogeneous composite or a cross-section of average properties. Just to the contrary. Only from the standpoint of the distinctive attitude symbolized by the detached perspective of distance is it really possible to distinguish one period from another. Only under this condition can each period be characterized in terms of a qualitatively continuous state which persists throughout the changing events of the hour and the day. Such a period resembles a sequence of differently constituted substantive fragments, each linked together by a thread or fiber that forms them all into one chain. Conceived by reference to the category of a state, individual facts acquire the coherence of an intrinsically homogeneous structure. They also acquire a certain stability which cannot be ascribed to the ephemeral rhythm of each of these individual facts insofar as they are represented autonomously.

In historical accounts insofar as they are considered here, it is clear that, in principle, the states of an epoch do not occupy a privileged status in comparison to the description of the singular facts. However the following point should be noted. Compare the domain of the historical consciousness with the domain of the consciousness of everyday life and its immediate contents. Within the former domain, the disposition to represent these data within the structure and against the background of a general state of the epoch is much more pronounced than it is in the latter domain. What differentiates historical import from anecdotal import is the context which extends from the single fact to all conceivable dimensions: time, causality, qualitative continuity, and self-evidence, a context which frees the single fact from its rigid, self-contained exclusiveness and its singular uniqueness. If the single fact is viewed within the perspective of a *state* (it does not matter whether this fact was only the ground on which knowledge of the state is based, a cognitive instrument for the identification of the state), then this process of disintegration, de-individualization, and interconnection is initiated or consummated.

Regardless of the data which we admit concerning Alexander or Caesar, Luther or Loyola, the possibility of understanding them historically invariably depends upon the following condition. It is necessary to situate them within an established state of a more narrowly circumscribed and more extensively defined temporal period. It is also necessary to determine how they are set in relief from this background. The circular relationship that is suggested here should not lead us to draw any mistaken conclusions. A temporal state is established on the grounds of fragmented individual events and processes. On the basis of this state, however, these events and processes acquire historical perspicuity and completeness. This is one of those circles that is quite typical of our mode of cognition. For example, we infer the character of a person from his actions; but we understand his actions on the basis of his character. We establish an abstract law on the basis of concrete observations; however the law itself provides a basis or foundation for the empirical facts. We infer the psychological nature of an individual from his bodily appearance and physical expressions; however we interpret his observable behavior as a consequence of his psychological nature. There are many other cases of this sort.

If the event and the state are the two categorial forms of the contents of life, then we can make note of the following consideration. As a phenomenon of immediate experience, our consciousness is primarily concerned with the rhythm of the event and its periodic modes of consummation. Insofar as its transcends the single event, this level of consciousness is more concerned with the discovery of the connection between one event and another. It is not occupied with the discovery of the deeper and more profound stratum of the contents of life, the general state in which these events are implicated. Suppose that consciousness becomes concerned with the discovery of this state. There are, of course, innumerable cases in which these two modes of consciousness are inextricably related. When this happens, a certain distance is established between consciousness and the emotions and excitations of the moment. One is no longer completely engrossed in the actual vicissitudes of the moment. The appearance of a more reflective disposition to harmonize and balance the singular data of immediate experience can be detected. Strictly speaking, this point could be stated in the following way. If the consciousness of the state begins to outweigh the consciousness of the event, or if the former consciousness begins to be stressed within the latter, then this is the first step in forming the historical configuration of life. If we take this step within the confines of our own life, then we create a foundation for the continuous process in which we become the historians of our own lives.

If the concept of a state is distinguished from the concept of an event, then, as an historical concept, the concept of a state becomes part of the process which, in the largest sense, represents the historicizing of experience: the transformation of the absolute and continuous succession of the sequence of events—the ineluctable flow of experience—into *one* image. On the one hand, there is a sense in which this image exhibits the structure of a self-contained framework. On the other hand, it juxtaposes elements and places them in relief from their location within the stream of time. This point may be articulated more precisely in the following way. The states and the contents of every life are always fluid; they are invariably inextricably interrelated. If we make reference to the phases of life or a cross-section of its development, or the periods of life and its moments of inactivity and stagnation, then these distinctions and periodizations have their source in values and concepts that do not lie within life itself. They are superimposed upon life. They do not lie within the natural rhythm of life itself. Put another way, these concepts are formed when we represent life—including our own lives—from the perspective of history, when life is conceived in terms of the a priori of historical form. It is obvious that history as a form necessitates the suspension of the continuity of life itself. On the one hand, history—by employing an integral idea as a principle—synthesizes data that are temporally discrete and fragmentary into a continuous whole. The continuity of this whole can only be ascribed to the historical construct. It is not a property of reality itself. On the other hand, history is obliged to destroy the real continuity which subsists within any given temporal process. It is even obliged to abstract this temporal process as a whole from the continuity of the cosmic and human sequence of events. All "preludes" or prehistories and epilogues not withstanding, any given historical theme is rigorously distinguished from past events, future events, and contemporary events. These distinctions destroy the smooth transitions of life itself. The truth of this proposition is based not only on the self-evident grounds of our own finite limits and the limits of our cognitive methodology in general. On the contrary, the transformation of the vital, organic event into the form of an image necessitates these distinctions.

Among all the scientific and scholarly endeavors, it is especially history which is most often compared with art. There are many more grounds for this comparison than we are usually led to believe. One of the most important foundations of this comparison is the following. There is a sense in which the historical idea grasps the dimensions of events—which are, of course, extremely variable—in *a single,* inner, penetrating gaze. The work of art exhibits this process most perfectly. Consider all the strands which bind the content of the work of art to the surrounding world: time and space, meaning and fate, quality and dynamics. All of these threads are cut and then laced together again at the focal point of the work of art. As a result, the work of art becomes a self-contained, insular entity. For this reason—and only for this reason—a perspicuous view of a work of art is possible in a single glance. The pictorial development of an extended temporal process may also be characterized by employing this symbolic expression. A drama may last three hours or a novel may spin out a fabric of human life as long as a decade. Nevertheless, the artistic perfection or consummation of the work is dependent upon a mode in which it is presented, the process by which it becomes accessible to us. This mode or process must satisfy the following condition: we can grasp it in a single act of perception. In the specific sense of the single act of perception which is at stake here, no object within the concrete process of life itself satisfies this condition. Within the domain of life, inner perception as well as external perception is led from one object to another without a break. The clear focus of the center of the perceptual field fades imperceptibly into its periphery. If we remain suspended, swimming in the raging stream of experience, if we are only immediately conscious of this stream of experience, then we have no genuine "image" or "representation." An image always requires a formal unity. And this sort of unity can only be produced by making a certain distinction between the phenomena that are integrated within this unity and the phenomena that are excluded from it.

The scale of mental structures which fall under this formal law attains its peak in the work of art. This is why the concept of a representation or an image has it real source in art. The historical image, however, is not very different from the artistic representation. If the historian is said to sketch an "historical portrait," then the profound point of this analogy does not lie in the substantive "similarity" between the portrait and the reality which it reproduces. On the contrary, it lies in the intimate relationship between the historical portrait and the definitive form of the work of art. It is obvious that the content of history cannot be defined within the rigorous limits of an image or representation as strictly as this is possible in the case of a painting, a piece of music, or a drama. Suppose that there were a mechanical correspondence between history and its object. In that case, no definitions or limits of an historical event would be possible. History itself would be a complete reproduction of the continuity of the processural event. This point exhibits even more clearly the criterion which is definitive for history. The complex of an event must be structured into one representation: that is to say, *one* image, which is formed when contents are—in a certain sense—concentrated or locked into one framework within the limits of this image (its upper, lower, and lateral limits). The satisfaction of this condition may be described as the constitutive formation of life and the event of immediate experience by an a priori. The foundation or the product of this a priori is expressed by the fact that we can acquire a perspicuous view of this complex in one inner gaze. However the immediate, nonhistorical idea of this complex is not grounded on the intellectual category of the "single gaze." On the contrary, consciousness is continuous with and temporally parallel to the complex itself. As it is opposed to this form of consciousness, so the historical is also diametrically opposed to everything that is anecdotal. The anecdotal phenomenon cannot be represented as a synthetically formed, self-contained entity. On the contrary, it can only be represented by employing the symbol of the episodic. It is not necessary to form the anecdotal phenomenon into an integrated, homogeneous entity. This is because, strictly speaking, the anecdote does not constitute a manifold.

Naturally the function and force of this form are not limited to art and history. Just to the contrary. Irrespective of all genuinely objective artifacts or creations, this form is invariably operative not only whenever we are life, but also whenever we have life. We see life as decomposed into periods, not from the perspective of the actuality of experience itself, but rather retrospectively, from the perspective of the total process of life. These periods resemble a collection of pictures each of which focuses upon a characteristic feature, a decisive event, or the concept of an epoch of life. In consequence, a framework which corresponds to these pictures is created. There is a sense in which each of these epochs of life fills one of the retrospective glances of the recollection in which they are surveyed. The transition from one epoch to another requires a new stimulation and motivation of the inner gaze. This is the form in which we see our own life as history. In the autobiography, the phases of life are self-evident products of the distinctions made within immediate experience itself. In history, however, these phases must be explicitly and self-consciously defined. The purpose and the conditions and limits of knowledge determine the substantive extension and the temporal range of data which are circumscribed within one coherent description.

The idea that this procedure is unproblematical is an utterly naive and superficial suggestion. On this view, the facts themselves—the "nature of the substantive data"—are responsible for structuring contents into integrated entities—periodizations, research areas, narrative structures, and so on. It is not the objective facts which have this constitutive function. On the contrary, it is the condition of the mind—in other words, the constitutive a prioris of history. The reign of a monarch, the breadth of a cultural period, the length of a war, or the oeuvre of an artist are employed to define a single, coherent domain of historical problems. This procedure is so self-evident that it may be safely and unhesitatingly employed for the purposes of historical praxis. That is because these dimensional units satisfy the conditions required of representations or pictures. This means that they can be surveyed in a single, internal gaze. What falls within the limits of a single gaze is, of course, dependent upon the powers of the gaze itself and the manner in which it is methodologically trained. The history of historiography indicates how many varieties are possible here. The syntheses produced by one historical epoch often seem to be singularly eccentric to another epoch. In consequence, they are collapsed into the continuous process of the events themselves. Then these events are re-integrated by the use of new representational entities. A constitutive idea represents the intellectual or theoretical analogue of the perspicuous view that is achieved by a single gaze in the perceptual domain. As an example of such an idea, consider the duration of the hegemony of a political power or trend. If it encompasses a span of twenty years, then it would be senseless to add ten years to this same historical representation or to subtract ten years from it. On the other hand, suppose that we consider the historical perspective of a period of religious reformation or a literary fashion. In the former case, a period of up to thirty years may constitute a single historical representation. In the latter case, an abbreviated period of no more than ten years may constitute such a representation.

The transformation of episodic time or the time of direct experience into historical time is in general not only a function of the analysis of time into structurally defined phases. On the contrary, the extent of a single historical unit, the concentration of historical data around a single centrifugal point, and the definition of the limits of the unit with reference to the extension of the lines of development which radiate from this centrifugal point are all specifically determined by the intentions, forces and motives, and available forms which at any given time have the status of historical a prioris. The raw material of history before it has been structured by the form of history may be more or less accessible to these a priori functions of history. However it acquires the rigorously defined status of a representation that we designate as historical only by reference to these a priori functions. Compared to the purely immanent meaning and rhythm of the event and life itself, the historical representation is a categorically new entity.

On the History of Philosophy

(from an introductory lecture)

In science, truth and error are related like the past and the future. Scientific theories are recognized as "outmoded" or "past" precisely insofar as they are acknowledged as false. The theories which are still regarded as true do not lie in the past. On the contrary, they are included within the inventory of contemporary science, even though aspects of these theories may become "outmoded" or "past" at some future point.It is inevitable that the contemporary stage of the development of any science seems to embody the objective truth. Every earlier stage which diverges from the present appears to have "only an historical interest."

Philosophy, however, does not follow this general rule of scientific development. It constitutes the exclusive exception to this model. From the perspective of the ultimate and most comprehensive problems of philosophy, the definitive philosophical criterion for truth entails that the philosophical theories of the past cannot be refuted or transcended in the same way that the geocentric theory was refuted or transcended by the heliocentric theory. This is because truth in philosophy is defined in such a way that the problems of philosophy cannot be objectively resolved.

It seems to be characteristic of any cognitive synthesis which, at least in principle, constitutes a necessary or a sufficient condition for objective truth, that it can only comprehend superficial or external properties or individual facts about the world. It seems that only individual strata of the mind respond to the total character of existence, the question of the source of becoming, and the question of the meaning of life. These individual strata of the mind seem to deny themselves access to a general understanding and the objective truth. The philosopher, however, is not like most men. His mind does not consciously respond to this or that detail. On the contrary, it constitutes a conscious response to the totality of existence. It is a response to an integrated whole. However the answer which the philosopher offers to the question of total existence possesses a kind of super-individuality that is not really susceptible to a precise theoretical description. This form of super-individuality is not a species of universal validity. On the contrary, it is comparable to the super-individuality of works of art. In addition to their extremely subjective nature, they can also exhibit this property.

Insofar as philosophy expresses this sort of response, its truth does not really constitute a form of correspondence with the object of the philosophical theory. On the contrary, it reproduces the properties of the subject, the philosopher. If a philosophy is considered as a set of propositions which refer to objective reality, then it is grounded on the historical process which replaces the errors of the past with the truths of the present. On the other hand, suppose that a philosophy is regarded as a world view: an expression of the existential relationship between a mind and the cosmos as a whole. In this latter case, the truth of a philosophical theory is immanent. It is grounded in the faithfulness or the integrity with which this mental facticity—the response of the philosopher's mind to the cosmos as a whole—is embodied in the philosophical theory. From this perspective, the significance of a philosophical theory lies in the dimensions and the profundity of this mind itself. If a work of art is "a fragment of the cosmos seen from the perspective of a certain personality," then philosophy is the cosmos as a whole seen from the perspective of a certain personality. Like a landscape, it is a *état d'âme*.

Philosophies, therefore, are not true in the same sense that the propositions of other sciences are true. It also follows that they cannot be false in the same sense that the propositions of other sciences are false. There are still minds today that find in Socrates and Plato, Thomas Aquinas and Giordano Bruno, Spinoza and Leibniz the decisions and the modes of release that bear upon their relationship to the world. Viewed from a more comprehensive or abstract perspective, these philosophical accomplishments of the past lie on the same plane as the philosophical activity of the present. This is precisely the reason why philosophy is constituted by its history. The history of philosophy gradually realizes the timeless domain of possible philosophical positions.

However it is necessary to counter the thesis that the history of philosophy is the only legitimate subject matter of philosophy and the claim that philosophers can only be understood "historically." Both ideas are products of the excesses of historicism, exaggerations that can be encountered in every intellectual domain today. Philosophy, however, may be the paradigmatic domain in which the splendor and ostentation of the trappings of this doctrine conceal its utter impotence. The concept of history has become an idol. Now it has acquired the status that was once occupied by the concept of nature: reality can be exhaustively structured within the form of history. The process and the interaction of individual and social causes and motives appear as the cause and motive itself. Historicism has been pushed to such excesses that today serious attention to the substantive problems of philosophy is regarded as an expression of confusion. This confusion can be resolved only if we turn to history, which can resolve all the problems of philosophy itself.

In reality, however, each progressive moment of every historical development has only been possible through emancipation from history; through dissatisfaction with the historically given conditions and the courage to begin anew, even if with intellectual techniques that are improved by degrees. In the absence of a present level of development, therefore, it is clear that anyone who wants to *become acquainted with* philosophy must have recourse to its history. It is not possible to learn philosophy substantively or objectively—by mastering its content—in the same way that it is possible to learn physics. However, whoever undertakes to *philosophize* cannot allow himself to be limited by the history of philosophy. This is because he encounters fundamental problems which hardly appear any different to him than they had already appeared to Plato and Kant. Philosophy, therefore, is a quite unique cultural phenomenon. If the activity of the philosopher is receptive, then the nature of philosophy is absolutely historical. But if the activity of the philosopher is productive, then its nature is absolutely ahistorical.

The other axiom of philosophical historicism is no less misleading. This is the thesis that philosophical theories can only be understood historically, as a consequence of their antecedent conditions and their historical context. In opposition to this thesis, my claim is the following: by employing this method, it is impossible to achieve a genuine understanding of philosophy, in quite the same way that it would be impossible to understand Phidias and Michelangelo, Dante and Goethe in exclusively historical terms. The consequences of this historicist thesis may be compared to a closed container which is passed from hand to hand without its contents ever being divulged. In other words, the genesis and development of the subject matter is understood, but not the substance of the subject matter itself. Suppose that every philosopher is conceived exclusively by reference to his location within an historical sequence: in other words, exclusively in terms of an inquiry into his predecessors and successors. This sort of account distorts our perspective. Such an account may be valid for the development of objective types of knowledge. However suppose that we understand all propositions about things as the form or the garb which conceals the mind of the philosopher that stands behind this external form. The mind of the philosopher—insofar as it embodies within itself the image and sense of existence—expresses the genuine essence of things. It follows that every great philosopher, like every artist, represents a beginning and an end in himself. From this perspective, it is of no consequence whether his historically determined techniques are quite primitive—like the methods of Heraclitus and Giotto—or subtle and refined, like those of Schelling and Whistler.

Even the manner in which philosophy and art are related to the general culture is not quite so important as the relationship between the general culture and other products of the human spirit. This is because philosophy and art are more a function of the personality. Compared to the predominance of the element of creativity in philosophy and art, the element of tradition plays a *relatively* modest role. Consider all the human capacities which, ultimately, are only *formed* by the influence of historical and societal conditions, structured in such a way that their style and expression are defined. In philosophy and art, these are the decisive capacities.

In the final analysis, these claims are all logical consequences of the individualistic character of philosophy. We may have rejected the individualistic conception of culture in other provinces. However the history of philosophy is the history of the great philosophers. The history of philosophy is a form of hero worship.

Moreover, the heroic character of the history of philosophy is transposed onto the elements of philosophical theories. Philosophy is exclusively concerned with the small number of genuinely great ideas within every philosophical system. Suppose that in the history of philosophy it is philosophy itself which is stressed. In that case, the essential purpose of the history of philosophy is to exhibit the ultimate and elemental root of philosophical systems, the ultimate ground of the system which is sometimes not expressed in the system itself. This is the basic rhythm and the fundamental motive force of a philosophical system. It transcends all the details of the system, the specifics which can only be developed on the basis of this foundtion.

Under these conditions, of course, a certain subjectivity of conception is inevitable, and this should be acknowledged from the very outset. This subjective perspective is not a deficiency that can be eliminated. On the contrary, it is the form and the necessary condition for constituting the raw material of given philosophies as a new structure: the history of philosophy. History is not a mechanical reproduction of the real properties of given data. Just to the contrary. It forms these data in conformity with the theoretical purposes of knowledge. History is an interpretation which satisfies a priori conditions. This same point also holds for the history of philosophy. As a province of the discipline of history, the history of philosophy cannot qualify as a mere reproduction. "Historical truth" is an intellectual activity or function. It transforms the object of historical investigation into something new, something that did not yet exist. This process of transformation is not simply a consequence of the fact that specific details are outlined and summarized. On the contrary, the history of philosophy confronts its raw material with questions. Like the other provinces of history, it comprehends the singular fact in a sense that often was simply not present in the consciousness of its "hero." The history of philosophy unearths meanings and values in its raw material. These meanings and values transform the data of the past into a structure which satisfies the criteria that *we* impose upon it.

However this personal character of every great philosophy is completely consistent with the following position: every consideration of the so-called personal life of the philosopher should be eliminated from the history of philosophy. This position is based on the consideration that biographical anecdotes concern precisely the impersonal characteristics of the philosopher. That someone may be rich or poor, handsome or ugly, English or German, married or single is a purely general fact which does not differentiate the philosopher from countless other persons. The springs of philosophy flow much deeper than this. On the view which is rejected here, philosophy can be derived from the currents which flow along the surface of life. It can be derived from "circumstances" of one sort or another, "conditions which are only circumstantial to life itself and which do not coincide with its innermost dynamic and the destiny of its nature."[4]

The personal characteristics of the philosopher insofar as we have a legitimate interest in them in this context lie exclusively in his philosophy. For it is only his philosophy that makes him unique and absolutely individual. This is the only feature that is peculiar to him.

Suppose that we infer the innermost properties of the personality of the philosopher from his philosophical accomplishments. And suppose that we also interpret his philosophical accomplishments as a consequence of these features of his personality. This sort of reasoning may seem to be circular. However it is one of those circular forms of logic that is indispensable to our thought. It only represents the total homogeneity of the phenomenon which it expresses: each of the elements into which this phenomenon is analyzed can only be understood by reference to all the other elements. The personality which is at stake here is exclusively the person who appears in *this* work, the author of *these* ideas. We understand the philosopher insofar as we understand his philosophy.

All these adventurers of the human spirit, these marvelous saints and sinners, have, of course, set down their most intimate and profound reflections in the form of objective images of the world. Consider the subjective passion with which life, the relationship between the mind and the foundation of all things, and the value and significance of the real and the unreal are experienced. On the other hand, consider the cool and passionless conceptuality, the sublimated abstraction in which this passion is formatively structured. It is exactly in such a form that this feeling makes a generally valid claim to represent what is most personal and intimate in each of us. One of the chief attractions of every significant philosophy lies in precisely this tension. The genius lives in a form of productive subjectivity which completely transcends his existence in the domestic, bourgeois sense. Our

[4]See my book *Kant:* Sixteen Lectures delivered at Berlin University.

task is to extract this productive form of subjectivity from the crystallizations and the frequently abstruse settings in which it is embedded until each philosophy can be understood as the objectification of a certain type of human being. This is the point at which each philosophy reveals the human psyche that is embodied in it. Every such philosophical structure represents the response of a certain type of human being to the total impression of the universe.

Index

This volume contains translations of four previously untranslated essays by Georg Simmel and a lengthy introduction by the translator which analyzes the principal theses of the essays and their methodological importance.

Simmel is here concerned with a closely related set of issues revolving around the questions: How does an event become history? Under what conditions is any event constituted as an object of historical knowledge? He also addresses the question of the status of the concept of interpretation which, in his view, is one of the definitive categories of the historical sciences. In the fourth and final essay, he applies the main doctrine of his philosophy of the historical sciences to the problem of understanding the history of philosophy.

Georg Simmel is increasingly recognized as one of the major intellectual contributors to the shaping of modern sociology. These essays are crucially relevant to those areas of sociological research—phenomenology, ethnomethodology, and existential sociology—which reject the empiricist framework of mainstream social science.

Guy Oakes is associate professor of philosophy at Monmouth College, New Jersey. He has translated Max Weber's *Roscher and Knies: The Logical Problems of Historical Economics* (1975) and *Critique of Stammler* (1977) as well as Georg Simmel's *The Problems of the Philosophy of History* (1977).